LA TRAPPE IN ENGLAND

HOLY CROSS ABBEY, STAPEHILL, DORSET

LA TRAPPE IN ENGLAND

Chronicles of an Unknown Monastery

By
A RELIGIOUS OF HOLY CROSS ABBEY
STAPEHILL, DORSET

With a Foreword by
FATHER DOMINIC DEVAS, O.F.M.

Hæc est generatio quærentium Dominum

LONDON
BURNS OATES & WASHBOURNE LTD
PUBLISHERS TO THE HOLY SEE

NIHIL OBSTAT:
Fr. Antonius Daly, O.C.R.,
Fr. Augustinus Arcand, O.C.R.,
Censores.

IMPRIMATUR:
Fr. Hermanus Joseph Smets,
Abbas Generalis, O.C.R.

Romae,
die 2a Julii, 1935.

NIHIL OBSTAT:
Georgius Ford, S.T.D.,
Censor deputatus.

IMPRIMATUR:
Cyrillus Mahoney,
Vic. Gen.

Plymuthae,
die 27a Septembris, 1935.

MADE AND PRINTED IN GREAT BRITAIN
FOR
BURNS OATES & WASHBOURNE LTD
1937

CONTENTS

PIÆ CISTERCII MATRI ET REGINÆ

FOREWORD

ENGLISH monasteries should be visited in November. There is no nonsense in our impressions then. There are no azure skies, no delicate summer dawns, no filmy mists of blue over the evening distances ; there are no soft breezes and bright sunshine, no flowers in bloom, birds in song, cool cloisters, ecstasy. But in the long black mornings, and swiftly approaching nights, amid wet fields and beneath grey, cloudy, wind-swept skies, the realities, not grim but solid, not melancholy but strong, may be sensed aright. It was in November that I made my first acquaintance with Holy Cross Abbey, Stapehill.

The writer of this book, in the *Conclusion*, quotes the words of Pope Pius XI on the value of the Contemplative Orders, words of such lapidary precision and emphasis as to form a fitting crowning scroll upon the edifice of the eulogies of the past, and to render wholly unnecessary here any attempt at emulation. Rather would I profit by the privilege offered me of writing these few lines to remind the reader of what to look for in the pages of this most interesting book.

Cîteaux is indeed a name to conjure with. The very word recalls a reaction towards the light from ideals, not sullied, but dimmed, a monastic home of a sanctity so splendid, a beauty so entrancing as to make one tremble as one reads of it, waiting for the inevitable decline. For religious history is as the history of Peter walking over the waves towards Christ. At one moment he is on the crests, and Christ is seen, at another he is in the trough of the waves, and the vision is veiled, and only faith, blind, implicit, in Him who calls—faith, too, in the way by which He calls us—can sustain the soul, till the Arms of Christ, near and supporting, are felt lifting her up and holding her in an ineffable embrace. Peter, in that great venture of his, symbolises not alone the soul that would jettison all at Christ's word, but Religious Orders themselves, for these too—each in its own measure—have left the substantial ways, the stolid, practical solidity of boat and sail and oars, to walk in the ways of protest against the false secular traditions around them : so that they too measure their progress down the centuries by crests and hollows.

As with the others, so with the Cistercians. Armand de Rancé—a difficult subject, more wisely handled far, in these pages, than in more expansive biographies—leads Cîteaux up the heights again ; and after him, out from the depredations of Revolutionary France, Dom Augustin de Lestrange —name redolent of the mountains of Switzerland and of that sweet monastic home hemmed in by them, La Val Sainte— re-lifts a fallen standard.

Out from all that turmoil emerges Stapehill, progeny of toil and sacrifice, and herself to know life's stormy course. She has had her periods of weakness and her periods of strength ; but to-day most happily hers is the very strength of parenthood, for from Stapehill in Dorset has sprung Glencairn in County Waterford. Over her history move figures of whose, till now unchronicled, greatness history has left us unaware ; and we are grateful for the example of courage their lives embody. Then from time to time, familiar faces of the Church in England during the nineteenth century—Baines and Collingridge, Hendren and Ullathorne —peep, as it were, for the moment, over the cloister wall, into this hidden house. The actual Abbey Church, for example, was consecrated by the Franciscan Bishop Hendren.

But wisely has the writer of this book devoted many pages to a preliminary review of Cistercian origins—admirably clear and concise pages too—that we may trace down the centuries the distant parentage of this one house of Cistercian Nuns in England. Worthy indeed of a chronicler is a house whose immediate origins take us more than a century back ; and—one may add—the house is happy in her chronicler. For well over a hundred years, then, has Stapehill held on its noble way, and realised Cistercian life amongst us. Often have her gates opened in welcome to souls ' seeking God,' and many are those who, beneath the white Cistercian cowl or the brown robe of the lay sister, in a life at once austere and homely, have watched the Object of their life's choice draw nearer to them, and themselves to Him. May He, in whose Hands are the hearts and wills of all, inspire many another to follow in such footsteps and to sanctify themselves in a life aloof from the very world to which they bring such effective aid.

DOMINIC DEVAS, O.F.M.

From HOLY CROSS ABBEY, STAPEHILL.
Feast of the Presentation of Our Lady, 1935.

INTRODUCTION

THE Cistercian life as lived at the present day by the monks and nuns of the Strict Observance is admittedly the most primitive form of monastic life now in existence in the Western Church.[1] It is impossible, therefore, to understand it rightly without some knowledge, however slight, of the origin and development of monasticism itself. The Cistercian Order is not a creation of the Middle Ages, but a branch of that mighty tree, the Monastic Order, which has its roots deep in antiquity, in the very earliest forms of Christian asceticism—the trunk being the Rule of St. Benedict, while the ramifications have covered the whole of Christendom. If we would understand the Cistercian life, therefore, we must first take a brief glance at those primitive beginnings from which the Monastic Order sprang. And this, more especially, because the Cistercian Observance has from the first stood for a return to the primitive simplicity of the Rule of St. Benedict. That Rule gathers up all that is best in the earliest monastic traditions, but by its breadth and largeness of view it has lent itself to developments not contemplated by the great legislator himself.

Cîteaux—that is, the Cistercian Order—represents, however, not the principle of development and expansion in the Rule, but rather the Rule as a perfectly ordered summary of the simplest forms of traditional monasticism. It stands for fidelity to the letter, not in any spirit of studied archaism or deliberate harking back to the manners of a bygone age, but from the desire to drink those life-giving waters of evangelical simplicity as close to their source as possible.

Certain later renewals of Cîteaux have gone back beyond the Rule of St. Benedict and drawn their inspiration from the Fathers of the Desert, but this was a mistake, and has

[1] Cf. *Catholic Encyclopædic Dictionary* : " Monasticism, Western."

xi

not been ratified by posterity. All that was best in Eastern monasticism is to be found in the Rule of St. Benedict, tempered with the Western spirit of order and moderation ; and in this form the essential elements of monastic life have been handed down through the ages. The so-called ' Trappists ' and ' Trappistines ' are simply those Cistercian monks and nuns who follow most closely the primitive observances of their Order ; the Cistercian Order itself was a return, at the end of the eleventh century, to the literal following of the Rule of St. Benedict ; the Rule of St. Benedict, written in the sixth century, was a summary of the earliest monastic traditions of East and West. This must be our apology for the following brief historical sketch, which seems to us an indispensable preliminary to any account of a Cistercian monastery and Cistercian life at the present day.

But there is perhaps a deeper reason, too. We live in an age in which the spirit of reverence is notoriously lacking ; an age of levelling, of criticism, when everything is brought to the bar and judged purely on its own merits. From this standpoint it might be said that the old religious Orders cannot live on their past ; they must justify their existence, and show by their fruits that the sap of life is still flowing in the old trunk. This is true ; otherwise they would merely be saying with the Pharisees : ' Abraham is our father,' and doing not the works of Abraham. Yet it is also true that the vital spirit of the old monastic Orders essentially implies that very reverence for antiquity which is thought so little of in our own days, so that the absence of this would prove indeed that the sap of life had ceased to flow. The customs and observances of monastic life are hallowed by the tradition of ages ; they have sanctified generations of saints throughout the Church's history ; they have, therefore, in a sense, a prescriptive right, and, like the laws of God, are ' justified in themselves '—*justificata in semetipsa*.[1] They ought, therefore, to be approached from this standpoint, distasteful as it may be at first sight to our modern generation. For, after all, a way of life which has adapted itself thus successfully to every age and every country of Christendom can hardly have lost its appeal, and the Cistercian Order

[1] Ps. xviii.

has preserved the old monastic tradition in its simplest form, which belongs to no one period or race, but is accessible to all. And, in point of fact, it is attracting souls to-day, in all parts of the world—in the Far East as in Europe and America—just as it attracted them in mediæval England or in seventeenth-century France.

There is at the present time a remarkable revival of devotion to the liturgy of the Church. More and more, souls are turning to the ancient hallowed formulæ of prayer for the nourishment of their devotional life, rather than to modern sources. The life of the old religious Orders has, like the liturgy, grown with the growth of the Church herself, and, like the liturgy, it ever contains, under forms which may at first seem antiquated, a spring of living waters at which souls can slake their thirst. And those who approach will perhaps be surprised to find, not the shackles of a conventional or formalist piety, but rather the freest and most untrammelled access to God, and a breadth and liberty of spirit like that of the Catholic Church herself.

LA TRAPPE IN ENGLAND

CHAPTER I

GROWTH OF MONASTICISM

Si revera Deum quærit—if he truly seek God.—This is the essential condition required by St. Benedict of those who seek admission to the monastery—the true test of vocation which implicitly includes all the others—for the soul that is indeed seeking God will be ready to embrace all that may be asked of her in God's service.

Yet, surely, all Christians are bound to seek God? Union with God, the perfection of charity, is the end to which every Christian is bound to tend, but he is free as to the choice of the *means* to that end. Hence the distinction between the precepts and the counsels. From the beginnings of Christianity there have been those who, not content to seek Him by the indirect means of the duties of their state, would embrace a more direct and a more rugged path—the path of evangelical renunciation—in order that, in St. Benedict's phrase, they might *by a straight course reach their Creator*—like the athletes of old, stripping themselves of all that might impede them in the spiritual warfare : laying aside temporal cares that they might occupy themselves solely with the *unum necessarium*. Such as these received from very early times the name of μοναχοί (*monachoi*), derived from the Greek word μονός (*monos*) : alone, unique, simple ; not merely as living solitary and apart, but as being men of unity, seeking God alone in simplicity of heart, and expressing this oneness of aim by external simplicity of life ; renouncing internal division and external multiplicity in order to concentrate all their forces on the one essential

I

objective—union with God in perfect charity—God, who, in the Divine Simplicity of His Nature, requires, says St. Bernard, a corresponding simplicity in the heart that seeks Him. It is in this sense that Denys the Areopagite explains the term ; monks are so called, he says, ' because of their single undivided life, which removes their spirit from the distraction of manifold interests, and by which they are borne towards the oneness of God and the perfection of holy love.'[1]

The earliest form which this seeking of God alone took was the vow of virginity, which is the very foundation of the religious state, and which implies in the first instance, according to St. Paul's teaching, this very ' undividedness,' freedom for the things of God ; though it has also a positive and higher significance, as the supreme expression of the union of the soul with God. In the early centuries ' ascetics ' and ' virgins ' were a recognised class in the Christian communities, leading in the seclusion of their own homes a life of prayer and self-discipline.

Later, these ascetics did not content themselves with leading this life of seclusion ; they left the cities and went into solitude. A second evangelical counsel, that of poverty, now comes into prominence. Antony hears read in church those words of the Gospel : ' If thou wilt be perfect, go, sell all that thou hast, and give to the poor . . . and come, follow Me '—takes them as spoken to himself, and instantly fulfils them. Thus began that *fuga mundi* which peopled the Nile valley and the deserts of Egypt and Syria during the fourth century. Persecution had ceased, and to the arena succeeded the desert as the stage on which Christian heroism displayed itself. The spirit of the martyrs now found its expression in the ascetic life, and those who embraced it did so in a certain vehemence of reaction against the corruption of the dying pagan civilisation around them. It was an age of prodigious bodily austerity, inspired by a spirit of intense individualism and holy emulation. This could be only a passing phenomenon, and the work of the great monastic legislators was to harness this undisciplined spiritual energy and guide it into ordered channels ; to

[1] *De Hierarchia Ecclesiastica*, c. vi.

work out by patient experiment and gradually accumulated wisdom a stable mode of life, which should be accessible not merely to giants of sanctity, but to all souls of good will possessed with the desire to seek God alone by prayer and sacrifice, in solitude and separation from the world. And so we have the gradual evolution of the anchoretic or eremitical life into the cenobitical life.

Among the solitaries of Egypt were men of spiritual genius, of whom St. Antony is the type ; such men, by their holiness and wisdom, attracted lesser souls, who came and placed themselves under the guidance of the master. To St. Antony is due the organisation of the anchoretic life, and from the beginning of the fourth century we find *groups* of solitaries, clusters of cells with a central church. But whether living singly or in groups, the solitaries were still solitaries. The real landmark is the year 322, when Pachomius, a solitary of the Upper Thebaïd, left his master, Palemon, and at Tabennisi established the first *cœnobion*—by the simple means of building an enclosure wall around the group of cells. The cluster of cells became a monastery ; the group of solitaries became a community, following a common Rule and subject to the authority of a Superior. Here we have two new elements, which we have become accustomed to regard as essential—or even as *the* essential— elements of religious life ; obedience to a Superior, which became the third religious vow, and common life, that is, the substitution of a fixed standard of living in place of individual initiative. This meant the levelling of all to a normal standard attainable by the majority, and consequently an inevitable lessening of bodily austerity.

Thus came into being that *fortissimum genus cœnobitarum*, as St. Benedict calls them—that most strong race of those who live the common life—κοινός βίος (*koinos bios*). The name implies the new element introduced, and which the wisdom of experience found to be the most potent form of self-discipline, calling for a more far-reaching self-renunciation than all the austerities of a Macarius or a Simon Stylites. Yet to these very cenobites the generic term μοναχός (*monachos*) comes to be applied, until ' monk ' and ' cenobite ' become synonymous terms—because nothing had been

lost of that ' one-ness ' of aim ; the monk was still pre-
eminently the man of unity, but he had found that for most
men, at least, the great means of achieving that ' one-ness,'
of attaining to the Divine Simplicity, lay rather in the
discipline and self-effacement of community life than in the
single combat of the desert.

Pachomius himself founded nine monasteries, and his
sister founded at Men a community of nuns following the
same Rule. The monastic life thus organised spread rapidly.
New monasteries, both of monks and nuns, were founded,
and many groups of ascetics embraced the Pachomian Rule.
Moreover, Pachomius not only established community life,
but organised the monasteries which embraced his Rule into
a congregation, with a central government to ensure uniformity. Later, in Asia Minor, St. Basil wrote his Rule,
which afterwards became universal in the Eastern Church,
and is distinguished from that of St. Pachomius by a new
element of intellectual culture with a view to apostolic
influence, and by a more marked spirit of discretion.

Egyptian monachism soon spread to the West. St.
Athanasius, the friend and biographer of St. Antony, exiled
from his see of Alexandria by his Arian opponents, carried
its fame to Rome and Trèves in 335. In 360 St. Martin
established monastic life in Gaul, at Ligugé, then at Mar-
moutiers. St. Jerome came to Rome in 382 and fostered
the seed sown by St. Athanasius. St. Augustine began
monastic life in Africa in 387, and soon afterwards we
find monasteries in the north of Italy, in Spain, and in
Provence. In 375 St. Honoratus founded the famous monastery of Lerins, from which, most probably, St. Patrick drew
the first inspiration of the great Celtic monastic movement of
the sixth century. About 415 the monastery of Marseilles
was founded by John Cassian, who in his youth had visited
the deserts of Egypt and gathered up from the lips of the
solitaries the quintessence of the monastic teaching of the
East, which in his famous Conferences and Institutions thus
became part of the spiritual heritage of the Western Church.[1]

---

[1] St. Benedict quotes from the writings of Cassian more frequently than
from any other book except the Holy Scriptures, and twice in his Rule
recommends them to his monks. Seven centuries later, they were the
favourite spiritual reading of St. Thomas Aquinas.

In all these countries, Egyptian monasticism became adapted and modified according to local needs and ideals, so that eventually a multitude of Rules came into being, though the general framework was that established by St. Pachomius. Western monasticism was to achieve its definite and permanent form only through the genius of St. Benedict, who gave to the Western Church the Rule which was to become *the* Rule *par excellence.*

The brief summary we have given above is necessary to the understanding of the Rule of St. Benedict. St. Benedict is the father of Western monasticism, but his Rule is not a new creation ; he was not an innovator, nor did he aim at originating a new form of religious life. His mind is steeped in the teaching of the earlier monastic writers, and his Rule is the mature and final expression of all that is best and most enduring in their principles and practice. He borrows constantly from the older Rules, even to their very terminology.[1] Yet the Rule of St. Benedict is far from being a mere compilation. In the first place, it bears on every page the stamp of a lofty spiritual genius. The depth and wisdom of the ascetic teaching contained in it surpasses anything in the older writers, and has raised it above the level of a mere code of regulations to that of a profound treatise on Christian perfection, so that even souls not called to the religious state have in all ages derived help and inspiration from it. Secondly, it stands supreme by reason of the legislative genius which has taken the traditional elements of monastic life, and with an unerring power of selection and co-ordination has welded them into a perfectly balanced scheme of life in which prayer and labour, action and contemplation harmonise, and in which all is regulated in that spirit of discretion and moderation which St. Gregory notes as the chief characteristic of St. Benedict's Rule. Thus was the traditional asceticism of the East transmitted to the Western Church in a form accessible to Western needs and habits of life.

And who was the man who achieved this work and merited

---

[1] This can be seen almost at a glance in Dom Butler's admirable edition of the Latin text of the Rule. (*Sancti Benedicti Regula Monasteriorum,* 2nd edition, 1927.)

the title of Patriarch of the Monks of the West ? Benedict, the son of Eutychius, was born in the year 480 at Nursia in Umbria, where his father possessed a villa. In early youth he was sent to Rome to pursue his studies, but he soon fled from the world and, aided by a monk, Romanus, who gave him the habit of religion, he concealed himself in a cave at Subiaco, where he dwelt for three years in solitude, prayer and penance. Disciples came to him, and he built a monastery; their number increased, and eventually twelve monasteries, each containing twelve monks, were built in close proximity to one another on the banks of the Anio—an organisation exactly modelled on that of the monks of Egypt. In 529 St. Benedict left Subiaco with a few disciples, and established himself on Monte Cassino, where he organised that form of cenobitic life which is described in his Rule. There, towards the close of his life, the great Patriarch is believed to have written his Rule, the ripe fruit of a life-time's experience of the ascetic life in all its forms, and a summary of all that was best in the monastic traditions of East and West. From his childhood St. Benedict had set himself, with an uncompromising fixity of purpose which is wholly characteristic of him, to seek God and God alone, and to break with everything that could turn him from that search. In his maturity he establishes a ' school of the Lord's service ' for those possessed of a like aim. To go to God—such is the one aim he sets before his disciples—and by what road ?—by following in the footsteps of Christ by humility and obedience. The external life as organised by St. Benedict comprises the three traditional monastic occupations—liturgical prayer, the *Opus Dei*, to which nothing is to be preferred ; *lectio divina*—that study of divine things and assiduous meditation of the Scriptures which had been from the first one of the dominant features of the ascetic life ; and manual labour, the value of which in a contemplative life was well known to the monks of the East. It is in the wise ordering of the alternation of these three occupations that St. Benedict's genius for organisation is so apparent. The whole is enveloped in an atmosphere of silence, liberating the soul and enabling it to commune with God. None of these elements is new. To them St. Benedict added the vow of stability, attaching the monk to the monastery of his profession. Moreover, he greatly strengthened the bonds of community life by his hierarchical system of government, and by a much greater insistence on uniformity of observance. With St. Benedict's Rule the common life acquires its full importance. The setting up of a common Rule inevitably meant, as we have seen, a lessening of bodily austerity—yet that very common life was found to be a most potent instrument of self-discipline. St. Benedict conceives spiritual progress—that is, the putting off of self, the one supreme obstacle to the reign of charity in the soul —as, above all, progress in humility. The chapter on the twelve degrees of humility, in which is condensed the whole of his ascetic doctrine, shows how this fundamental virtue is both acquired and exercised in all the various circumstances of community life. The two chapters on mutual obedience and on that 'good zeal,' which is only another name for brotherly love, complete this doctrine, and show how, in the continual contact of community life, the exercise of charity demands the complete effacement of the *ego*, the elimination of that selfishness which most of all holds the soul back in its ascent to God. St. Benedict's conception of obedience—the chief manifestation of this fundamental humility—is also wholly his own. He regards it not so much in a negative light, as a means of mortification, but positively, as the great means of union with God, an act of love, effecting directly that union of the human will with the Will of God which constitutes sanctity—' knowing that by this way of obedience they will go to God.' ' To return to God by the labour of obedience ' is the whole programme he sets before his disciples—*imitans Dominum*—following in the footsteps of Him Who became for us obedient unto death—and always out of love—*pro Dei amore*. The exercises of the ascetic life thus acquire in St. Benedict's view an essentially unitive character. The whole life of the religious is bathed in the light of faith, and inspired by the motive of love. In his Superiors, in his brethren, in the guests, in the sick, he sees Christ, and loves, serves and obeys Christ in their person. The common things of life are thus invested with a supernatural significance, and yet withal everything is ordered with a practical good sense and administrative ability which makes of the monastery a complete social organism.

In that epoch, when chaos seemed to reign in place of the law and order of ancient Rome, we can well realise how a monastery like Monte Cassino stood out as an oasis of peace and order, while all around the insurgent waves of barbarism seemed about to sweep away the last feeble and corrupt remnants of Roman culture. Side by side, under St. Benedict's wise legislation, Roman patricians, freed slaves, and converted barbarians lived together in peace and harmony in this ' school of the Lord's service,' where there was no respecting of persons, because ' whether bond or free, we are all one in Christ, and bear an equal burden in the army of one Lord.' The monastery was a kind of citadel, containing within its walls, as far as possible, the necessary means of production ; for separation from the world by monastic enclosure was an essential element in St. Benedict's scheme, and was the safeguard of that vow of stability which cut off so many abuses at the root.

' A school of the Lord's service,' where everything was ordered with one sole end in view—the sanctification of souls for the glory of God, by a life of prayer and labour— labour which had no external or secondary aim, but was solely for the good of the monk's soul and the support of the community. This was all that St. Benedict had in view —yet Divine Providence made use of his institution for the good of the Church and society in ways undreamed of by the holy legislator.

In 590, less than half a century after St. Benedict's death, a Benedictine monk was elected to the See of Peter. This was St. Gregory the Great, who, in his youth, had converted his palace on the Cœlian Hill into a monastery. As Pontiff his task was a gigantic one. The Western Empire had perished ; Italy was devastated by the Lombard invasions ; the Church was torn by schism and heresy, and ecclesiastical discipline was at a low ebb. Gregory saw that the future lay in the hands of the barbarian races who had overrun the provinces of the Roman Empire, and who were either pagan or Arian. He determined to send missionaries for their conversion, and it was to the monks of St. Benedict that he entrusted this vast project. The great Christian centre of Northern Europe had been the Celtic countries of Britain, Ireland, and Brittany ; but, except in the West, Britain had relapsed into paganism as the result of the Anglo-Saxon invasion. To England, therefore, in 596, St. Gregory sent St. Augustine and his companions, a band of monks from the monastery on the Cœlian Hill. This was the beginning of the world-mission of the sons of St. Benedict. As a result of the Benedictine mission to England, a new centre of Christian civilisation came into being. Monasteries, both of monks and nuns, covered the land, and became centres of culture as well as of religion. It was from these monasteries that missionaries went forth to evangelise the Germanic peoples of Northern Europe. Chief of these missionaries was Boniface of Crediton, ' the Apostle of Germany,' who, says a recent historian,[1] ' had a deeper influence on the history of Europe than any Englishman who has ever lived.' And all this missionary enterprise was carried on chiefly by means of the establishment of monasteries, of nuns as much as of monks, who implanted in the rural pagan populations the knowledge not only of the Faith itself, but of agriculture, learning, and the arts. In the words of the writer just quoted, ' it was the Anglo-Saxon monks and above all St. Boniface, who first realised that union of Teutonic initiative and Latin order which is the source of the whole mediæval development of culture.'

Besides carrying the Faith to the still heathen races, the monks also did much to bring about the reformation and renewal of the decadent Church of the Franks, and the formation of that alliance between the Frankish monarchy and the Papacy which culminated in the coronation of Charlemagne as Roman Emperor in the year 800. Charlemagne became the patron of the great revival of letters and the arts known as the Carolingian Renaissance, which was diffused throughout the Empire chiefly by means of the great monastic centres. In short, during these centuries when, from the chaos which followed the downfall of the Roman Empire, European civilisation slowly and painfully emerged, the most potent formative influence in the develop-

[1] Christopher Dawson, *The Making of Europe*, p. 211.

ment of that civilisation was indisputably that of Benedictine
monasticism—and these centuries have justly gained the
title of 'the Benedictine centuries.' The great Celtic
monastic movement of the sixth century had also been
marked by extensive missionary enterprise, and by the
growth of centres of culture like Luxeuil, but the wisdom and
discretion of St. Benedict's Rule caused it eventually to
supersede all others. Gradually the monasteries of St.
Columbanus became Benedictine, and the movement of
expansion spread southward to Italy, as well as eastward to
the Slavonic peoples, so that by the end of the eighth century
Benedictine monasteries covered the whole face of
Europe.

In the course of this expansion an immense change had
come over monastic life. 'The Carolingian abbey,' says
Mr. Dawson, 'was no longer a colony of self-supporting
ascetics; it was a great social and economic centre, the
owner of vast estates, the civiliser of conquered territories,
and the scene of a many-sided and intense cultural activity.'[1]
The apostolic activity of the monks was temporary and
local; but the work of civilisation which went hand in hand
with it was to endure. The monasteries were the schools
and universities of those times, and to the labour of monastic
scribes and scholars the world owes the preservation of pagan
classical literature. The care of the poor and the sick was
in the hands of the monks. Immense tracts of barren and
marshy land had been brought under cultivation by their
labour; the monasteries thus became great landowners, and
in this way they became an integral element in the new
social fabric which was gradually being built up, until we
find the mediæval Abbot taking his place among the great
feudal lords of the realm. Thus, insensibly and by force of
circumstances, a complete change had taken place. The
monastery, instead of being a place of solitude, apart from
the activities of the world, had become the chief centre
of those activities. The desert had become the city. Those
who sought to serve God apart from their fellow-men had
become centres of attraction to whom all men flocked. Yet
at all times there were souls who longed for the desert, and

[1] *Op. cit.*

for the primitive simplicity of the earlier monastic life. Moreover, inevitably with this vast expansion, there came about a certain relaxation of discipline. St. Benedict had been right in fearing for his monks the consequences of frequent contact with the outside world. By the beginning of the ninth century the need of reform was being felt, and also the need of some kind of external bond between the monasteries to ensure fidelity to tradition. St. Benedict had made no provision in his Rule for any such unification, and it was not until 817 that the first attempt was made to bring it about. St. Benedict of Aniane was the first Benedictine ' reformer.' In the monasteries which he founded he introduced an observance more austere than that of the Rule of St. Benedict. He cut off all external ministry, and reinstated manual labour to some extent, but by his additions to the liturgical duties he destroyed the equilibrium which St. Benedict had established between the three monastic occupations. The Emperor Louis the Pious entered into Benedict's views, and at the Council of Aix-la-Chapelle (Aachen), convoked by him in 817, he brought together an assembly of abbots, with a view to establishing uniformity of observance throughout the monasteries of the Empire. The scheme of absolute uniformity devised by Benedict of Aniane never came into effect. Nevertheless, a body of *Capitula* was accepted by the Council of Abbots as a basis of common observance, and Mr. Edmund Bishop says of these that ' the decree of this meeting of Aachen, in which Benedict was as well the author as the life and soul, was a turning-point in the history of the Benedictines, forming the basis of later legislation and practice. After the great founder himself, Benedict of Nursia, no man has more widely affected Western monasticism than did the second Benedict, he of Aniane.'[1]

The year 817 is, therefore, a landmark in monastic history. But the work of Aniane did not endure. During the ninth century the disorder of the times, the invasions of the Danes, Northmen and others, had a disastrous effect on the monastic houses. The next landmark is the foundation of Cluny in the year 910. Cluny, lineally descended from Aniane, in-

[1] *Liturgica Historica*, p. 213.

herited also its spirit. St. Odo aimed at returning to a life of silence and separation from the world, of prayer and austerity. Manual labour, however, was left to the dependents of the monastery, the time of the monks being almost entirely absorbed by liturgical duties. Multiplication of Offices, prolongation of psalmody and lessons, made the *Opus Dei* not merely the principal, but almost the only work of the Cluniac monk. The solemnity of the liturgical offices was further enhanced by elaboration of ceremonial, perfect execution of the chant, and magnificence in vestments and in the architecture and ornamentation of the churches. It was really a new conception of monastic life, in which, in the words of a Cluniac monk, the labour of the long psalmody took the place of manual labour. Nor was intellectual work much cultivated ; liturgical prayer and spiritual reading filled the day. This conception of monasticism became universal in the two following centuries under the influence of Cluny. For Cluny succeeded Monte Cassino as the centre of monastic traditions, and for two centuries wielded a tremendous power throughout Christendom. Cluny proudly claimed the title of ' a second Rome,' and the Abbot of Cluny was the leading figure in the Western Church, after the Pope. This was partly due to the personal ascendancy of the six great Abbots who ruled Cluny in succession for two centuries—four of them canonised saints—and partly to the highly centralised system of government for which Cluny stood. Every monastery founded from Cluny, or placed under its jurisdiction, was directly subject to the Abbot of Cluny, who appointed at will the local Superior, the latter bearing the title, not of Abbot, but of Prior. This was a complete departure from St. Benedict's conception of the monastery as an autonomous unit, an organism complete in itself, a family of which the Abbot was the Father. And this, no doubt, was the weakness of Cluny, and the cause of its decline, once the era of the great Abbots was at an end. But in the eleventh century Cluny reigned supreme, and besides the two thousand houses directly under its jurisdiction, a large number of monasteries throughout Europe had adopted the Cluniac observance, while remaining independent abbeys, or being simply affiliated to Cluny. One such abbey, a small monastery only forty miles from Cluny, where the Cluniac observance was followed, but which was not under the jurisdiction of the Abbot of Cluny, was *Molesmes*, from which issued the new monastic influence which was to rival and finally to eclipse that of Cluny—CÎTEAUX.

CHAPTER II

ROBERT of Champagne, Abbot of Molesmes, was born in 1017, of noble parentage, and at the age of fifteen entered the Benedictine monastery of St. Peter-la-Celle, near Troyes. Soon after his profession, while still the youngest of the community, he was chosen Prior. His reputation for wisdom and holiness spread beyond the walls of his monastery, and the monks of the Abbey of St. Michel de Tonnerre, on the borders of Champagne and Burgundy, asked for him as their Abbot. The monastery was in a relaxed condition, and Robert consented with reluctance. His efforts to re-establish regular discipline failed completely, and finding the monks obdurate, he returned to La Celle. He was then elected Prior of St. Aigulphus, but did not remain there long. A group of seven hermits, living in the forest of Colan, had determined to found a community under the Rule of St. Benedict, and made up their minds to obtain Robert for their Superior. They even appealed to the Holy See, and Alexander II granted their request. In these fervent solitaries St. Robert found more congenial material for his efforts to establish exact observance.

When the numbers of the infant community reached thirteen, they removed to the forest of Molesmes, in the diocese of Langres in Burgundy. There they built a small wooden oratory, and round it a group of huts roughly constructed from the branches of the trees they cut down. This ' monastery ' was dedicated to Our Lady, on Sunday, December 20, 1075. The produce of the land which they had cleared, and which was granted to them by a neighbouring baron, was their only source of livelihood. The spot was remote and difficult of access, and few found their way thither in the early days. Among those few, however, was a young English pilgrim, returning on foot from Rome. This was Stephen Harding, who was destined to become the legislator of the Cistercian Order and the spiritual father of St. Bernard. Brought up from childhood in the Benedictine Abbey of Sherborne in Dorset, he went to study in Scotland (or, as some think, Ireland) and Paris, and then proceeded on foot with a companion to visit the tombs of the Apostles. He set out again from Rome in the same manner, intending to return to Sherborne, but turned aside from his path—from what motive we know not—to visit the newly founded monastery of Molesmes. Here he found the ideal he was seeking. He threw in his lot with Robert and his companions, and never returned to England.

The first years at Molesmes were spent in extreme poverty and hard work, but Robert's trust in Providence was never deceived. Gradually numbers increased; alms came to them in abundance, and daily bread was no longer a constant anxiety. But with prosperity, the first fervour waned; a new generation saw no object in continuing to work with their hands when not compelled by necessity; more costly clothing came into use, and some of the fasts were dispensed with. So it came about that after twenty years of existence, while the founders were still living, reform was already being spoken of. There is no reason to suppose any extreme decadence, and we shall do well to bear in mind, when speaking of monastic reforms, the words of a Cistercian historian, D. Canivez : ' To certain people this word (Reform) conveys a somewhat sinister impression. It seems to evoke the idea of a desperate situation, made up of crying abuses, and total neglect of the essential duties of the religious state.' On the contrary, it often happened that ' the Christian and religious life remained intact in their essential elements ; the question was only one of a greater or lesser degree of intensity in the warfare against the tendencies of (man's) sensual nature. The real fault was to have allowed a little comfort in an existence which should have been fixed in a perpetual holocaust.'[1] This would appear to have been the case at Molesmes, and the innovations were no doubt justified

---

[1] D. Joseph-Marie Canivez, *L'Ordre de Cîteaux en Belgique* (1926), pp. 22, 27.

by an already long tradition and by the example of most contemporary monasteries. At the same time, Molesmes had been founded by St. Robert and his thirteen solitaries as a house of strict observance, and the Abbot had the right to require his monks to observe the customs originally established. This they declined to do, at least the majority of them, for the community was divided. The more fervent, led by Alberic, the Prior, supported Robert in his efforts at reform, but the opposition was of so violent a character that the Abbot retired for a time to Hauz, a farm or hermitage belonging to the monastery. Left in charge, Alberic, who was of a more fiery temperament, and seems to have been the animating spirit of the reforming movement, pursued the fight, but had to suffer for his tenacity, and was even imprisoned. Such a state of things could not long continue. The Abbot was recalled and the Prior released, but they realised now that internal reform was an impossibility, and that the only remedy was the sword of separation.

From this point we have the authority of a precious document, entitled *Super Exordium Cisterciensis Cœnobii*— ' Of the beginnings of the Monastery of Cîteaux '—drawn up in the very life-time of the founders. The object of this document is clearly stated at the outset. Its author, Stephen Harding, speaks not in his own name, but in the name of the founders of Cîteaux, of whom he was one. ' We, the first founders of this Church of Cîteaux, by this present writing do make known to those who shall come after us all that concerns the beginnings of this monastery, and the manner of life led therein, the canonicity, authority, persons and period of its foundation, in order that, the facts being made known with exact truth, they may have a greater love of the place, and of the observance of Holy Rule which by the grace of God we have begun therein.' The *Exordium* is unique among works of the kind by its conciseness, simplicity, and sobriety of style. The facts are briefly recorded, and the canonical documents approving the foundation are cited in full, ' in order,' St. Stephen writes, ' that our successors may know with what prudent counsel and by what authority their monastery was founded.' Above all, the motive of the foundation is made perfectly clear.

' These men, while still living at Molesmes, moved by the grace of God, often spoke together concerning the transgression of the Rule of St. Benedict, Father of monks. They sorrowed and lamented, seeing that they and the other monks had promised by their solemn profession to observe that Rule, and yet they did by no means observe it. *For this reason . . . they came to this solitude, in order that they might fulfil their profession by the observance of the Holy Rule.*'

Their first move was to obtain ecclesiastical sanction for the step they were about to take. Early in 1098 Robert, Alberic, and five other monks, of whom Stephen the Englishman was one, approached the Papal Legate, Hugh, Archbishop of Lyons, and solicited his authority to withdraw from Molesmes to a place where they could observe in its integrity the Rule to which they were bound by their profession. The Legate received them sympathetically, and afterwards sent them a letter giving the desired authorisation. The tenor of this letter is as follows : ' . . . You have declared to Us that you have formed the project of following henceforward more strictly and more perfectly the Rule of St. Benedict, which at Molesmes is observed only with negligence and tepidity. But since, for manifold reasons, it is impossible for you to carry out this holy resolution in that monastery . . . it seems expedient to Us that you should establish yourselves in some other place . . . where you may serve the Lord in greater quietness and to your souls' health. . . . When you came to submit to Us your design, We rejoiced thereat and counselled you to remain faithful to it ; but now We *enjoin* you and all those who shall join you, to persevere in your noble enterprise.'

Thus fortified by canonical approbation, Robert and his companions, to the number now of twenty-one, left Molesmes, carrying nothing with them but the sacred vestments and vessels for the celebration of Mass, and the books required for the Divine office. Their destination was the solitude of Cîteaux in the diocese of Chalon-sur-Saône, in Burgundy, fifteen miles south of Dijon ; *Cistels—Cîteaux—Cistercium—* a place of virgin forests, inaccessible, the home of wild beasts ; a marshy soil through which ran a stream called *Sansfonds* or *Centfons*. A small rough church existed there

for the use of the scattered peasantry who dwelt on the lands of Raynald, Viscount of Beaune, by whose leave the monks established themselves there. They cleared a site, dug a well, and with the timber they had felled put together some rough buildings, which they called *Novum Monasterium*— ' the New Monastery '—the Church of Our Lady. Cîteaux was founded. Absolute poverty marked its beginnings, but the Legate appealed to Odo, Duke of Burgundy, on behalf of these new dwellers on his lands. The Duke, ' delighted,' we are told, ' at their holy fervour,' sent workmen to complete the building of the wooden monastery, and from that time forward was their chief benefactor, supplying them with the necessaries of life, and endowing them with lands and flocks.

The solemn inauguration of the monastery took place on March 21, 1098, the Feast of St. Benedict, which in that year fell on Palm Sunday. The *Novum Monasterium* was canonically erected into an Abbey by the Bishop of Chalon, and Robert was elected Abbot, Alberic being appointed Prior, and Stephen Sub-Prior. A year later Robert, whom the Order of Cîteaux honours as its founder, disappears from its history. Recalled to Molesmes at the petition of his former community, granted not too willingly by Urban II, he left his newly-founded monastery at the call of obedience. His name brings before us a picture of silence, self-effacement, utter obedience—a living model of a Rule whose whole spirituality rests on that triple foundation of silence, humility and obedience ; a fitting foundation-stone, on which others were to raise a great edifice.

Alberic was elected to succeed him. Always the active, enterprising spirit, it fell to him to organise and consolidate the work—Alberic, whom the *Exordium* characterises in a phrase which condenses the portrait of the perfect monk— *amator Regulæ et fratrum*—' a lover of the Rule and of the brethren.' Gifted with ' wondrous prudence,' his first care was to obtain the protection of the Apostolic See for his Abbey, ' that it might for ever remain in quiet, and safe from all molestation, whether on the part of ecclesiastical or secular persons.' Two monks, John and Ilbodus, were sent to Rome, armed with letters from the two Cardinal Legates then in France, from the Archbishop of Lyons, and from the

Bishop of Chalon. The result was a Bull issued by Paschal II on April 18, 1100, granting the *Privilegium Romanum* to Alberic and his successors in perpetuity, and ' forbidding any person whatsoever to introduce the least change into their way of life '—which was exactly the motive for which the Privilege had been sought.

The enterprise being now solidly established on a canonical basis, the conventual Chapter met, in order to define exactly the manner in which the Rule of St. Benedict was to be observed at Cîteaux. Their programme is thus set forth in the *Exordium*: ' This Abbot (Alberic) and his brethren, mindful of their promise, unanimously determined to establish and to maintain the observance of the Rule of St. Benedict in that place, rejecting all that was contrary to the purity of the Rule. . . . And hence, taking the integrity of the Rule as their standard for the whole conduct of life, they conformed with exactitude to the path traced out by it. . . . And having thus put off the old man, they rejoiced to put on the new.' In these words we have the summary of what may be called ' the Cistercian Idea.' Nothing more nor less than this : the integral observance of the Rule of St. Bene-dict. Robert and Alberic were not innovators. They never dreamed of ' founding an Order.' No new ideal had dawned on them like Francis' ' Lady Poverty ' ; no vision had appeared to them like Dominic's ' Sign of God ' seen from the hill-top of Fanjeaux. They had promised fidelity to the Rule of St. Benedict, and they were resolved to carry out their promise, rejecting all developments, however legitimate —because in the integral and literal observance of that Rule they believed that everything necessary to monastic perfec-tion was to be found, and all the means for attaining that union with God which is the sole end of the monastic life. Again and again the phrase is repeated—*puritas Regulæ*— the Rule pure and simple, with no admixture of foreign elements ; and *rectitudo Regulæ*—the straight line of the Rule without deviation. Certain minds may criticise this zeal for the literal observance of the Rule in its least precepts as mere formalism. This would, however, be a misunder-standing. It is clear from the passage quoted above, and from many others, that the ideal of the founders of Cîteaux

c

was no mere slavish adherence to a dead letter. To them the letter was precious indeed, but only as being the vehicle of the spirit—and the spirit was none other than that spirit of evangelical simplicity which is so peculiarly St. Benedict's. By observing the Rule in its purity they sought to '*put off the old man,*' and so doing '*they rejoiced to put on the new*'— to be clothed with Jesus Christ, and thus to attain to union with God. In these words we have their true aim expressed —and that simplicity of aim, that singleness of purpose, is expressed in simplicity of life. If we wished to sum up in one word the spirit of primitive Cîteaux, it would be, as a recent General Chapter of the Order has pointed out,[1] in this word: SIMPLICITY. Yet this Simplicity was not a self-conscious or deliberately chosen ideal; the guiding principle was, as we have said, the return to *tradition;* but the dominant feature of that return was Simplicity. And is not that very devotion to tradition, that very desire to live in accordance with the Rule they had professed, one form of simplicity?—a simplicity which in reality is nothing else but that spirit of truth, of sincerity, so characteristic of St. Benedict, who always requires that the reality should correspond with the name, whether he is speaking of the Abbot, who is to 'fulfil by his deeds the name he bears,' or of those unworthy monks who 'lie to God by their tonsure'; or of the oratory of the monastery, which is to '*be what it is called,*' a place of prayer. Their return to the 'purity of the Rule' might be equally well expressed by the term 'the simplicity of the Rule,' which is the simplicity of the *unum necessarium*—the seeking of God alone in the footsteps of Christ. And to attain this ideal of interior simplicity they rejected all additions, all modifications, embracing in its primitive simplicity that traditional monastic life which St. Benedict had organised with such genius, and which in its very simplicity has proved itself to be of no one age or country, but possible in every age and in every place.

The *Instituta* or 'Regulations of the Monks coming from Molesmes,' drawn up under St. Alberic, and completed under

---

[1] 'L'Esprit de Simplicité, caractéristique de Cîteaux,' etc. (Westmalle. 1928).

his successor St. Stephen, have been handed down to us in the *Exordium*, and we thus have detailed and authentic information as to the manner in which the Holy Rule was actually observed at Cîteaux. They began by suppressing all that was not to be found in the Rule or life of the Patriarch and by re-establishing all that he directly ordains. There are points, however, where St. Benedict does not descend to details, and where there is room for divergence of interpretation. In such cases their interpretation is always on the side of austerity, poverty and simplicity. These primitive Regulations deal with four points, all of which relate to monastic simplicity.

First, in the matter of clothing and bedding, rejecting the use of furs and linen and costly materials of any kind ; and in food, forbidding the use of flesh meat, or of anything beyond what St. Benedict prescribes, either in quantity or quality.

Secondly, in the matter of temporal resources ; and here the reform was even more radical. In an age when monasteries derived their revenues from ecclesiastical benefices, from tithes, farms, and the labour of serfs, and when manual labour had fallen into disuse, Cîteaux renounced all these sources of income, retaining only as much land as the monks themselves could cultivate around the monastery, and at a distance, with the assistance of lay brethren, or *conversi*, and of hired workmen. The principle was clearly laid down, that the monks were to live by their own labour (chiefly by agriculture and the rearing of cattle), and the assistance of lay brethren and workmen was permitted, not to dispense them from this, but to ensure the better observance of Rule in two respects : first, to provide sufficient resources for the fulfilment of the great monastic duty of hospitality and charity to the poor ; and secondly, for the care of granges distant from the monastery, in order that the monks might live within their enclosure, and devote themselves without interruption to the Divine Office and the other regular exercises—' for, according to the Rule, monks ought to dwell in their cloister.' Moreover, to safeguard still further this spirit of separation from the world, the monasteries were to be built in solitary places, remote from towns or even villages.

The law of enclosure was also restored, the Duke of Burgundy himself and other nobles being forbidden to hold their court in the monastery on great festivals, as had been the custom. Unworldliness could hardly go further than thus to incur the risk of alienating for ever their chief benefactor, on whom at the time they were practically dependent.

Lastly, the return to simplicity and poverty was extended to the church itself and to all the ornaments used in divine worship. The sacred vessels were not to be of gold, but of silver gilt, and the censers of brass ; a single candlestick, and that of iron, was permitted. The chasubles were of wool or linen, instead of silk, or gold or silver tissue. Gold or silver crucifixes were forbidden, and wooden crosses, painted in a life-like manner with the Figure of the Crucified, took their place. All these and other similar details may perhaps seem trivial or exaggerated to modern minds, but it must be remembered that each of them was a deliberate protest against the excessive elaboration of the Cluniac churches, as being opposed to monastic poverty and humility. The intention of the founders of Cîteaux was ' that in the House of God, where they wished to serve God with devotion, day and night, nothing might remain which savoured of pride or superfluity, or which might injure that poverty, the guardian of the virtues, which they had voluntarily embraced.' This word ' poverty ' constantly recurs ; these ' new Knights of Christ ' were to be ' poor with the Poor Christ '—*cum paupere Christo pauperes*—phrases which seem like a foreshadowing of the Franciscan ideal. But there is a difference. Cistercian poverty is not the ' beatitude of destitution ' of the mendicant friar, begging his bread along the highways of the world, but rather that absence of superfluity to which St. Benedict so constantly recurs. Though ecclesiastical revenues and feudal dues were forbidden, St. Stephen himself notes with joy the rapid extension of farm lands and vineyards at Cîteaux, ' *without any detriment to regular observance.*' For St. Benedict, individual poverty was complete ; but while owning nothing, the monk was to hope for all things necessary from the Father of the monastery, and the community, therefore, must be sufficiently provided with temporal resources. Simplicity rather than actual want was the Cistercian form of poverty—just what nature requires, neither more nor less.

Simplicity in food and dress and the externals of daily life ; solitude and separation from the world ; manual labour for the support of life ; liturgical prayer still the chief, but no longer the only work of monks, and shorn of its gorgeous setting ; such are the main lines of the Cistercian reform as outlined in its earliest document ; and they are no other than the traditional features of the older monasticism. As M. Guignard points out,[1] ' it is precisely those primitive regulations ' drawn up by St. Alberic and St. Stephen, ' that were henceforward to distinguish the White Monks or Cistercians from the Black Monks or Cluniacs,' and it is in them, therefore, that we find ' the particular spirit, the special character ' of the new Order. The principles were thus clearly established from the outset, and had only to be applied, when the expansion began, to other departments, such as architecture, which are not specifically mentioned in the *Exordium* itself. Unity of purpose, simplicity of aim, the power of concentrating on essentials and eliminating everything non-essential, characterised the founders of Cîteaux. They did not discard external means of leading the soul to God, but they combined an unerring selection of just those means which really served their purpose, with a drastic curtailment of mere accessories and trimmings. In architecture, for instance, it would be a mistake to see in the austere simplicity of the earlier Cistercian churches a rigid puritanism or an enmity to the beautiful. It is rather the concentration on beauty of line and proportion, to the exclusion of a mass of ornamental detail and elaborate carving, which only served to arrest the eye and keep it from following the soaring lines of column and vaulting, so fitted to lead the spirit Godward.

It was only by degrees, however, that the full consequences of the principles they had started from were perceived. The Cistercian ideal did not come into being all at once, but was gradually evolved during a period of twenty years or more. This is clearly seen in the works produced in the

---

[1] *Monuments primitifs de la Règle Cistercienne* (Dijon, 1878), Preface, p. xxix.

scriptoria of the early Cistercian monasteries. It is remarkable that the earliest manuscripts of Cîteaux—including the great Bible—though produced amid extreme poverty, were richly ornamented with decorative initials and exquisite miniatures. Gradually, however, it came to be seen that this was inconsistent with the principles of the reform ; the decorative work was therefore simplified, and the rule came into force—though only finally laid down by the General Chapter of 1134—that the initial letters were to be ' of one colour only, and without paintings.' The typical Cistercian manuscript has the beauty of simplicity, with its clear and well-formed script, and its graceful capitals in plain colour, whereas in the elaborately illuminated manuscripts the ornamentation often served rather to obscure than to embellish the written text.

In all this, the early Cistercians were truly men *pulchritudinis studium habentes*—' studying beautifulness '—but of material beauty they sought only that which was apt to raise the mind to its Creator, and not merely to charm the senses or captivate the imagination. To them, the monastery was exactly what St. Benedict intended it to be, ' a school of the Lord's service,' where no other art was practised for its own sake, but only as subservient to the art of arts— that of forming souls to the perfect likeness of Christ.

In the Cistercian chant we find the same principles. The Cistercians did not, like the Carthusians, deliberately restrict their melodies, but they sought out the authentic Gregorian chants in their purest form, omitting the elaborate ornamental passages which in some cases had been introduced ; this, however, less from ascetic motives than from the desire to conform to the most authentic traditions—but here, again, tradition meant simplicity.

For this simplicity in externals went hand in hand, or, rather, was one thing with that passion for authenticity, which showed itself as much in matters liturgical as in questions of regular observance. And so it came about that this handful of monks, dwelling in wooden huts in a marsh, and engaged in wresting a scanty livelihood from a hitherto untilled soil, undertook the gigantic task of making a complete revision, not only of all the liturgical texts and chants,

but of the entire Bible. The initiative as well as the execution of the revision of the Bible is generally, and no doubt
rightly, ascribed to St. Stephen. The work was, however,
almost entirely carried out while St. Alberic was still Abbot
of Cîteaux, being completed in 1109, the year of his death.
We can only allude in passing to this remarkable achieve-
ment, which has its own place in the history of the text of
Holy Scripture.[1] Not only did St. Stephen carefully collate
all the Latin versions he could discover, but he compared the
New Testament with the original Greek, and for the Old
Testament, distressed at the variations in the current
versions, he consulted some learned Jewish Rabbis, to
ascertain the readings found in the Hebrew and Chaldean
texts. No pains were spared to obtain the most correct and
authentic text possible—*ut veraciorem sequeremur*, as St.
Stephen himself expressed it—and this is simply another
manifestation of that same spirit of truth, of sincerity,
which had led the founders of Cîteaux to return to the exact
following of the Rule of St. Benedict.

This chapter may fitly be concluded with the summary
of the Cistercian ideal given by a Benedictine historian, Dom
Berlière :

' The Cistercian programme was simple and clear : the
return to the letter of the Benedictine Rule, without any
compromise with the customs introduced in the course
of ages, the practice of poverty in the daily performance of
manual labour, a life of penance in the pure and simple
acceptance of the Rule laid down by St. Benedict, a life
of prayer in the celebration of liturgical offices restored to a
greater simplicity, an interior life in solitude, without heed
to any other intellectual occupation than that of nourishing
the soul with holy reading, total self-abnegation, complete
sacrifice of the things of the world, entire surrender to the
service of God ; in short, the ideal of Cîteaux was to leave all
things in order to seek God alone.'[2] *Si vere Deum quærit !*

---

[1] Cf. note by Fr. Thurston, S.J., to ch. XV of his edition of the *Life of
St. Stephen Harding*, by Fr. Dalgairns (1898). The Bible, a sumptuous
work in four volumes, is preserved in the Municipal Library at Dijon.
The fourth volume, with two other contemporary MSS. from Cîteaux, was
exhibited at Burlington House in 1932, in the Exhibition of French Art.

[2] *L'Ordre Monastique*, p. 272.

CHAPTER III

THE ORDER OF CÎTEAUX

In the life thus established at Cîteaux, Alberic, Stephen and their companions found peace and contentment of heart, and that supernatural joy which is the lot of those who have chosen God alone for their portion. Though they were reduced at times to the extremity of poverty, this troubled them little; their only sorrow was that so few came to join them. To their contemporaries their ideal seemed an impossible one, and beyond human strength to attain, and those who came to see their way of life, or even heard of it, rather fled in horror from them than sought their fellowship. In the monastic world of the day their enterprise was the common subject of gossip, and its failure was confidently predicted—*de perseverantia titubare non cessabant*. Alberic died in 1109 without seeing the fruit of his labours. The *Exordium* thus records his death: ' Now the man of God Alberic, having been happily exercised in the school of Christ by the discipline of the Rule for nine and a half years, departed to the Lord, a man glorious in faith and virtue.' Stephen's discourse in Chapter on this occasion has been preserved; in it he laments the loss ' not only of a father and ruler, but a friend, a fellow-soldier, and a mighty warrior in the battles of the Lord.' Alberic was never canonised by the Church, but by the devotion of the faithful; the Cistercian Order keeps his feast on January 26, the day of his death. Stephen Harding was unanimously elected to succeed him. One of the evidences of Stephen's authorship of the *Exordium* is the striking contrast between his praises of Alberic and the brief allusion to his own election. He describes himself merely as ' a certain brother, Stephen by name, English by race, who had come with the others from Molesmes to Cîteaux, and was a lover of the Rule and of the monastery.'

He appears to have been in no way discouraged by the declining state of the New Monastery. On the contrary, with an imperturbable trust in Divine Providence, he continued the work of consolidation on the original lines. It was under his rule that the *Instituta* or Statutes, of which we have spoken above, were completed, by the regulations concerning ecclesiastical ornaments. No compromise here in order to attract recruits. The exclusion of the Duke of Burgundy and his court was a still bolder challenge to Providence. Stephen's faith was to be rewarded, but it was first to be tried to the uttermost. In 1111 a severe epidemic broke out in the community, and Stephen saw his sons carried off one after another by the hand of death. For a moment even his confidence was shaken. Was it a sign from God that the reform was not pleasing to Him? Were the critics of Cîteaux right after all, and was the mortality a punishment for their presumption in attempting to live more strictly than others? He would seek from God the answer to his fears. At the deathbed of one of his monks, in presence of the assembled community, Stephen commanded the dying brother by virtue of obedience, ' in whatever way the grace of Our Lord may determine, that thou return to us and give us information touching this our state, as far as His mercy will allow.' A few days after the death of the brother, Stephen was working in the fields with his brethren. During the interval for rest the dead brother appeared to him in glory and gave him the assurance he sought. ' Lay aside all doubt,' he said, ' and hold it for certain that your life and conversation is holy and pleasing to God. Moreover, thy grief at thy want of children shall very soon be turned to joy and triumph ; for even yet the children of thy barrenness shall cry in thine ears, " the place is too strait for us, make us room to dwell in." For, behold, the Lord will send unto you many noble and learned . . . and like bees swarming they shall fly away and spread themselves through many lands.'

The prophecy was soon fulfilled. In April, 1112, thirty-two young men, of the noblest families of Burgundy, knocked at the gates of the *Novum Monasterium* and demanded admission to the novitiate. The tide had turned. And not only had that steady stream of novices, which never afterwards ceased, begun to flow, but Cîteaux had gained the apostle she needed, for at the head of the band was Bernard of Fontaines, then twenty-one years of age.

Bernard was born at the Castle of Fontaines-lès-Dijon in 1091. His father Tescelin and his mother Aleth belonged to the *haute noblesse* of Burgundy; but Aleth was also a saint, and from her Bernard drew his early piety. The third of seven sons, his physical frailty and precocious intelligence marked him out as better suited to a learned than a military career, and he was sent to study humanities at Châtillon-sur-Seine, under the Canons of St. Vorles. At twenty years of age, his studies completed, his mother dead, he was about to proceed to Germany for a course of higher studies. But he had already heard the call of God, and in the autumn of 1111 his final decision was made. No further opposition could move him. He would be a monk, and a monk of Cîteaux. Bernard was not one to do things by halves. There was a vehemence, a precipitancy in his character, which impelled him to the most complete holocaust. Nor would he enter alone. He became the apostle of Cîteaux before entering the novitiate. His uncle, Gaudry, a married man and the father of a family, was his first conquest; then his four brothers, Bartholomew, Andrew, Guido, and Gerard, Guido likewise a husband and father; friends and other relatives—soldiers, clerics, students, men of the world—thirty-two in all—for Bernard's powers of persuasion were irresistible. All these he brought together in his father's house at Châtillon, where for six months they lived in retreat, a kind of community life, with Bernard, of course, as Superior. The thirty-three took the road to Cîteaux on that April morning of the year 1112; one, however, lost courage at the eleventh hour, and Bernard's cousin, Robert, a boy of fifteen, was considered by Stephen too young for admittance.

Bernard gave himself unreservedly to the life he had chosen; he set himself to achieve monastic perfection with the same whole-heartedness and tenacity with which he would have devoted himself to any other profession. During his novitiate he constantly asked himself the question: *Bernarde, ad quid venisti?* This unremitting pursuit of the end in view was wholly in accordance with the spirit of Cîteaux. In humility and obedience, in silence and recollection, none could equal him. In the manual labour he was less successful. His first efforts in the harvest fields resulted in exhaustion to himself and peril to any who came within range of his scythe or reaping hook. He was put to sweep the monastery or chop wood, but his indomitable perseverance was such that in the end he excelled in the fields as everywhere else. In him, certainly, genius could be defined as an infinite capacity for taking pains.

This novitiate of Bernard's must never be allowed to be eclipsed by the achievements of his maturity. If any man ever exemplified Christ's saying : ' Unless the grain of wheat falling into the ground die, itself remaineth alone. But if it die, it bringeth forth much fruit,' that man was Bernard of Fontaines. In entering Cîteaux he turned his back for ever, as he sincerely believed, on fame or greatness of any kind, to bury himself in an obscure, despised, and apparently moribund foundation, thus carrying out first in his own life the *Ama nesciri* which he was afterwards to preach to others. His name has evoked a chorus of admiration and praise from writers of every creed and none. For the most part, they admire and praise in him that which was only secondary and accidental : the greatness of his gifts, his influence and his achievements ; more rarely, as in the case of the Positivist, Frederick Harrison, the perfect beauty of his character. Almost all forget that those great gifts of his, he deliberately and with open eyes offered in sacrifice to God, to remain for ever unused, and that that perfection of character was the finished product of the very monastic discipline to which, at the most plastic age, he wholly yielded himself. It was in the novitiate of Cîteaux, under the guidance of St. Stephen, that that fine steel was so finely tempered. In one short year Bernard fulfilled a long course, and himself became the personification of that ideal of the Cistercian religious to which he was afterwards to draw multitudes of souls.

At the end of the year's probation, all but one of the novices made their profession. Then the foundations began : La Ferté (Firmitas), to the south of Cîteaux, in May, 1113 ; Pontigny, to the west, a year later— Pontigny, where two great Archbishops of Canterbury, St. Thomas and St. Edmund, were to take refuge in their exile and to receive the Cistercian habit. In June, 1115, Clairvaux and Morimond—Clairvaux to the north, Morimond to the east—so that the four eldest daughters of Cîteaux lay at the four points of the compass, each becoming in turn the centre of a further expansion. Bernard, scarcely two years professed, was placed at the head of the colony sent to found Clairvaux, which consisted, according to Cistercian usage, of twelve religious with a Superior, representing Christ and His apostles. Among the twelve, St. Stephen included Bernard's uncle, his four brothers, and two cousins—a detail which of itself is enough to show how far the spirit of the early Cistercians was from any kind of harsh rigorism, and how full, on the contrary, of humanity and Christian charity. In them the love of God did not destroy but only supernaturalised and therefore strengthened the bonds of human affection. Bernard's father Tescelin and his youngest brother Nivard were soon to join him at Clairvaux.

The reform of Cîteaux, based as it was on a clearly conceived idea, had now taken root and begun to flourish. But Stephen knew by long experience that it was easier to make foundations than to keep up strict observance, when the primitive fervour had begun to wane. He had no mind to leave the four daughter houses to share the fate of Molesmes, and he began to think out a means of maintaining unity of observance among them. He began by convoking an annual assembly of the Abbots at the mother house— a General Chapter, in fact. The first of these was held in 1116. This, however, was not enough. As the number of monasteries increased, the need was felt of a Constitution which should form a bond of union between the different houses, and thus maintain intact the observance of Cîteaux. Stephen gradually matured his project, which reached its decisive form in the *Charta Charitatis*,[1] promulgated by

---

[1] i.e. ' Charter of Charity,' usually, by a Gallicism, called in English the ' Chart of Charity.'

the Chapter of 1119, when the houses already numbered twelve or more. The purpose of the *Charta Charitatis* is stated in the opening words, with characteristic clarity and conciseness. ' Seeing that we all acknowledge ourselves to be the servants, however unworthy, of one true King, Lord, and Master, therefore we do not impose on the Abbots and brethren of our monasteries . . . any temporal exactions. . . . But we nevertheless desire to retain the care of their souls for the sake of charity : so that if at any time they should attempt to turn aside from their holy purpose and the observance of the Holy Rule (which God forbid), they may through our solicitude return to uprightness of living.' . . . ' Now, therefore, we will and ordain that they observe in all things the Rule of St. Benedict as it is observed in the New Monastery. Let them not introduce any other meaning into the text of the Holy Rule, but as our holy fathers and predecessors, that is, the monks of the New Monastery, understood and observed it, so let them also understand and observe it.'

Cîteaux itself had been a return to tradition, and St. Stephen's object now is the maintenance of that tradition. The Chart of Charity is his chief title to fame, and by it he ranks as one of the greatest of monastic legislators. The idea of unification in itself was no novelty, as we have seen. From St. Benedict of Aniane onwards it has been the constant problem in Benedictine history. St. Benedict's conception of monastic government is patriarchal ; the monastery is a family, of which the Abbot is the Father. This essentially carries with it the idea of the independence and autonomy of each monastery. At the same time, there is in all human institutions an inevitable tendency to decadence and to a falling away from their first principles, and this required some check. From the eighth century onwards, attempts were made to solve this problem, but it was reserved for the genius of St. Stephen to achieve the blending of the two ideas—to effect a real vital union between the different monasteries without sacrificing anything of the independent family life of each. The *Charta Charitatis* was not the imposing of a code of regulations by a superior authority, such as was attempted by

Benedict of Aniane ; neither was it the setting up of a centralised monarchy like Cluny. It was simply the application of St. Benedict's conception of family life and abbatial authority, extended to the wider family, the Order. For by the Chart of Charity the monasteries of Cîteaux were formed into a religious Order properly so called, and it is in the Chart of Charity that we find the expression ' our Order ' used for the first time in the modern sense.

The government is still patriarchal in character. Each foundation, or rather *filiation*, while becoming an autonomous abbey, is to remain in certain respects under the supervision of the Abbot of the mother house—the *Pater Abbas* or *Pater Immediatus*—who is to make an annual Visitation, but solely with a view to ascertaining that regular observance is maintained intact. Cîteaux itself is to be visited by the Abbots of the first four foundations—La Ferté, Pontigny, Clairvaux, Morimond. The Abbot of Cîteaux, therefore, while holding a certain rank of pre-eminence, is in no sense a monarchical ruler like the Abbot of Cluny. The supreme authority of the Order rests, not with him, but with the General Chapter, which is to meet annually, and which all the Abbots of the Order are under strict obligation to attend. The General Chapter is to treat of what concerns the good of souls ; to maintain regular observance, and to correct abuses ; and to strengthen the bonds of peace and charity. The ultimate legislative power thus rests solely with the Abbots of the Order, *ex officio*, and the family life of the monastery remains intact. The *Pater Abbas* may not interfere with the temporal affairs of his filiations, much less dispose of their *personnel*. He is simply to exercise a paternal vigilance, and to see that they remain faithful to the family traditions. Thus the Cistercian ideal of unity is attained : ' that we all live united in the observance of one and the same Rule, according to the same customs and in a common charity.'

It was not a theoretic scheme, conceived first and then applied ; it grew from the historical circumstances. With the growth of the Cistercian family came the solicitude for maintaining the bond of union and the spirit and traditions of the family ; and to meet this desire the

Chart of Charity was framed. 'Maintained in this union by the duties of a mutual deference, they form a single Church, a single Order, a single Body in Jesus Christ'; while at the same time each individual monastery is a 'church'—*Ecclesia*—an organic body of which the Abbot, representing Christ, is the Head, and which possesses the principle of fecundity common to all organic life. St. Stephen's genius lay in the application of this principle to the constitution of an Order. The union between the houses is not an artificial bond, or a merely geographical aggregation; it is the living bond of filiation, based on the natural law of fecundity. In an audience granted in 1926 to the then Abbot General of the Cistercians of the Strict Observance, His Holiness Pope Pius XI congratulated the Order on the example of union it now presents to the Church, and expressed his admiration of that union, based as it is on the 'Hierarchy of Mother Houses and Daughter Houses, which brings into religion that which is most profound and most vital in nature.' This union was to be the strength of the Order of Cîteaux and the source of its immense influence and expansion during the first two centuries of its existence, as it was also to be the vital principle of all the later movements of renewal and reform. The observance of the Chart of Charity has ever been the touchstone of the vitality of the Order.

The Chart of Charity was presented by St. Stephen to the General Chapter of 1119, and accepted unanimously. The next step in the work of consolidation was to obtain Papal approbation, and the Bull granting this was issued by Callixtus II at Saulieu on December 23, 1119. Together with the Chart of Charity, Stephen presented to the Pope the *Exordium*, of which we have spoken above, which contained the primitive Statutes of Cîteaux, with an historical statement of the circumstances of the foundation. These Statutes 'touching the manner of observing the Rule of St. Benedict' were approved and confirmed by Callixtus II at the same time as the *Charta Charitatis*.

One of the fundamental points of the Chart of Charity was the maintenance of uniformity in the observances. To ensure this, the *Liber Usuum* or *Consuetudines* was drawn up, probably between 1120 and 1125, regulating both the order of celebrating Mass and the Divine Office, and in general, all the customs of monastic life. On this book all the subsequent regulations of the Order have been based, and its ordinances are still faithfully carried out in every Cistercian monastery.

The Order of Cîteaux was now firmly established and could expand freely ; the spread of the Order during the first century of its existence is unparalleled in monastic history. At the death of St. Stephen in 1134, thirty-six years after the foundation of Cîteaux, there were already seventy-seven houses ; twenty years later, at the death of St. Bernard, there were 343, and within the second century of its existence the Order was to number 742 houses of monks and 900 of nuns. This fertility may be ascribed to two causes : first, the extraordinary ascendancy of St. Bernard's personality and the extent of his influence ; and secondly, the fidelity to tradition ensured by the Chart of Charity with its system of annual Visitations and General Chapters.

St. Bernard's power of drawing souls to God was not to remain inactive after his entrance at Cîteaux. Yet, even as Abbot of Clairvaux, the field of his influence would have been a restricted one, but for the providential circumstances which drew him out of his cloister in the interests of the Church. We are not concerned here with his manifold activities as counsellor of Popes and Emperors, peacemaker between states, destroyer of heresies, preacher of the Holy War ; incessantly journeying, his heart ever with his children at Clairvaux, and his soul with God, for, as his old biographer tells us, he carried with him everywhere his interior solitude, and while wholly occupied with external labours, never withdrew his attention from God within. He himself bitterly lamented this life of action imposed on him by obedience, and described himself as ' the chimera of his age, neither clerk nor layman, wearing the habit of a monk and living like a worldling.' His journeyings on the affairs of the Church, however, became the providential means of a still more fruitful monastic apostolate. Wherever he went, the charm of his personality and the splendour of his sanctity drew all hearts to him ;

vocations and foundations multiplied, and the Cistercian ideal, with all its austerity, spread like a contagion throughout a Christendom which had only too much need of the salt of penance to preserve it from corruption.

And St. Bernard was not merely the propagator of the Order, but its animating spirit. He who had imbibed so thoroughly the spirit of Cîteaux in his novitiate was afterwards to impress his own spirit on the entire Order. For the spirituality of the Cistercian Order was—and ever has been, when the Order has been true to its traditions—the spirituality of St. Bernard. The predominant devotion to the mystery of the Incarnation, which has left so strong an impress on the Cistercian liturgy and ceremonial; the devotion to the Person of Our Lord, to His Sacred Humanity, and above all, to His Passion and Death; the place given to the honouring of the Mother of God; —all these, which became the distinguishing features of Cistercian spirituality, owe their primary inspiration to the spirit and writings of St. Bernard. It was in his sermons in the chapter house at Clairvaux that he gave his inmost soul to his spiritual sons, mingling the sublimest teaching on divine love with the most homely details of domestic life in the monastery. In the Sermons on the Canticle of Canticles, St. Bernard describes the ascent of the soul to the highest mystical union with the Word—a union which he always conceives as a union of wills. It is the conformity of the human will with the divine which ' marries the soul to the Word '; [1] and the road to that union is the love of the Humanity of Christ; ' the healthful love of His Flesh,' which ' leads, little by little, to spiritual love.'[2] This love is acquired, above all, by the contemplation of the Sufferings of Christ: ' This is my sublimest philosophy—to know Jesus, and Him Crucified.'[3] Divine love is the whole burden of his spiritual doctrine, and this was the secret of that power of attraction, that *élan*, which made it possible for such countless souls to embrace a life so austere and hard to nature. ' The world sees our cross,' says St. Bernard,

[1] *In Cantica Canticorum, Sermo LXXXIII*, 3.
[2] *Ibid., Sermo XX*, 6.
[3] *Ibid., Sermo XLIII*, 4.

D

' but not the unction which renders the cross sweet.' That
unction was the love of Christ. A young Cistercian monk
who fell in Flanders in 1917 showed himself a true son of
St. Bernard when he wrote in his note-book as a novice :
' Our religious life is not *something* ; it is *Someone* : it is
Jesus—Jesus and His service.'[1]

At Clairvaux seven hundred monks and lay brothers lived
under the immediate influence of St. Bernard, and during his
government no less than sixty-eight foundations were made,
in almost every country of Europe, so that the extent of his
influence can hardly be exaggerated. Copies, moreover, of
his sermons and writings were multiplied and passed from
one monastery to another. A whole school of Cistercian
spiritual writers during the twelfth and thirteenth centuries
reflects the teaching of St. Bernard—William of St. Thierry,
Blessed Guerric, and others, and in our own country St.
Aelred of Rievaulx and Gilbert of Hoyland. Gilbert was a
disciple of St. Bernard, and seems to have especially imbibed
his spirit, so that he was asked to continue the explanation
of the Canticle of Canticles where St. Bernard had left off.

The Cistercian ideal took firm root in England at a very
early date, and proved to be particularly congenial to the
English character. The monasteries of the Order in Great
Britain and Ireland outnumbered those of every other
country except France. The first coming of the Cistercians
to England was due to William Gifford, the Norman Bishop
of Winchester, who obtained a colony of monks from
L'Aumône in the Orléanais (a filiation of Cîteaux), and established them at Waverley, near Farnham in Surrey, in
November, 1128. Waverley Abbey became the mother of
eleven other monasteries. The next foundation was Tintern,
in Monmouthshire, in 1131. Rievaulx was founded either in
1131 or in 1132, by a colony sent from Clairvaux by St.
Bernard himself, and headed by Bernard's secretary William.
The place chosen for the new monastery was a deep and
gloomy valley called Blackmore, through which ran a stream
called the Rye—hence *Rievaulx*—a damp and marshy spot,
like Cîteaux itself. While the foundation was still in its

[1] Octave Daumont : *Une Ame Contemplative : P. Maxime Carlier* (1921),
p. 139.

earliest stages of poverty and obscurity, a young Saxon of noble birth, who had been brought up at the court of David, King of Scotland, entered the novitiate. This was Aelred, who has been called the 'English Bernard,' and who, like Bernard himself, gave up everything the world has to offer, to bury himself and his great gifts in an obscure Cistercian monastery. Abbot William, however, discerned his abilities and made him Novice-Master, and in 1142 sent him to found the Abbey of Revesby in Lincolnshire. A few years later, on the death of William, he was elected Abbot of Rievaulx, where he remained till his death in 1167, ruling over a community of three hundred monks. St. Aelred was canonised in 1191 by Pope Celestine III. He has left ascetical works of great merit, the most important of which is the *Speculum Charitatis*—' Mirror of Charity '—and many of his sermons are extant. He also wrote the *Life of St. Ninian*, and other biographical and historical works. His eulogy was pronounced by his friend Gilbert of Hoyland, Abbot of Swineshead in Lincolnshire, who, on receiving the news of his death, interrupted his discourse on the Canticle of Canticles to draw a beautiful portrait of Aelred's character and virtues.[1]

Fountains Abbey, also in Yorkshire, was founded in 1132 by a group of monks from the Benedictine Abbey of St. Mary's, York. These monks, fired by the example of the Cistercians of Rievaulx, determined to carry out the Rule of St. Benedict in its integrity. They had to suffer bitter persecution from the community of St. Mary's, but Archbishop Thurstan took them under his protection, and settled them in a wild valley called Skell-dale, near Ripon. The Saxon word *skel* means ' spring,' and the Latin name of the Skell-dale Monastery was *Sancta Maria de Fontanis*— hence Fountains Abbey. The chronicler describes it as ' a place uninhabited for all the centuries back, thickset with thorns, lying between the slopes of mountains and among rocks jutting out on both sides; fit, rather, to be the lair of wild beasts than the home of human beings.' In this unpromising spot the twelve monks settled in midwinter,

[1] See the delightful study of St. Aelred by the late Father Bede Jarrett, O.P., in *The English Way* (1933).

building for themselves a rough shelter around the trunk of a great elm which stood in the midst of the valley, roofing it with turf spread over the branches of the elm. Such were the beginnings of most of the Cistercian monasteries, and the beautiful fertile valleys in which they stood only took their present aspect as the result of hard and prolonged toil on the part of the monastic settlers. Richard, the ex-Prior of St. Mary's, York, was elected Abbot, and it was decided to send two monks to Clairvaux, asking St. Bernard to receive the new community into the Order of Cîteaux, and to send someone to instruct them in the Cistercian mode of life. St. Bernard received the messengers with the utmost kindness, and sent a letter of congratulation to Fountains, in which he wrote : ' This is the finger of God, working with subtlety, sweetly renovating, healthfully changing ; not making the bad good, but the good better. Oh, that I might go and see this great sight ! For the advance from good to better is no less admirable than the change from bad to good. Indeed, it were more easy to find many men of the world converted to good, than one religious passing from good to better. He is a *rarissima avis in terra* who ascends even a little above the degree he had attained in his first fervour.' Moreover, St. Bernard sent back with the messengers his secretary Geoffrey, a monk of age and experience, who had already been employed in many foundations. Geoffrey instructed the monks in the Cistercian chant, as well as in monastic customs, and under his guidance a temporary monastery of wooden huts was built, according to the Cistercian plan. Not till 1135 was the stone monastery begun, the ruins of which, at least those of the earlier portions, remain as the most perfect example in England of the best period of Cistercian architecture.

Rievaulx and Fountains both gave rise to many new monasteries. The earliest foundation from Fountains was Newminster in Northumberland, the first Abbot of which, St. Robert of Newminster, formerly a monk of Whitby Abbey, had joined those who seceded from St. Mary's, York.

Soon the Cistercian monasteries spread throughout the land, especially in the north—in Yorkshire alone there were eight Cistercian Abbeys. Lincolnshire possessed five ; in

Leicestershire there was Garendon, near which has sprung up the present Cistercian Abbey of Mount St. Bernard. Buckfast in Devon and Quarr in the Isle of Wight have both risen up again, rebuilt by the Black Monks. There were Netley and Beaulieu in Hampshire, Bindon in Dorset, Cleeve in Somerset, where the monastic buildings still stand, typically Cistercian in their solid simplicity ; Buildwas in Shropshire, Boxley near Rochester, and many others ; some whose beautiful ruins are yet in existence, recalling their past glories, others of which little or no trace remains. ' The Order,' writes Fr. Dalgairns, ' seems to have thriven in St. Stephen's native air . . . (it) took to itself all the quiet nooks and valleys, and all the pleasant streams of old England, and gladdened the soul of the labourer by its constant bells. Its agricultural character was peculiarly suited to this country, though it took its birth beyond the seas.'[1] And an old monastic chronicler records how ' the simple folk wondered to see the hooded race performing at certain hours the Work of God, and at others occupied with rural labours.'

St. Stephen died in 1134, and Waverley, Tintern, Rievaulx, Fountains, Buildwas, and Garendon at least were in existence before his death. Furness, founded by King Stephen in 1127, did not become Cistercian till 1147.

The total number of Cistercian monasteries in England and Wales was seventy-five. In Scotland there were eleven, Melrose being the first. Melrose, Jedburgh, Kelso, and Dryburgh were all founded by King David between 1136 and 1153, in that troublous Border country. The Cistercian Order was introduced into Ireland by St. Malachy O'Morghair, Bishop of Down, the friend of St. Bernard. The Abbey of Mellifont in Co. Louth was founded by him in 1142, the first monks having been trained at Clairvaux under St. Bernard, who sent some of his own monks with them to assist in the foundation. Five foundations were made from Mellifont during St. Bernard's life-time, and at the time of the dissolution there were forty-two houses of the Order in Ireland, and two monasteries of Cistercian nuns, one in Down and one in Derry. In England and Wales there were

[1] *Life of St. Stephen Harding* (1898), p. 203.

twenty-six houses of Cistercian nuns, ten of which were in
Yorkshire alone.

One and all were swept away in the sixteenth century,
from the great abbeys whose wealth attracted the King's
greed, down to the humblest priories, like that little priory
of nuns which stood on Wintney Moor in Hampshire, the
annual value of which was estimated at £52 5s. 8d. There
were ten nuns there at the time of the dissolution, ' by
reporte of good conversation, which trooley desieren to
contynue in the same religion.'[1]   But King Henry's Commissioners cared little for their desires, and all alike were
ruthlessly thrust out of their silent cloisters into a world
which they had long since left for God.   In the case of the
Cistercians, the breach with the past was complete ;   more
than two and a half centuries were to elapse before Cistercian
life was resumed on English soil, brought back by the
victims of a yet fiercer persecution than that of Henry Tudor.

[1] J. C. Cox, *Hampshire* (1929), p. 128.

CHAPTER IV

CISTERCIAN NUNS

WE saw how in the beginnings of cenobitic life, communities of women were formed under the Rule of St. Pachomius, following in all things the life led by the monks. Among them were personalities such as that ' attractive and virile Mother Sarah, who, disgusted with the ways of the monks about her, used to say : " It is I who am a man and you who are women." '[1] St. Pachomius' sister was the foundress of these nuns, and in a later age St. Benedict's sister, St. Scholastica, was likewise to share her brother's work. St. Gregory tells us that she consecrated herself to God from her childhood, and when St. Benedict founded Monte Cassino, she settled at Plombariola, about five miles distant, where she ruled over a community of nuns who were evidently under St. Benedict's authority. Parallel with the spread of the monks of St. Benedict was that of the nuns who followed his Rule, and we have seen how the Anglo-Saxon nuns shared even in the missionary labours of the monks. A common feature of early English monasticism was the establishment of double monasteries, the Abbess being often the chief ruler.

When St. Bernard's irresistible powers of persuasion carried with him to Cîteaux so many of his kinsfolk and friends, it was but natural that the women of the family should become fired with the same enthusiasm. There was as yet, however, no monastery of nuns following the observance of Cîteaux to which they could retire. They entered, therefore, Benedictine monasteries, chiefly that of Jully, in the diocese of Langres, which was under the jurisdiction of Molesmes. St. Bernard's only sister, Humbeline, was the last of the family to respond to the call of grace ; however,

[1] Fr. Bede Jarrett, O.P., *The Religious Life* (1919), p. 147.

41

a visit to Clairvaux brought about her conversion in 1117. She could not leave the world without the consent of her husband, and for several years lived a retired and austere life in her own home. At last her husband gave his consent, and she, too, retired to Jully. Succeeding her sister-in-law, Elisabeth, the wife of Guy, as Superior, in 1130, she retained that office until her holy death, some years later. Blessed Humbeline herself lived and died a Benedictine, but during her administration Jully gave rise to the first community of Cistercian nuns, and this, perhaps, is the reason why she has sometimes been spoken of as the foundress of the Cistercian nuns.

In 1125, the project was first formed of a community of nuns carrying out the integral observance of the Rule of St. Benedict as practised at Cîteaux. The project was due to the initiative of St. Stephen, and the place chosen for the foundation was Le Tart, near Dijon, at no great distance from Cîteaux itself. The monastery was, however, only finally established in 1132, by a colony of nuns from Jully. According to a memoir written about the year 1685, ' the Monastery of Notre-Dame de Tart has always been considered in the Church as the parent stem of all the houses of nuns of the holy Order of Cîteaux.' Vocations multiplied, and many foundations were made from Tart. The Cistercian nuns soon spread into all parts of Europe, the expansion following a parallel course to that of the monks. From the beginning, the nuns formed an integral part of the Order of Cîteaux ; equally with the monks, they were subject to the authority of the General Chapter, and their spiritual direction was entrusted to the monks of the Order. Their life was the same in all respects as that of the monks, and they followed the *Consuetudines* of Cîteaux, no special regulations being drawn up for them. A manuscript of the thirteenth century, preserved at Dijon, contains a French translation of the Rule of St. Benedict and the *Consuetudines*, for the use of a community of Cistercian nuns.[1] The translator calls himself *le povre frere Martin*, and was presumably chaplain to a monastery of nuns. In his preface he says that he has altered nothing in the text, except that in

[1] Printed by M. Guignard, *op. cit.*, Appendix I.

certain places he has changed words which apply to men, replacing them by words which apply to women ; as, for instance, abbess for abbot, nun for monk, and so on, ' because I am doing this work for women.' He also omits from the *Consuetudines* certain chapters which apply only to monks, chiefly those dealing with the functions of the priesthood. The same principle has been observed in all subsequent legislation of the Order concerning nuns. It is clear from this that the Cistercian nuns are in no sense a distinct Order, but that their history is bound up with that of the whole Order of Cîteaux, and cannot therefore be treated as a separate subject.

At the same time, though the nuns were under the jurisdiction of the General Chapter, the principle of filiation which formed the bond of union between the monasteries of monks could not, obviously, be fully applied in the case of nuns. There were, however, two cases in which it was thus applied, and in which a certain measure of self-government was granted them. The first Spanish foundation was that of Tulebras in the kingdom of Navarre, in 1134. Many others followed, the most famous being the Monastery of Santa Maria la Real, commonly called *Las Huelgas de Burgos*, founded in 1187 by Alfonso VIII, King of Castile. Owing to the entrance of King Alfonso's own daughter Constance, and other members of the royal houses of Castile and Aragon, Las Huelgas rapidly attained a position of pre-eminence among the Spanish houses, and in 1189 the Abbesses of thirteen dependent monasteries were authorised to assemble there each year in General Chapter, on the feast of St. Martin. In the following year, 1190, a similar authorisation was granted to the eighteen filiations of Tart. The Abbess of Tart presided at these General Chapters, side by side with the Abbot of Cîteaux or his delegate. They were held on the Feast of St. Michael, shortly after the General Chapter of Cîteaux, the enactments of which they adapted to the requirements of the nuns. They also issued statutes specially concerning the nuns, corrected abuses, and imposed penances. Severe penances were imposed on Abbesses who absented themselves from the Chapter without giving a sufficient reason or sending a delegate. The few acts of the Chapter of Tart which have been preserved belong to the latter half of the thirteenth century, and contain strict regulations regarding simplicity in dress and abstinence from meat ; abuses were evidently creeping in, but were promptly dealt with. The Abbesses of Tart and Burgos also made the Regular Visitation in the houses of their filiation, and had full power to correct and punish any deviations from the Rule, provided that they did not ordain anything contrary to the regulations of the Abbot Visitor. These General Chapters and Visitations held by nuns continued uninterruptedly until the Council of Trent, when the laws of enclosure then established forbade the Abbesses to leave their cloister even for such purposes.

The monasteries of Cistercian nuns increased so rapidly in numbers that the Order found it impossible to continue to take the responsibility of their government. The General Chapter of 1228 decreed, therefore, that no further monasteries of nuns subject to the jurisdiction of the Order were to be founded or associated to the Order. Not wishing, however, to stand in the way of this great spiritual movement, which was drawing so many souls to a life of perfection, the Chapter added that they did not forbid any monasteries of nuns to adopt the Cistercian observances, but that they could not undertake the care of their souls or the duty of visitation. It thus came about that in addition to the nine hundred monasteries of nuns under the jurisdiction of the Order, there was an even greater number which followed the Cistercian observance, while remaining under the jurisdiction of the Bishops. These monasteries were especially numerous in the north-east of Germany, and it is now generally admitted[1] that among their number was the famous Abbey of Helfta in Saxony, where St. Gertrude and St. Mechtilde lived their wonderful lives of mystical union —lives which drew their whole inspiration from the liturgical celebration of the Mysteries of Christ, and were characterised by an ardent and tender devotion to the Sacred Humanity. The influence of St. Bernard is particularly marked in the writings of St. Gertrude, and she had a great devotion to

[1] Cf. G. Ledos, *Ste. Gertrude* (Collection ' Les Saints '), Ch. I. P. Pourrat, *Christian Spirituality*, Vol. II (Eng. trans., 1924), p. 85.

him whom she called her *sanctissimus pater*. From St. Bernard she drew the inspiration of that devotion to the Sacred Heart, of which St. Gertrude was the herald, four centuries before St. Margaret Mary.

The Cistercian nuns also flourished especially in the Low Countries, where from the beginning of the thirteenth century there was not only an astonishingly rapid multiplication of foundations, but also a great efflorescence of mystical life, centring chiefly around the Abbey of Villers-en-Brabant, ' the Clairvaux of Belgium,' which governed a large number of houses of nuns. In these monasteries of the Netherlands we find a whole group of mystics, whose lives present very much the same features as those of the nuns of Helfta. Chief among them is St. Lutgarde of Aywières (1182–1246), who died ten years before St. Gertrude's birth, and to whom Our Lord likewise revealed the secrets of His Heart. The vision of Our Lord showing her His Pierced Heart, which turned Lutgarde in earliest youth from earthly to divine love, is the first recorded revelation of the Heart of Jesus.[1] This initial favour was followed by many others, notably that of the ' exchange of hearts ' with Our Lord, afterwards recorded of other saints who have been the confidants of the Sacred Heart—St. Gertrude, St. Mechtilde, St. Catherine of Siena, St. Magdalen of Pazzi, St. Margaret Mary. St. Lutgarde's most famous vision, however, and the scene in which she is most often represented in art, is that of the Crucifix, when the carved Figure of the Crucified came to life, and detaching His Right Arm from the cross, drew the saint towards Him and pressed her against His Heart. All these visions took place while she was still in the Benedictine monastery of St. Catherine at St. Trond in her native Flanders. In 1206 she passed to the Cistercians of Aywières in Brabant, where the remainder of her life was spent as a victim of expiation for the evils

---

[1] M. Georges Goyau writes: ' When Thomas of Cantimpré, Coadjutor Bishop of Cambrai, then Prior of the Dominicans of Louvain, wrote in the thirteenth century his memories of Lutgarde, who had just died, he little knew that he was writing the prologue of a story which reached its culminating point with St. Margaret Mary, four centuries later : the story of the Heart of Christ revealing itself to men and speaking to them.' (*Libre Belgique*, Nov. 1, 1925 ; article reprinted in *La Belle Vie de Ste. Lutgarde*, par l'Abbé Lambert, Curé, Ways, Brabant, 1927.)

of the Church and the conversion of sinners, of whom she was specially called to be the advocate. By this life of penance and suffering she entered more and more deeply into the Mystery of Christ's Passion, to which she became conformed even to the extent of receiving the *stigmata*—the wounds of the Nails and the Crown of Thorns. Her spiritual influence and the fame of her miracles spread far beyond the walls of her monastery, and she is regarded as one of the national saints of Belgium. Her tomb at Aywières was a place of pilgrimage up to the time of the French Revolution, and after the destruction of the Abbey her relics were translated in 1827 to the parish church of Ittre, where they are still venerated.[1]

Others of this group are the three Idas—Blessed Ida of Louvain (d. 1300), who received the stigmata in early youth, and whose subsequent life of suffering and ecstasy was passed at the romantically named Abbey of Roosendael (Val-des-Roses), near Malines ; Blessed Ida of Nivelles (d. 1231) ; and Blessed Ida of Léau, whose life, like St. Gertrude's, combined a familiar intimacy with Our Lord and an ardent love of the liturgy and the science of the Scriptures—*felix amica studii*, her biographer calls her. The two latter were both nuns of La Ramée in Brabant, which became a great centre of sanctity and letters, and was famous for its Scriptorium, where the work of transcribing the liturgical books was carried on. At La Ramée also was trained Blessed Beatrice (d. 1268), spiritual daughter of Ida of Nivelles, and afterwards Prioress of Nazareth, near Lierre—a lover of the Eucharist and Holy Scripture, and likewise favoured with the stigmata. Blessed Aleys of Scharbeek (d. 1250), nun of La Cambre, near Brussels, suffering in a solitary cell the lingering martyrdom of leprosy, healed by her touch others struck with the same fearful malady.

To this school of spirituality belongs also St. Juliana of Mont-Cornillon, at Liége, to whom the Church owes the institution of the festival of Corpus Christi. She was not a

---

[1] Dom Columba Marmion, on one occasion, accompanied Cardinal Mercier to Ittre, and astonished and edified the Cardinal by shedding tears of devotion as he kissed the relics of the saint. (Cf. Dom Raymond Thibaut, *Dom Columba Marmion*, Ch. XII.)

Cistercian, but an Augustinian ; she had, however, deeply imbibed the spirit of Cîteaux, and knew by heart many of St. Bernard's Sermons on the Canticle. Forced to leave the monastery of Mont-Cornillon, of which she was Prioress, owing to the storm of persecution which broke over her on account of her revelations, it was to the Cistercian nuns that she turned for shelter. Four of their monasteries received her in succession, the last being that of Salzinnes, near Namur, but each time she was compelled to flee. She died at Fosses in 1258, assisted by her friend, Blessed Imaine, Abbess of Salzinnes, and at her own wish was laid to rest at Villers, among the monks who had aided and supported her in her many trials.

Blessed Jeanne, daughter of Baldwin, Emperor of Constantinople, and Countess of Flanders—*notre bonne comtesse*, as she was called by her devoted subjects—ended her days as a Cistercian nun in the Abbey of Marquette, near Lille, which she had founded.

Another Cistercian saint of royal origin is St. Hedwig, patroness of Poland, who after the death of her husband, Duke Henry of Poland, entered the monastery of Trebnitz, where her daughter was Abbess, and spent her remaining years in prayer and penance.

These are but a few among those whose lives were marked by exceptional graces or singled out for the honours of canonisation. Besides these, a countless multitude of holy souls have sanctified themselves under the Cistercian rule during the ' Golden Age ' of the Order and throughout its history. Their lives were ' hidden with Christ in God,' known to Him but unknown to men.

CHAPTER V

THE expansion of the Cistercian Order during the first century of its existence extended to every country of Europe, and even to the Near East : northward into Scandinavia, southward to the islands of the Mediterranean, westward to Ireland and Portugal, eastward to Russia and Syria. And this rapid and vast expansion was no mere passing phenomenon—a sudden blaze soon to be extinguished. For two centuries the Order remained at the height of its fervour and prosperity, thanks to its admirable constitution and the vigilance of its General Chapters. The Regular Visits, carried out according to the *Charta Charitatis*, ensured fidelity to the observances, and this fidelity was the secret of that sanctity which was undoubtedly the greatest power of attraction and the source of the immense influence of the Order during its ' Golden Age.' Rarely, surely, in the history even of religious Orders has sanctity been in danger of becoming cheap by reason of its frequency. Yet so it was, for in 1228 the General Chapter decreed that in future no fresh causes of canonisation were to be introduced, *ne multitudine Sancti vilescerent in Ordine*—' lest the Saints of the Order, being too numerous, should fall into disrepute.' Seven centuries later, this Decree was revoked by the General Chapter of 1920.

The wisdom of the *Charta Charitatis* was thus tested by experience, and the General Chapters of Cîteaux became a model which was imitated by the Premonstratensians and other Orders. The Fourth Council of Lateran imposed the holding of General Chapters on the Black Monks ; the Abbots of each kingdom or province were to meet in a triennial assembly, and two Cistercian Abbots were to take part in the initiating of these Chapters, that all might be carried out ' after the manner of the Order of Cîteaux.'

Throughout the ' Golden Age ' the authority of the General Chapter was unquestioned ; its decrees were everywhere obeyed, and its sentences submitted to by all. The Statutes of the General Chapters of this period show a constant endeavour to maintain the observance of the spirit and letter of the *Exordium*, so that a Cistercian historian writes : ' In spite of the abuses which tended to creep in, the Order wished to remain faithful to the poverty, simplicity, and discipline of the early days.'

Insensibly, however, decadence set in. It was a gradual process, to which no definite date can be assigned, and to which many different causes, internal and external, contributed. We will briefly enumerate the chief of these. First and foremost, that which lies at the root of almost every instance of relaxation, whether in a single monastery or in an Order or Congregation—the decline of the spirit of poverty. This was especially ruinous in the case of the Cistercian Order, the very foundations of which had been laid in the practice of poverty and simplicity. That devotion to labour which had been the strength of Cîteaux resulted in a temporal prosperity which in the end proved fatal. The monasteries became wealthy, and Cistercian simplicity inevitably suffered. This can be seen clearly in the development of Cistercian architecture. Simplicity of living could not long survive in an atmosphere of wealth and grandeur, and little by little relaxation crept in. Moreover, the Cistercian Abbots became more and more implicated in secular affairs, to the detriment of the souls committed to their charge. But above all, the General Chapter lost its authority and prestige, and was powerless to check the growing abuses. The very expansion of the Order had carried with it the seeds of decay, since it became impossible to preserve the bonds of unity and the observance of the Chart of Charity when the monasteries were at such immense distances from Cîteaux and often from their own mother house. Regular Visitations and annual attendance at the General Chapter became impracticable in those days of slow and difficult travelling, rendered still more difficult and dangerous by the condition of Europe, torn asunder as it was by wars and strife. External causes contributed to hasten the decadence : the rise of the Mendicant Orders and their growing popularity, which drew to them all that spiritual ardour and enthusiasm of youth which had peopled the monasteries of Cîteaux in the preceding age, the evangelical poverty of the Friars contrasting sadly with the magnificence in which too many Cistercian Abbots lived. Temporal disasters such as the Black Death and the Hundred Years' War, with their consequences of depopulation, famine, and devastation ; the neo-paganism of the Renaissance, with its insidious naturalism infecting men's minds ; the Protestant Reformation, which swept away at a blow all the monasteries of England, Scotland and Ireland, of Holland and Scandinavia, and almost all those of Germany and Switzerland. Lastly, perhaps the most deadly of all, the institution known as the *Commende*, by which an Abbey became a benefice in the royal gift, and was presented to any cleric or layman, or even to a woman or child, who drew the revenues, whilst the monastery was allowed to fall into a state of material and spiritual decay.

Nevertheless, in many of the monasteries efforts were made to react against the forces of decadence and destruction, and during the fifteenth, sixteenth, and seventeenth centuries we find such monasteries forming themselves into Congregations, thus effecting the work of reform, but at the cost of separation from the Order. The same decadence, and the same efforts at reform, appear among the Cistercian nuns. The most famous of the reformed Congregations was that of the Feuillants in France, founded in 1577 by Jean de la Barrière and approved by Sixtus V in 1587. In 1588, Marguerite de Polastron founded the first monastery of Feuillantine nuns, at Mont-Squiou, near Toulouse, these nuns following the same rigorous observance as the Feuillant monks. These reforms, however, are outside the Order, not merely as to jurisdiction, but also in their spirit and observances.

In 1615 we have the beginnings of a revival within the Order itself. Denis Largentier, Abbot of Clairvaux, struck to the heart by the contrast between the Clairvaux of St.

Bernard's day and that of his own, cried out as he knelt at St. Bernard's tomb : *O abbas et abbas !*—' What an Abbot— and what an Abbot ! ' ' Without asking any of his monks to follow him in the way of sacrifice . . . he began to cut off everything that St. Bernard would have condemned in his person and his way of life. On the other hand, he added all the monastic virtues and observances of primitive Cîteaux, its profound piety and traditional austerities. . . . Three months later, he saw himself followed by all his monks . . . pressing close behind him in the rugged ascent back to the ancient observances.'[1] This was the origin of the so-called ' Strict Observance.' Other monasteries followed the example of Clairvaux, and for half a century two Observances existed side by side within the Order—the Mitigated or Common Observance, and the Strict Observance. The latter was slowly but surely gaining ground, until by 1660 sixty-two monasteries of monks and seven of nuns had returned to the primitive observance of Cîteaux. A Vicar General was appointed to govern these houses, remaining subject, however, to the General Chapter. But feeling ran high between the two parties, and the controversy at times became acrimonious. It was a situation which could not continue indefinitely. The Abbot of Cîteaux, Dom Claude Vaussin, proposed a compromise with a view to union, and Alexander VII favoured the project. Each Observance was invited to send representatives to Rome, and the thirty-two Abbots of the Strict Observance met in Paris on September 1, 1664, to appoint the deputies who were to defend the interests of the Reform. Their choice fell on the Abbot of Val Richer and the Abbot of La Trappe—de Rancé —then a neophyte in the Order, but on whose eloquence and *savoir faire*, no less than on his reforming zeal, the Strict Observance chiefly built its hopes.

Born in 1626, of good family, godson and namesake of Richelieu, Armand Jean le Bouthillier de Rancé was destined by his ambitious father for a career of ecclesiastical dignities. He received the tonsure at the age of ten, and at eleven was Canon of Notre-Dame, and held *in commendam* five Abbeys and a Priory, the combined revenues of which

---

[1] D. Canivez, *op. cit.*, p. 44.

provided him with a substantial income. Of brilliant intellectual gifts, and educated in Paris under the best masters, he rapidly acquired a vast and varied erudition ; at thirteen his Greek scholarship was remarkable, even in that age of Hellenism ; at the same time he loved dress and fashion, society and hunting. A priest who had a profound knowledge of men, the Abbé Huvelin, has summed up de Rancé's character in the word ' insatiability '[1] : an eager, ardent, active temperament, needing to know everything and experience everything for himself. He obtained brilliant successes at the Sorbonne, outstripping even his rival and life-long friend, Bossuet. To satisfy his father, who had a bishopric in store for him, he reluctantly received holy orders, becoming a priest in 1651. The priesthood affected his outward life but little ; he slightly—very slightly—modified his dress, but continued to hunt and entertain as before at his beautiful country house at Veretz. His conversion took place suddenly in 1657, but six years were to elapse before he could decide to embrace that monastic state of which he had always had a horror. Little by little, however, he broke all his worldly ties, and surrendered his benefices, retaining only the ancient Cistercian Abbey of La Trappe, where he established the Strict Observance, himself remaining commendatory Abbot. In 1663 he took the final step, and entered on his novitiate at the reformed Abbey of Perseigne. He made his profession in June, 1664, and the following September set out for Rome as deputy of the Strict Observance.

The result of the negotiations was disappointing ; the Brief of Alexander VII, while praising and encouraging the Strict Observance, made it subject to the Common Observance, and legitimised the principal mitigations of the latter. De Rancé's mind was made up ; he was not a man for half measures. If he could no longer hope for the reform of the entire Order, in his own Abbey at least he would restore the primitive observance of Cîteaux. The remaining thirty-six years of his life were dedicated to this work. In 1662, six monks who were monks in name alone,

---

[1] *Some Spiritual Guides of the Seventeenth Century*, Eng. trans. (1927), p. 148.

lived as they pleased in the half-ruined monastery ; at his death in 1700 de Rancé left a community of between eighty and ninety monks whose regularity, fervour, and sanctity made La Trappe famous throughout Europe. Much has been written of late concerning the man who accomplished this work. In his own day and down to the present time, de Rancé has had, alike, impassioned admirers and bitter enemies. His was one of those vivid, forceful personalities which inevitably inspire either attraction or repulsion, but seldom mere indifference, and with all such characters it is difficult for a later age to recapture from the pages of historians and biographers anything of that personal charm which made so vivid an impression on their contemporaries. Judged, however, by the Gospel standard of ' By their fruits you shall know them,' de Rancé's claim to greatness can hardly be questioned. He carried out the work he had set himself to do, and that was to revive in the France of Louis Quatorze the times of St. Stephen and St. Bernard. He was not, therefore, as is so often erroneously supposed, the ' founder ' of an ' Order of Trappists ' ; neither did he ever dream of composing a Rule. His one aim was to restore the integral observance of the Rule of St. Benedict as it had been practised at Cîteaux in the twelfth century. He re-established silence, manual labour, and many penitential practices which had fallen into disuse. Even de Rancé's ardour for penance, however, could not succeed in restoring the full austerity of the primitive observance—contrary to what is often supposed. The fasts as laid down in the Rule of St Benedict proved impossible in seventeenth-century France ; the hours of manual labour were shortened ; even the silence was mitigated by weekly conferences. But if in bodily austerity La Trappe did not equal primitive Cîteaux, in the spirit of penance it went far beyond, especially in the practice of methods of humiliation which savoured rather of the Thebaïd than of the discretion of St. Benedict. In the infirmary the penitential spirit reigned supreme, as we see in the *Relations* of the deaths of the monks of La Trappe, composed by de Rancé himself. Reading them, we feel far indeed from the spirit of St. Benedict's ' Before all things and above all things let care be had of the sick, that they

be served in very deed as Christ Himself.' Yet it is hardly
fair to lay the blame on the Abbot, when we know that the
patients themselves sent him messages like the following :
' I respectfully take the liberty of asking you to continue the
permission you have already granted me to follow out the
common life until I die. For the love of Jesus Christ, I
beg you to forget that I have a body.' Yet these heroes of
penance, even—or perhaps especially—those whose lives
had stood in greatest need of expiation, died in the most
touching dispositions of childlike confidence and supernatural joy. And their filial affection and devotedness to
their Abbot is beyond all question, and is perhaps de Rancé's
best eulogy.

But de Rancé's influence was by no means confined to
his own community. Many other Cistercian monasteries
were inspired by the example of La Trappe to embrace the
Reform, and sought de Rancé's counsel and help—Sept-Fons,
Orval, Tamié. The nuns of Les Clairets placed themselves
under his guidance and adopted the Regulations of La Trappe
—La Trappe became, in fact, a beacon-light in the monastic
world of the day, and not in the monastic world alone, but
in that world of court and society which had known de Rancé
in his earlier days. La Trappe was the sensation of the hour ;
all Paris went out into the desert to see this marvel, and
many who went merely out of curiosity or for the sake of the
sensation were struck by grace. Some entered La Trappe to
end their days in penance ; others changed their lives
without changing their state—royal princesses like Anne of
Gonzaga, Bishops like Le Camus, army officers who wore hair
shirts beneath their uniform. De Rancé had an ever-
widening circle of such penitents in the world, whom he
directed by correspondence. The devout, too, of all classes
flocked to La Trappe as to a place of pilgrimage. The exiled
James II of England loved to visit it, and to follow the
monastic exercises during his stay.

The man who accomplished all this was certainly a great
man—a great monk and a great reformer—and his greatness
was recognised even in that *Grand Siècle* which so admired
and appreciated greatness, and produced so many great men
in every department of life. There is, however, in de Rancé's

character and work a certain note of exaggeration which is repellent to some minds, but was quite in keeping with the age in which he lived, and was understood by his contemporaries. It was an age of extremes, of sharp contrasts ; there were no half-tones. Only extreme penance could counterbalance the extravagances of worldliness and luxury in that pleasure-loving age. Monasticism, sapped of its vitality, had reached its lowest ebb, and strong measures were necessary if a genuine revival were to be brought about. De Rancé was a child of his age, and his work responded to the needs of that age. He was also himself a penitent, and that need of expiation felt by his ardent nature inevitably led him to emphasise the penitential or negative aspect of the Cistercian life, rather than its contemplative or positive aspect. This is the root of the difference, we cannot help feeling, between the spirit of La Trappe and the spirit of the early Cistercians. To turn from the writings of St. Bernard to those of de Rancé is to pass into another spiritual climate. The difference has been well summed up by Dom Chautard, Abbot of Sept-Fons.[1] ' De Rancé,' he says, ' certainly bears in mind that the commandment to love God is the first of all the commandments. From the point of view of orthodoxy, his teaching is irreproachable. He speaks of divine love in many passages of his works ; he even dwells at length upon the subject. As literary theses, these passages are excellent, but they somehow lack unction. From the point of view of the good to be done to souls he is incomplete. He makes us esteem love, but does not communicate it. Now, in the life of a Cistercian, love is everything ; his exterior actions have no value unless they proceed from love and lead to it. A monastic legislator should lay stress on love above all things, and de Rancé does not do so sufficiently. He states the doctrine, but does not give it all its practical applications. His charity does not radiate widely enough. Whereas the flame of love should have burnt more ardently in his abbey so as to create a love for the stricter observance, this fundamental virtue does not sufficiently animate the whole of the life ; it does not become the real lever of the

[1] *Les Cisterciens Trappistes : L'Ame Cistercienne* (Conférence de Drac, 1931).

monk's existence, and this is the reason why the spiritual doctrine of the Abbé de Rancé is wanting in the warmth that dilates the heart and aids the soul's ascension. It was not thus that our true masters formed their disciples . . . St. Bernard does not ignore the cross ; indeed, he likes to emphasise the crucifying conditions for the attainment of perfection, but he mingles so much love with them, that beneath his pen the bitterest things appear sweet as honey —he has been called the '' Mellifluous Doctor.'' He reminds us that the sacrifice God loves is that made with joy, because also with love. He was never better inspired than when commenting on the Canticle of Canticles, that mutual love-song of the soul and its God. Thus the cross itself as presented by St. Bernard becomes desirable—we see in it only a proof of love for the Crucified and a means of loving Him more.'

With regard to the much-quoted controversy on the subject of monastic studies, we must again bear in mind, in the first place, de Rancé's own passionate love of the classics, and the need he felt to renounce this as an obstacle between his soul and God ; and secondly, that the vehemence of his protests was provoked by the exaggerated classicism of the age, when the *Grand Monarque* was endeavouring to revive the glories of Imperial Rome, and monastic scholars were devoting their lives to studies in pagan mythology. Though couched in violent and paradoxical terms, de Rancé's protest is, in reality, based on what has always been a fundamental Cistercian principle, that of only admitting such studies as really conduce to the attainment of the main end of monastic life, that is, which help the soul to contemplation and union with God. In his application of the principle, however, de Rancé departed from the best traditions of Cîteaux. He was careful to restore the *lectio divina* made in common, which is so essential a feature of the Rule of St. Benedict, but he limited its subject matter in a way never intended by St. Benedict, and it was this which provoked Mabillon's protest. The details of the controversy do not concern us here. Rather would we dwell on the scene of reconciliation between the saintly Maurist scholar and the fiery reformer, on the occasion of

Mabillon's visit to La Trappe, as he himself has recorded it for us—a scene which recalls the friendship between St. Bernard and Peter the Venerable, the two protagonists in the even more acrimonious controversy between Cîteaux and Cluny. In both cases we see that virulence on paper does not necessarily imply any personal vindictiveness, and all reformers are liable to such excesses, for reform is in itself a reaction, a protest against an existing state of things.

The Reform of La Trappe, therefore, in spite of certain divergences due in the main to the circumstances of the time, remained fundamentally Cistercian in character. And de Rancé's work was not the result of a mere passing wave of enthusiasm ; it was solidly established, and was to prove enduring. Such was the impetus he gave to his Reform, that of all the Cistercian monasteries La Trappe alone retained sufficient vitality to weather the storm which broke over France a century later.

CHAPTER VI

In the year 1780 a young priest, Louis-Henri de Lestrange, entered the novitiate of La Trappe, and took the name of Frère Augustin. Born in 1754, Louis-Henri was the four-teenth child of the Marquis de Lestrange, an officer in the army of Louis XV, who had fought at Fontenoy; his mother was of Irish extraction, her father having accom-panied James II into exile in 1688. At sixteen, Louis-Henri entered the Seminary of St. Irénée at Lyons, and thence proceed for his theology to St. Sulpice, where his piety earned for him the nickname of *le petit saint*. Ordained priest in 1778, his brilliant talents and rare holiness of life marked him out for rapid advancement in the Church. At twenty-six he was already designated for the episcopate, but, alarmed at the prospect which was opening before him, he fled from the world and presented himself as a postulant at the Abbey of La Trappe. There, too, his exceptional qualities were soon appreciated, and not long after his profession he was appointed Master of Novices. His sound judgement and experience led him to foresee the impending cataclysm, and from the very beginnings of the Revolution he had no illusions as to the gravity of the situation as far as the religious Orders were concerned. When, in February, 1790, the National Assembly issued the Decree proscribing the religious state, many were hopeful that La Trappe would be spared; Dom Augustin, on the contrary, urged the immediate necessity of providing a refuge out of France, in case of expulsion. His project met with nothing but contempt and opposition; his correspondence was inter-cepted, and he was deposed from his office, but he met these trials with that tranquil confidence in Divine Providence which was to characterise him throughout his stormy life.

A fresh decree of the Assembly, however, in November, 1790, expressly included La Trappe in the general suppression. There was no longer any room for hope, and Dom Augustin once more laid his project before the Prior (the Abbot of La Trappe had died on February 7, 1790, six days before the first decree). Only one of the letters written by Dom Augustin had reached its destination, and in reply to it he had learned that a refuge might be found in the Canton of Fribourg in Switzerland, if a request to that effect were signed by some of the religious and presented by him in person to the government of the Canton. The petition was already prepared, and Dom Augustin had now no difficulty in obtaining from the Prior all the permissions he required. He lost no time ; six of the community willingly gave their signatures, and he started on his mission. Further obstacles sprang up, but all were finally surmounted, and he set out for Switzerland with the full authorisation of the Abbot of Cîteaux, the Bishop of Séez, and, to his great joy, of the Father Immediate of La Trappe—Dom Louis Rocourt, Abbot of Clairvaux, who, under the influence of misrepresentation, had deposed him from his office as Novice-Master, but now generously acknowledged his mistake and gave him every encouragement.

The Senate of Fribourg consented to receive the monks, but only to the number of twenty-four, and assigned to them the deserted Carthusian monastery of La Val-Sainte. Dom Augustin accepted the offer and returned in haste to La Trappe. All opposition had vanished, and the most incredulous were now the most anxious to join the colony. Only twenty-four could be accepted, however, and the seven who had signed the petition chose those who were to accompany them into exile. Before leaving, the twenty-four unanimously elected the ex-Novice-Master as their Superior, and their choice was confirmed by the Father Immediate, the Abbot of Clairvaux, who, by an act of May 3, 1791, appointed Dom Augustin Superior of the new monastery, giving him practically abbatial powers. In spite of the imminent danger and consequent need of haste, all, therefore, was done in perfect order and with full canonical approbation. The Abbot of Clairvaux not only authorised the venture, but encouraged and furthered it in every way, urging them almost wistfully to maintain the traditions of La Trappe by their fervour and austerity of life—an exhortation which was to be surpassed in the fulfilment. In the person of the successor of St. Bernard, the Order of Cîteaux, which seemed, in France at least, to be at the point of death, gave its blessing to the little group of monks who were destined to perpetuate its life. For in that group of monks the corporate existence of the Order was, in fact, maintained, amid the general destruction. All the other Cistercian monasteries in France perished, but this new foundation, sprung from La Trappe, was to become the nucleus of a great revival—what is now called the Order of Cistercians of the Strict Observance. Monks of La Trappe they were ; ' Trappists ' they were nicknamed ; and this explains how that name of ' Trappist ' became attached to the whole Strict Observance, even to the point of superseding the ancient name of Cistercian, and still clings to the Order, though it has no longer the same official significance. It thus came about that whereas in the case of most of the religious Orders an entirely new beginning had to be made in France, when the revolutionary period had passed—as was done, for instance, by Dom Guéranger and Lacordaire—the Order of Cîteaux, thanks to Dom Augustin's initiative and firmness, knew no real break in its history ; not merely did it survive, but new life even was infused into it.

In the end, three of the twenty-four who had been chosen remained in France, so that the number of those who actually set out for Fribourg was twenty-one—the exact number which had left Molesmes six centuries earlier to found Cîteaux—just as the seven who had signed the petition corresponded to the seven monks of Molesmes who had sought the protection and authority of the Papal Legate—coincidences which the Trappists noted with joy, as signs of God's blessing on their enterprise.

Taking with them nothing but the barest necessaries, the twenty-one professed, with several novices, left La Trappe on April 26, 1791, in a covered waggon, which served them as a kind of travelling monastery. Silence was strictly

DOM AUGUSTIN DE LESTRANGE

Facing p. 60

observed, and all the regular exercises carried out, as far as
possible : Divine Office, reading, and manual labour, all at
the appointed hours ; even the chapter of faults was not
omitted. Thus, not only community life, but regular
observance and the performance of the Work of God were
continued uninterruptedly from La Trappe to Val-Sainte.
And this extraordinary exodus took place almost without
hindrance. Through the midst of revolutionary France the
Trappists passed unmolested in their strange caravan,
wearing their religious habit. As they passed through, the
roads closed behind them ; even a few days later, they
could only have departed secretly and in disguise. Rejoicing
in this visible protection of Providence, they reached the
Swiss frontier in safety, and after spending a week at the
Cistercian monastery of Hauterive, finally reached Val-
Sainte on June 1, 1791. There they found themselves con-
fronted with poverty and hardship such as can only be
paralleled by the early days of Cîteaux, Clairvaux or
Fountains. Living on roots and leaves, with black bread
as a rare delicacy, sleeping on the bare floor without cover-
ings, they passed ten or twelve hours a day in the hardest
toil, trying to render fruitful a soil which to a depth of
two feet was only a mass of stones. Little by little their
labours were rewarded, and regular observance was fully
established. But they relaxed little in the austerity of their
way of life. It seemed to them that they could not do
enough to show their gratitude to God, Who amid the
general destruction had granted them the grace of preserving their religious state. Not only did they accept
with joy the hardships imposed on them by necessity, but
they desired to establish an even stricter observance of
the Rule than that of La Trappe ; to restore, in fact, in
its entirety the primitive observance of Cîteaux, which de
Rancé, owing to the difficulties of the time, had not succeeded in doing. On the eve of the feast of St. Stephen
Harding, July 15, 1791, they laid their desires before their
Superior, who lost no time in putting them into execution.
After a Solemn Votive Mass of the Holy Spirit, some days
were spent in prayer, and the study of the Holy Rule ; on
the 19th was held the first of a series of Chapters in which

the new reform was inaugurated. Each Chapter of the
Rule of St. Benedict was read in turn, and each religious
was invited to give his opinion on the manner of carrying
it out. The regulations drawn up as the result of
these deliberations were then put in practice, and slowly
matured during the next three years ; only in 1794 were
printed the *Règlements de la Val-Sainte*, a work which is
now extremely rare.[1] It forms two well-printed quarto
volumes, with wide margins, in which are inserted the
corresponding passages of the Rule of St. Benedict,
the *Consuetudines* of Cîteaux, the Cistercian Ritual, and the
Regulations of de Rancé, showing exactly whence every
detail of observance is derived. Prefixed to the Regulations
is a full account of the foundation of Val-Sainte, and also
the text of all the canonical documents approving the
Cistercian Order, from the Bull of Paschal II onwards.
We see here the same spirit as in the *Exordium* of Cîteaux,
the same desire to define their aims clearly and do all with
full authority. In the *Avertissement* which precedes the
Regulations, the programme of the new reform is clearly set
out. After alluding to the false idea which was current,
that the life led at Val-Sainte was something entirely new,
and different from that of the early Cistercians, the Trappists
proceed to demonstrate their position by the simile of a
great river : the source of the river is the Rule of St. Benedict ; the main stream is primitive Cîteaux ; and the
Reform of La Trappe, of which the Reform of Val-Sainte is
only the completion, is a great arm of this river—but the
waters are the same throughout. ' All that we have pur-
posed,' they go on, ' is to revive in our times the great days
of St. Bernard, to approach as nearly as possible to our
fathers, to restore all the observances of the first monks of
Cîteaux.' In compensation, however, for certain observances
which they were not able to carry out, they added further
austerities, such as sleeping on a plank bed, covered only
by a serge cloth ; and also, practices of devotion which
were not altogether in the traditions of the Order. The

---

[1] Abbé Maire describes it as *presque introuvable*. A copy exists at
Stapehill, the two volumes bound in one, forming a bulky tome, which
the nuns nevertheless must have carried with them through all their
subsequent peregrinations.

choir offices were much longer than in the time of St. Benedict, and this led to a diminution of the time appointed for sleep, as well as of that given to manual labour. With these exceptions, the Regulations of Val-Sainte reproduce in the main the primitive Usages of Cîteaux.

Only a few days after the arrival of the Trappists at Val-Sainte, the Bishop of Lausanne, in an act dated June 3, 1791, gave his permission for the foundation of the monastery and the establishment therein of the 'primitive observance and constitutions of the Order of Cîteaux,' confirming to Val-Sainte all the rights, privileges and immunities granted to the Order by the Holy See. Three years later, by a Brief of Pius VI, Val-Sainte, now a flourishing community, was erected into an Abbey, and Dom Augustin de Lestrange, unanimously elected Abbot, was installed on December 8, 1794. The same Brief gave Dom Augustin authority over all communities sprung from Val-Sainte (which were thus formed into a congregation) and also praised and encouraged the reform undertaken.

For, notwithstanding the remoteness of situation, and the poverty and austerity of the new monastery, postulants flocked to it, as to an ark of salvation in the midst of the revolutionary deluge—souls animated with the same fervour and thirst for sacrifice as the founders themselves. So numerous was the influx of vocations that Val-Sainte was soon able to send out colonies, and between 1793 and 1796 no less than five foundations were made—the first was that of Santa Suzanna in Spain; then Westmalle in Brabant,[1] Mont-Brac in Piedmont, Lulworth in Dorsetshire, and, lastly, Saint-Branchier in Bas-Valais. Moreover, Christian education having been wholly suppressed in France, many parents begged Dom Augustin to take charge of their children. At first these children were received into the monastery, but they became so numerous that it was necessary to organise a separate establishment for them. To meet this need, Dom Augustin founded a 'Third Order' of teaching Brothers, who made simple vows, and followed a less austere régime than that of the monks.

---

[1] This community was shortly afterwards removed to Darfeld in Westphalia.

Many nuns, also, of various Orders, who had been expelled from their convents and forced to return to secular life, turned to Dom Augustin in the hope of finding some means of forming a religious community. For these nuns, Dom Augustin opened a house in Bas-Valais, close to the recent foundation of Saint-Branchier. The new monastery, which was dedicated to ' La Sainte Volonté de Dieu ' (the motto of Val-Sainte) was opened on September 14, 1796, and was soon filled to overflowing with nuns, who desired at all costs to maintain their religious state. One of the first members of the community was Dom Augustin's sister. The Superior during the first year was a certain Mère Marie, who is difficult to identify—in a letter written to her mother shortly before her profession she speaks of having been ' in a mitigated Order.' The Sub-Prioress and Mistress of Novices was Mère Sainte-Marie, a former Sacramentine nun. Dom Augustin prudently weighed the question of the Rule to be adopted by the new community, but the nuns themselves quickly solved the problem by unhesitatingly demanding to embrace the Regulations of Val-Sainte in their full rigour, even desiring to add further austerities, which were not, however, permitted. Thus was founded the first community of so-called Trappistines, which became the mother of almost all the houses of the Cistercian Nuns of the Strict Observance, and the eldest daughter of which is the monastery of Stapehill.

The austerities of the new Reform were followed at La Sainte Volonté without mitigation, but their severity was not accompanied by any spirit of rigorism. The devotion of the Reform of Val-Sainte was the devotion to the Sacred Heart, and the reigning virtue, without doubt, was the virtue of charity, which should be the fruit of that devotion. There are many instances of the affectionate union which reigned among the religious, both monks and nuns. This supernatural charity was especially needed at La Sainte Volonté. At Val-Sainte there had been from the beginning a nucleus of fervent and exemplary Cistercians ; at the monastery of Valais, on the other hand, there was a hetero-geneous assemblage of professed nuns of different Orders, with secular postulants also, in a tiny house, consisting only of four walls, the regular places—choir, refectory, and so on—being separated merely by wooden partitions. Here, as at Val-Sainte, Dom Augustin adhered firmly to the principle of refusing no subjects for want of space or of temporal resources, and the little monastery was soon filled to overflowing, the nuns sleeping on tables and benches and on the bare floor, rather than turn away postulants who showed signs of a genuine vocation. Notwithstanding these trying conditions, a perfect union of hearts reigned in the community. Mère Sainte-Marie writes to a friend : ' How could God be pleased with our manner of life if we had not His holy love in our hearts, and if the charity which ought to unite us did not reign amongst us ? Yes, by the mercy of the God of Charity, this divine virtue is the sacred bond which keeps closely united persons of different nationalities, and so diverse in age and condition, that it can truly be said that charity alone could bring about the happy state of things that is to be found in this house.' While admitting that ' it seems surprising that in a novitiate composed of persons of every age and condition, religious and seculars, all should be contented,' she goes on to affirm that ' more than twenty-six novices who are under my charge will bear witness with me that on entering here they have begun to experience a joy, a peace, a happiness which had hitherto been unknown to them.'

Among those who sought admittance was the Princess Louise-Adelaïde de Bourbon-Condé, first cousin of Louis XVI. For several years she had lived in exile at Fribourg, and there finally decided to embrace the religious life. Her one desire was to find a monastery where she could serve God in obscurity and austere observance. After several ineffectual attempts, she at length found what she sought at La Sainte Volonté de Dieu, where she entered in September, 1797, just a year after the foundation, and received the habit under the name of Sœur Marie-Joseph. She was then forty years of age, of mature judgement and experience, so that her letters form a valuable testimony as to the life led at the new monastery. She writes, a month after her arrival : ' This place is holy, God is truly here. I have found at last that real religious life for which my

heart was longing, and which is so different from the kind
of life led in most convents at the present day. . . . This
venerable Order of Trappists is indeed not known as it
really is, even by those who do it most justice. I myself
had not a right idea of it. The sweetness found in it infinitely
surpasses all that can be said of it. . . . To my mind,
perfection exists in a community all of whose exterior
exercises have God as their unceasing object, the Gospel
precepts as their basis, and as guides, exemplary and zealous
Superiors, filled with the spirit of their state.' She likewise
speaks with enthusiasm of the unselfish charity which reigns
in the community, of the peace and recollection, the silence
and regularity she found there. But her greatest joy was
the chanting of the Divine Office by day and night : ' In
chanting the *Benedicite* this morning at Lauds, I laid up
in my heart a provision of joy and happiness for my whole
day. What does the rest of the day matter, when I have
begun it by praising the Lord in the company of His angels
and saints ? '

Rightly to understand the spirit of this first community
of Trappistines, we need to recall the circumstances of the
time. Then, as always, persecution rekindled the flame of
fervour. These nuns had witnessed the indescribable horrors
of the Reign of Terror, and many of them had risked the
guillotine rather than compromise their loyalty to the Church
and their fidelity to their religious state. They were the
sisters of the heroic Carmelites of Compiègne, and of those
thirty-two nuns martyred at Orange in the same month
of July, 1794, and beatified by Pope Pius XI in 1925. Among
the latter were two Cistercian nuns of the ancient Abbey
of St. Catherine at Avignon, which was united to the Order
of Cîteaux by St. Bernard himself. These were Marguerite-
Eléonore de Justamond (Mère Marie de Saint-Henri), and
her sister, Madeleine-Françoise (Mère Madeleine du Saint-
Sacrement). Driven out of their monastery in 1790, they
returned to Bollène, their native town, and for two years
enjoyed the sisterly hospitality of the Ursuline community
of that town, where their aunt and elder sister, both Ursuline
nuns of other houses, had already taken refuge. After the
suppression of the Ursuline convent, the nuns continued to

live in community in a house in the town, until they were arrested for refusing to take the oath of *liberté-égalité*. Together with the Sacramentines of Bollène, they were taken to Orange on May 2, 1794, and imprisoned there with some other religious of different Orders. Thereupon, all the imprisoned nuns—they numbered fifty-five in all—unanimously agreed to live as one community under a single rule. They put their money, clothes, and all they had into a common stock, and organised a regular life, in which the day was filled by spiritual exercises. A perfect union reigned among them, and a wonderful spirit of charity and joy. They had no thoughts except to prepare for martyrdom. When the executions began on July 6, and the fatal cart departed daily with its victims for the guillotine, those who remained behind recited the prayers for the dying ; but as soon as the executions were over, they rose and sang the *Te Deum, Laudate*, and *Magnificat*, and encouraged one another to die in their turn. The judges were amazed at the calmness with which they received the death sentence, and their immovable firmness in refusing to take the oath. They set out for the scaffold ' with a heavenly joy, as if going to a marriage feast,' and their executioners, we are told, were stupefied at the sight of these women who ' laughed as they died.'

Of the same stamp as these heroic religious were those who formed the first community of Trappistines, and in this light we are better able to understand the life led at La Sainte-Volonté. There is the same union of hearts, for persecution drew closely the bonds of charity, and petty divisions were a thing impossible. There is also the same supernatural joy amid sacrifice and suffering ; these nuns had not been privileged to shed their blood for Christ, but at least they were determined to sacrifice themselves by a life of austerity and penance. Many motives urged them to this : first and foremost, gratitude to God for the grace of preserving their religious state amid the general devastation ; then, the urgent need of expiation and reparation for the appalling blasphemies and sacrileges which were defiling their native land. They thought, too, of the hardships to which so many of their compatriots, priests,

F

religious and others, were still exposed ; wandering without shelter, and lacking even the necessaries of life. All this must be taken into account before we can venture to tax with exaggeration and indiscretion the Reform of Dom Augustin. The times were extraordinary, and extraordinary penance was needed, in order to avert the anger of God from guilty France. And it is hardly to be wondered at that those who had endured prison and exile, hunger and thirst, for their Faith, found little or no hardship in the austere life of the new Reform.

Throughout Europe, the eyes of Catholics were turned in admiration to Switzerland, where the sons and daughters of Dom Augustin were reviving the fervour and austerity of the golden age of monasticism. At the same time, enemies and detractors were not wanting. As in the beginnings of Cîteaux, gossip was rife : *titubare non cessabant ;* many false rumours were in circulation regarding the life led by the Trappists. It was said that the austerities were excessive, and that in reality the religious were discontented with their state. To refute these calumnies, Dom Augustin proposed, at the time of the erection of Val-Sainte into an Abbey, that each of the monks should draw up a declaration of his love and appreciation of the life he had voluntarily embraced. These declarations were presented to Pius VI, and printed as an appendix to the *Règlements*. But the reports continued to be spread after the foundation of La Sainte Volonté, and when the first professions had taken place, the nuns drew up similar declarations, a number of which are preserved in a manuscript at Stapehill ; probably they were never printed. We quote in full one which has for us a special interest, being that of Sœur Rosalie Augustin de Chabannes, a former Cistercian nun of the Abbey of Saint-Antoine, near Paris, who was afterwards to be the Foundress and for forty-two years the Superior of the Monastery of Our Lady of the Holy Cross, Stapehill. She writes :

' I regard it as a great privilege to have an opportunity of making known my sentiments regarding my holy state. I should like to ascend the house-tops, to go into all the public places, and to cross the seas, in order to make known to the whole universe the happiness which I enjoy. It is so great that the strongest expressions could give only a faint idea of it ; I am sometimes unable to contain the feelings with which it inspires me. I can easily believe that anyone who is called happy in the world, if he had once tasted the satisfaction, the peace which is found in the different practices of our holy state, would not hesitate for an instant to change his condition. Let men cease, then, to regard as unhappy victims all those who retire here. They are indeed victims, but voluntary victims, and their sacrifice is accompanied by so much sweetness that I sometimes feel afraid that I am having my reward here below. I declare and bear witness to the whole world that I do not believe there can be in existence a being happier than I am ; all those austerities which so alarm everyone are my greatest consolation ; those constant vigils, those long fasts, which, so they say, destroy the health, have produced an exactly contrary effect, as before I entered La Trappe I had no health, and as a religious of the same Order, though, to my shame, very relaxed, I could not support even that amount of regular observance. I wish also to make known the difference in my feelings in my first and second profession. In the former, although I made it with joy, I could not resist an impression of terror which penetrated me entirely ; in the second, peace, joy and happiness filled me instead. In short, we bear the yoke of the Lord with joy, and there is no day on which I would not wish to be able to add something to the austerities.

' I am penetrated with so lively a gratitude at having been admitted, that I am unable to express it. I am ready to sign my declaration with my blood.'

Some account must now be given of this remarkable woman, who by her zeal and labours in the work of the Reform was to merit the name of ' the eldest daughter of Dom Augustin.'

CHAPTER VII

A MONASTIC ODYSSEY

MARIE-Rosalie de Vergèzes de Chabannes was born at Langogne, capital of Gévaudan, on May 19, 1769, of a family of *petite noblesse* of that province, her parents being described in the baptismal register as ' *noble Antoine de Vergeses* ' and ' *dame Marianne Clavel.*' She was baptised the same day, the god-parents being a cousin, Pierre Clavel de Monteil de Bavès, and a sister, Marie de Vergèzes du Maze. Dedicated by her parents to Our Lady from her infancy, at the age of five the child was sent for her education to the Cistercian Abbey of Saint-Antoine-des-Champs, on the outskirts of Paris, where her elder sister was already a professed religious and directress of the pensionnat. A few words must be said about this historic Abbey, from which Stapehill, through its foundress, can claim, in a sense, to be descended.

Saint-Antoine was founded about the year 1191, on a spot to the east of Paris, where a small chapel dedicated to St. Antony formerly stood. The district was then open country, and for the sake of security the monastery was surrounded, like a fortress, by strong walls and moats. In 1204 the Cistercian observance was adopted, and the monastery erected into an Abbey. In 1227 St. Louis granted to Saint-Antoine the title of Royal Abbey, and in 1223 the Abbey church was solemnly dedicated by the Bishop of Paris, Guillaume d'Auvergne, in the presence of the King and the Queen-Mother, Blanche of Castile. In the summer of 1339, the Holy Crown of Thorns, obtained by St. Louis from Baldwin II, Emperor of Constantinople, was brought to Paris in a magnificent procession, which halted at Saint-Antoine, the Sacred Relic being exposed for the veneration of the faithful outside the monastery Church. St. Louis and his brother Robert, bareheaded and barefooted, carried on their shoulders the casket containing the Holy Crown, from Saint-Antoine to the Sainte-Chapelle, where it was deposited in the shrine prepared for it. The Feast of the Reception of the Holy Crown is still kept in the Cistercian Order on August 11.[1] Nine years later, St. Louis came to hear Mass at Saint-Antoine on the eve of his departure for the Crusade.

Situated as it was, at the very gates of Paris, Saint-Antoine had a somewhat troublous history, and the peace of the Cistercian cloister was often disturbed by external events. Twice the monastery was sacked and pillaged: in 1573, by the soldiers of the League, and again in 1652, during the troubles of the Fronde, the religious being compelled to take refuge within the walls of Paris. In 1572 the Abbey fell *in commendam*, but for a time, at any rate, it appears to have suffered less than many religious houses from this disastrous system. Renée de la Salle, who governed the community from 1600 to 1636, established strict enclosure. She was succeeded by Marie le Bouthillier, daughter of Claude le Bouthillier, and cousin of de Rancé, under whose wise administration the Abbey prospered both spiritually and temporally; she died in 1652. In 1670 some of the religious conceived the desire of embracing a stricter observance, in accordance with the Brief of Alexander VII; but their project met with nothing but opposition on the part of Superiors and others, and they were subjected to all kinds of persecution and calumny. They were encouraged, however, in their line of action by de Rancé, who took on himself their defence, with the result that after three years their patience and perseverance were rewarded, and the Reform according to the Brief of Alexander VII was established at Saint-Antoine.

[1] By a happy coincidence, soon after the foundation of Stapehill, a precious relic, consisting of a portion of one of the Thorns from the Holy Crown, was presented to Mme de Chabannes, and is still preserved at Stapehill and venerated yearly on the Feast. This relic was detached from the Holy Crown when the latter was removed to St.-Denis, after the suppression of the Sainte-Chapelle, and was presented by the Superintendent of the Treasury of St.-Denis to an émigré priest, Abbé Lefevre, who gave it to Mme de Chabannes. It was duly authenticated by Bishop Collingridge in 1814 and the authentications were again examined and confirmed by the late Bishop Keily in 1924.

The commendatory system, however, still held sway, and in the eighteenth century the monastery fell on evil days under the rule of a princess of the blood royal, Marie-Anne-Gabrielle-Eléonore de Bourbon-Condé, who, according to Saint-Simon, was the scourge of Saint-Antoine, as she had previously been of Fontevrault and Val-de-Grâce, and who was removed from office by the King at the request of her own family. She died in 1760, and was brought back to Saint-Antoine for burial. Her successor, Gabrielle-Charlotte de Beauvau-Craon, was destined to be the last of the long line of Abbesses. Under her administration the Abbey prospered once more ; between 1767 and 1770, the greater part of the monastic buildings was rebuilt, and the Abbey school, in which about twenty girls of good family were educated, was in a flourishing condition. It was Madame de Beauvau who received the little Rosalie de Chabannes, about the year 1774. In later years, Madame de Chabannes used to relate an incident that occurred on her arrival and demonstrates the firmness and independence of character already possessed by this child of five. When the Abbess led her to her sister, and told her that the latter would be her mistress, the child drew back in the most determined manner, and declared : ' Mama says that one sister cannot exercise authority over another,' showing plainly her unwillingness to submit to the arrangement—greatly to the amusement of the Abbess and all present. This sister, however, lavished on her such motherly affection and devoted care, that it was afterwards to prove a source of temptation to Rosalie, and she would even threaten to leave the monastery on account of a possibly too human attachment. But she never executed this threat, and when the time came for her to leave the pensionnat, at the age of fifteen, she elected to enter the novitiate immediately. On June 3, 1787, she made her profession, taking the name of Sœur Augustin.

The young religious was not long to enjoy the peace of her Cistercian cloister. The storm-clouds were already gathering, and scarcely two years later the storm broke. We can only conjecture the forebodings which must have filled the hearts of the nuns of Saint-Antoine on that fateful fourteenth of July, 1789, when the storming of the

Bastille, so close to their Abbey, announced the end of the *ancien régime* and the opening of the revolutionary era. In 1790, the Commissioners presented themselves at the Abbey to make the inventory which was the preliminary to the work of spoliation. There were at that time twenty-four choir religious in the community, and eleven lay sisters. The prestige and supposed wealth of the ancient Royal Abbey made it a desirable prey : the nuns, too, belonged to noble families, and so were marked out for special hatred. We know little, however, of the details of the suppression. In 1795, the new buildings of the monastery were converted into a hospital : in September, 1796, the old Gothic Church was completely demolished, as also the ancient chapel of Saint-Pierre, where formerly the bodies of the Kings of France were exposed, before being translated to Notre-Dame and thence to their final resting-place at the Royal Abbey of Saint-Denis. In 1798, the great enclosure was sold in lots, but the site of the Abbey itself is still occupied by the Hôpital Saint-Antoine, and part of the buildings erected by Madame de Beauvau still stands. The only relic of an earlier period is a foundation stone let into the wall, bearing the following inscription : *Pozé par Madame Marie de Bragelone en présence de Madame Marie Bouteiller, abbesse de céans, du règne de Louis XIII*, 1643. The memory of the old Cistercian Abbey is preserved, too, in the name of the Rue de Cîteaux, adjoining the hospital, as well as in that of the Faubourg Saint-Antoine itself. For the Faubourg does in fact owe its origin to the group of dwellings which in feudal times clustered beneath the shelter of the Abbey walls. From this nucleus there gradually grew up in the seventeenth and eighteenth centuries a flourishing industrial district, still under the domain of the Abbess, who firmly defended the freedom and initiative of the craftsmen who came under her authority as territorial ruler.

Of the fate of the religious, thrown out on the world after the suppression of the Abbey, we have but little record. The Abbess retired to the house of her brother, Maréchal de Beauvau, and probably most of the other religious also returned to their families. Whether some of them continued to live in community, and thus incurred the odium of the Revolutionary Tribunal, we do not know, but it is certain that during the Reign of Terror some of the nuns of Saint-Antoine, Madame de Chabannes among them, were thrown into one of the Paris gaols, there to await their so-called trial, with its inevitable sentence to the guillotine. During the month of July, 1794, they were awaiting their sentence, and expecting to share the fate of the Carmelites of Compiègne and the nuns of Orange, when the course of events suddenly changed. On the famous ' 9th of Thermidor ' (July 27, 1794), all the prisoners in the Paris gaols lived in hourly expectation of a general massacre, and during that fearful night, when the sound of the tocsin, the roar of artillery, and the clamour of the mob resounded incessantly outside, the Cistercians of Saint-Antoine prepared themselves for Eternity, and encouraged one another to die bravely. In the morning the gates of the prison were opened, but it was to announce the fall of Robespierre ; the Reign of Terror was at an end, and the prisoners were set free. We do not know where Madame de Chabannes and her companions took refuge, or what befell them during the next few years. Doubtless it was on hearing of the establishment of the monastery of nuns in Valais, in 1796, that they decided to make their way thither. They travelled disguised as peasants, but suspicion was easily aroused, and they were forced to avoid the towns and to travel by by-paths, finding shelter as best they could, and often sleeping in the open air. Now and then they met a priest who, like themselves, was making his way to the frontier in disguise, and made their confession to him as they went along the road. At length, after many days of weary travelling, and countless dangers and hardships, they crossed the Swiss frontier. Madame de Chabannes has herself recorded in the earliest register of Stapehill, that she entered the monastery of La Sainte Volonté de Dieu on June 21, 1797, and received the habit on the 29th of the same month. As she was already a religious of the Order, her novitiate was shortened, and she made her profession on October 29, six weeks after the profession of the first novices and a month after the arrival of the Princess de Condé. She threw herself heart and soul into the work of the Reform, and almost immediately after her profession

Dom Augustin nominated her Superior. Scarcely three months were to elapse before she was again to take the road of exile, with the religious entrusted to her.

At the beginning of the year 1798, the armies of the French Republic invaded Switzerland. The exiled French religious could hope for no mercy from the invaders, nor indeed a continuance of hospitality from the Swiss. The event was sudden, and there was no time to make arrangements ; their only possible safety lay in flight. Dom Augustin could not resign himself to the dispersal of his communities, now well established and flourishing as they were, and he resolved on a heroic undertaking, trusting to Divine Providence to make possible what humanly speaking appeared impossible. He led the two hundred and forty-four persons under his care— monks, nuns, children—out into the unknown, making himself responsible for providing them with food and shelter and all necessaries. He at first intended to send the children back to their families, but nearly all of them implored to be allowed to follow the community, and in most cases the parents consented to this. The exiles traversed Switzerland in three separate groups, and made their way by various routes towards their first resting-place at Constance, from whence they proceeded into Bavaria. Most of these long and difficult journeys were performed on foot, and for food and lodging the wanderers were dependent on the charity of the inhabitants of the countries they passed through. As far as possible they sought shelter for the night at some religious house, but often they had to lodge at an inn. The most kindly hospitality was shown to them in Germany, both by religious and by lay people. At several large monasteries, such as Klosterwald, an abbey of Cistercian nuns, they were able to make a longer stay, which enabled the other groups to overtake them. The most remarkable feature of this ' monastic Odyssey,' as it has been called, was that both monks and nuns maintained throughout the observance of their Rule. Silence was strictly kept ; at midday a two hours' halt was made, during which the religious recited the Day Hours, while the lay brethren prepared dinner for the sick and the children. The others did not break their fast till evening, for it was Lent. At nightfall, wherever they might be, they never failed to close the day with the singing of the *Salve Regina*, which made an ineffaceable impression on those who heard it. Sundays and festivals they were always able to spend in some town or village where the priests could say Mass and all could receive Holy Communion.

The only European country which at that time seemed safe from the danger of war was Russia, and Dom Augustin hoped to find a refuge there. The Czar, Paul III, had in pre-Revolution days known and admired Princess Louise-Adelaïde at her father's château at Chantilly, and the Princess, now the novice Sœur Marie-Joseph, consented to write to him and beg him to receive the Trappists into his Empire. In her letter, she reminded him of the far-off days of Chantilly, and begged ' the amiable Comte du Nord ' (the name under which the Czar had visited France) ' to be her advocate with the Emperor.' This letter was despatched before the departure from Switzerland. While awaiting the Czar's reply, Dom Augustin hoped to receive hospitality in Catholic Bavaria, and the whole band advanced to Augsburg, where they were generously received by a rich merchant. The Elector Karl, however, influenced by infidel advisers, would not allow them to remain long in his dominions. He received Princess Louise and a limited number of her companions temporarily in his palace at Furstenried, while the remainder found hospitality in or near Munich. Meanwhile, the Czar's reply was received, in March, 1798. It was disappointing. He could not, of course, refuse to give shelter to the Princess, but made it quite clear that he offered a temporary refuge only, and did not intend to establish the Trappists permanently in his dominions. He limited the number to fifteen monks and fifteen nuns, whom he promised to settle in two monasteries at Orsza in Russian Poland. Unsatisfactory as this was, Dom Augustin decided to accept the terms, and prepared to advance towards Russia through Austria, where he hoped to establish the remainder of his religious. The different groups all assembled on the banks of the Danube, and embarked in two large barges, or rather house-boats, which the Elector had had constructed to transport them to Vienna. Borne by the stream, these two vessels moved slowly down the great river, the monks in one and the nuns in the other, the Divine Office being sung in two choirs when the barges were near enough to each other. Each night they moored the barges near some village or town, and landed to seek lodging and provisions, for the rough shelter of boards which had been put up on the barges was only sufficient to house the sick. After considerable delay on the frontiers of Austria, owing to difficulties regarding passports, they reached Vienna, where they received hospitality at the Visitation convent, the nuns being admitted into the enclosure, while the monks were lodged in the guest-house. The nuns entered the city by quiet by-roads, so as not to attract notice, but the monks and children walked in procession through the main streets. The whole population turned out to see them, and gave them an enthusiastic reception. The sixty little oblates in their white habits, walking two and two with a grave and recollected demeanour, aroused sympathetic interest everywhere. During the stay at Vienna, the Divine Office was sung in two choirs in the chapel of the Visitation, immense crowds flocking to hear it ; the Emperor Francis II himself was present on several occasions. Encouraged by this favourable reception, Dom Augustin, in an audience granted him by the Emperor, petitioned for an establishment in Austria. Francis II was willing to grant this, and offered the Abbot a property in Bohemia, but he was in the hands of the Council of the Regency established by Joseph II, and the members, for the most part rationalists, would only sanction the donation on condition that no novices should be received. This Dom Augustin could not agree to, and once more the Trappists had to look elsewhere for a home. Dom Augustin resolved to appeal personally to the Czar. He selected the two communities of fifteen who were to form the foundations at Orsza (Princess Louise of course being of the number) and himself accompanied them to Russia, at the end of July, 1798. After a long and difficult journey, they reached their destination, in the north-east of Russian Poland, not far from Smolensk. The Abbot went on to St. Petersburg, where the recommendation of Princess Louise won for him a favourable reception. The Czar promised him several monasteries in the Polish provinces which had become annexed to his Empire since the third Partition of Poland in 1795—the Palatinates of Brzesc, Volhynia and Podolia—countries still Catholic and adjoining the Austrian dominions. Five months passed in these negotiations, and during Dom Augustin's absence a storm of persecution had sprung up against the Trappists in Austria and Bohemia. On hearing of this, Dom Augustin sent orders to them to depart immediately for Poland. In October and November they set out, in several detachments, those from Vienna making their way to Cracow, those in Bohemia to Lemberg, where the nuns were hospitably received by the Benedictines of the Perpetual Adoration. Here they spent the rest of the winter, and here Dom Augustin, disregarding the snows which rendered such a journey all but impossible in midwinter, came from St. Petersburg to bring them news of the promises he had received from the Czar. In the spring of 1799, the main body of the Trappists set out for Russia. These journeys through the desolate plains and endless forests of Poland were the most painful of all. Monasteries, and indeed dwellings of any kind, were few and far between, and they had to spend many nights without shelter, encamping as best they could. When hospitality was available, however, it was of the most cordial and generous kind; the heroic Catholic Poles, impoverished and oppressed as they themselves were, could not do enough for the exiled religious. In August, the whole company was united at Terespol, where the River Bug formed the frontier between the Austrian and Russian dominions. Crossing the bridge, they found themselves at Brzesc, the Russian frontier town. Dom Augustin then divided them into five groups, and settled them in the five monasteries granted by the Czar. The nuns were established in a castle not far from Brzesc, and a community of monks in the same district; two communities of monks in Volhynia, and one in Podolia.

For the first time since they left their monasteries in Switzerland, the Trappists found themselves in a settled abode, and they were full of thankfulness to God. All they wanted was to be allowed to live in peace and observe their Rule, supporting themselves by the labour of their hands, and this was just what had been denied them elsewhere.

They had, however, further hardships to undergo in the rigours of the Russian climate. The two communities at Orsza had already endured a Russian winter, in spite of which they had maintained the full observance of their Rule, though the thermometer fell at times to thirty-two degrees below zero, and a chafing dish had to be placed on the altar in order that Mass might be celebrated. A passage had to be dug through nine feet of snow to enable the Superior to reach the house of the nuns, although it was quite close. In Volhynia and Podolia also, though very much further south, the winter was exceedingly severe, so that the wine often froze in the chalice, and the all-invading snow penetrated into the church through every crevice. Once the thaw had set in, however, the country was fertile enough ; the inhabitants, moreover, showed themselves kindly disposed to the Trappists, and there seemed every prospect of a permanent settlement. Suddenly all their hopes were dashed to the ground. In March, 1800, the Czar issued a decree ordering all French refugees to leave his dominions. Paul III had prudently changed his policy, and now ranged himself on the side of Bonaparte, whose power was becoming more and more formidable. The Trappists were included under this decree. The Czar's benevolence towards them had, in fact, cooled somewhat, as a few months previously the novice Sœur Marie-Joseph had left the Order, and the concessions to the Trappists had all along been merely an act of deference to the Bourbon princess. The latter had borne all the austerities and hardships with admirable courage and forti- tude, but as the time of her profession approached, the Czar was making arrangements with the Catholic Metro- politan that she should immediately be made Abbess, and it appears to have been partly in order to frustrate this project, and partly in obedience to her own strong interior attraction to the work of Perpetual Adoration, that she decided to leave the Order. She did so with the approval of the Superior at Orsza, Père Etienne Malmy, and never ceased to speak with enthusiasm of the Trappists and of Dom Augustin. After a short sojourn at a monastery in Lithuania, she entered the convent of the Benedictines of the Perpetual Adoration at Warsaw, where she made her profession under the name of Sœur Marie-Joseph de la Miséricorde. Once more driven into exile, she spent nine years in England with the Benedictine nuns of Montargis (now at Princethorpe), and after the Restoration returned to Paris, where she founded at the Temple the monastery of the Benedictines of the Blessed Sacrament (now in the Rue Monsieur), in reparation for the crimes of the Revolution, dying there in 1824.

The Trappists had no choice but to evacuate Russian territory without delay. The two communities in the Palatinate of Brzesc proceeded at once to the frontier, to that same spot where the River Bug separates the towns of Brzesc and Terespol. Forced as they were by the Czar's officials to leave Brzesc, they were prevented by the orders of the Austrian Emperor from entering Terespol. Their only resource was to descend the river into Prussian territory, but for this passports were required, and it would take time to obtain them. There was, however, in the middle of the river a deserted island, which neither of the rival powers had troubled to claim, and here they took refuge, the nuns remaining in a boat moored to the shore, while the monks encamped on the island itself. They received their provisions by means of a ladder set up on the island and reaching to the bridge above. There these servants of God, cast out by the kingdoms of this world, celebrated the Feast of Pentecost in the year 1800, the two communities united singing High Mass on the island, in honour of the inauguration of the invisible kingdom of Christ by the coming of the Holy Ghost.

The exiles remained on the island six weeks, their wants being charitably supplied by the Capuchins of Terespol. Then, having obtained passports for Prussia, they proceeded by water to Danzig, where they received the warmest of welcomes from the Lutheran authorities and people, and were given hospitality at the monasteries of the Bridgettine monks and nuns. There they were rejoined by the two communities from Orsza, and the three from Volhynia and Podolia, who had all made their way to Brzesc by various routes, and had likewise descended the Bug and the Vistula by boat. The Trappists could not, however, remain at

Danzig, and after a few weeks' stay, the whole company embarked for Lübeck on July 26, a rich Lutheran merchant placing three ships at their disposal for the voyage—one for the monks, one for the nuns, and one for the children and their masters. Hardly had they set sail when a violent storm arose, and for twenty-four days the religious, many of whom were suffering from dysentery and fever, endured all the horrors of seasickness, together with scarcity of food and water, as the voyage should only have taken two or three days. At length they reached Lübeck, and after a few weeks' stay proceeded by land to Hamburg, where they took up their abode for the winter in several houses rented for them in the environs of the city.

Meanwhile, Dom Augustin made a journey to England, in order to investigate the possibilities of making foundations in America. He met with a most hospitable reception in London, and learned that the British Government was willing to grant to his religious the same pension as that granted to the émigré priests since the beginning of the Revolution. He determined, therefore, to send a colony of nuns to England, there being already an establishment of monks of the Reform at Lulworth in Dorsetshire.

On the Abbot's return to Hamburg, separations took place which, this time, were destined to be final. For three years the Trappists and Trappistines had wandered homeless throughout Europe, driven from one country after another on account of their faith and religious profession, yet rejoicing in the midst of their sufferings, because they shared the lot of their Master, the Son of Man who had not where to lay His head. The time had come for separation, and the partings were deeply felt, for suffering draws closely the bonds of charity.

In March, 1801, Mère Augustin de Chabannes sailed for England with three companions. Soon afterwards, another group of nuns settled near the monks of Darfeld in Westphalia ; this foundation was not destined to be permanent, but gave rise later to the monastery of Ste.-Catherine (now the Immaculate Conception) at Laval. The remainder of the nuns afterwards settled at La Riedra in Switzerland, but returned to France after the fall of Napoleon and made

a number of foundations. The English monastery of Stapehill was thus destined to be the first permanent foundation
of Trappist nuns after the Revolution. A colony of monks
refounded Westmalle in Brabant, and in 1802 Dom Augustin
was able to regain possession of Val-Sainte.

CHAPTER VIII

ENGLAND

MADAME DE CHABANNES and her companions disembarked at St. Catherine's Docks, London, in March, 1801, and were met by a Mr. Wright, a Catholic banker, who devoted himself generously to the relief of the French émigrés and especially the religious. He drove the four Cistercians to his own house, where they received every kindness and attention, until the house which had been rented for them—Blyth House, Brook Green, Hammersmith—could be made ready. They remained ten months at Blyth House, and received three postulants, only one of whom persevered.

Meanwhile, efforts were being made to obtain a permanent dwelling for them, where they would have the assistance of the monks of their own Order. It has already been mentioned that a community of Trappist monks had been established at Lulworth in Dorsetshire. The origin of this foundation was as follows. In 1794, Dom Augustin sent a small colony of monks to London, with a view to their proceeding to Canada. Owing to various circumstances, they gave up this project and remained in England, gratefully accepting the generous offers of that great Catholic, Thomas Weld of Lulworth Castle, to whom the Superior, Père Jean-Baptiste, had been introduced by Dr. Milner, then Catholic pastor at Winchester. The little community of six were established in a small house in Lulworth Park, while their monastery was being built. In 1796 it was finished and dedicated under the title of St. Susan, and the monks took possession of it. This monastery, the first to be built in England since the Reformation, was in the Early English style, and, though small, was perfectly planned. It was situated in a sheltered spot to the south-east of Lulworth Castle, about half-way between the Castle and the sea-

shore. In this remote corner of Dorset, the county of St.
Stephen Harding, the Cistercian Order returned to England,
after more than two hundred and fifty years.   Only a few
miles distant were the ruins of Bindon Abbey, an ancient
Cistercian house, founded in 1172 by Robert de Newburgh
and Maud, his wife.   Though little remains of the buildings,
the foundations are still intact, and the ground plan of a
typical Cistercian monastery is plainly discernible.   It was
on the same plan, though on a much smaller scale, that
Mr. Weld had had the new monastery constructed,
so that Lulworth sprang up almost under the shadow
of Bindon, and like a miniature replica of the ruined
abbey.

The foundation gradually took root ; several novices
joined the new community, and in 1796 three monks were
sent from Westmalle to increase the numbers.   When it
was decided to send a colony of nuns to England, it was
naturally desired that they should be established within
reach of Lulworth, and no doubt Dom Jean-Baptiste
interested Mr. Weld in the project. About twenty miles
to the north-east, in an obscure hamlet called Stapehill,
was a small property belonging to the estates of Lord
Arundell of Wardour, another of those noble Catholics
who showed such generous kindness to the French refugees.
The Welds of Lulworth were connected by marriage with
the Arundells of Wardour, and it was evidently through
Mr. Weld's influence that Henry, eighth Lord Arundell of
Wardour, came to make his generous offer of this property
for the purpose of establishing a community of Cistercian
nuns. Stapehill had been used by the Jesuits as a place of
retirement since the early penal times, but this was the
period of the temporary suppression of the Society, and the
Fathers of the English Province were no longer able to
maintain all their missions.

Stapehill is situated in the Parish of Hampreston in the
Hundred of Cranborne, and was formerly included in the
Manor of Hampreston, which belonged to the Arundells
of Wardour from the sixteenth to the nineteenth century.
The spot was admirably adapted as a place of retreat, being
situated in the heart of that great tract of barren moorland,

covered with heather and gorse, which, intersected by the valley of the Stour, occupies the south-eastern portion of Dorset, stretching westwards of the New Forest and forming part of the ancient Selwood Forest. The property consisted of twenty-five acres of land, on which stood a small farm-house with two or three cottages, and a long narrow barn-like edifice which served as a chapel. The little group of buildings stood on the edge of the heath land, where the moors slope down into the valley, looking south-west over the green meadows watered by the Stour. On the south-east it was sheltered by a low heather-covered ridge, jutting out into the valley and forming a kind of promontory ending in a somewhat abrupt declivity ; this is said to have given the name of ' Steep Hill ' (whence *Stapehill*) to the neigh-bouring hamlet.[1] To the north stretched Hampreston Heath, to the east Parley Common and Herne Common, while southwards across the Stour the expanse of Canford Heath and Poole Heath lay between Stapehill and the coast, ten miles distant, where only a desolate line of sandbanks marked the site where the town of Bournemouth, the resort of health and pleasure seekers, was to spring up in the latter half of the nineteenth century. The whole country-side has changed greatly since 1802, and although the open heaths still remain, residential districts are growing up along the roads which traverse them, while Bournemouth is pushing its spreading suburbs further and further inland. Stapehill is no longer a lonely hamlet, but a growing village, and the motorbuses between Wimborne and Bournemouth pass the Abbey gates. The Abbey itself, however, stands well back from the high road, surrounded by its own fields, and the noise of modern traffic does not reach it. A fir plantation now clothes the ridge, forming a picturesque background to the monastic buildings, and the outlook over the peaceful valley of the Stour is unchanged, scarcely a house being visible even now from the quiet pastures of the monastery. In the middle of the enclosure garden there are two ancient yew trees, under which tradition says that Mass was celebrated during the penal times, while a

[1] The form " Steep Hill " is found in old maps and in the early records of the Abbey.

small boy, perched among the branches, kept a look-out
for the pursuivants.

Stapehill appears to have been served from the early
penal times by the Jesuit missioners of the District or
' College ' of St. Thomas of Canterbury, which was formed in
1633. This District comprised the counties of Sussex,
Wiltshire, Hampshire, and Dorset, and for purposes of
secrecy went by the name of ' Mistress Hants.' The origin
of the mission of Stapehill is probably closely connected
with that of the neighbouring mission of Canford. The
Manor of Canford was purchased in 1611 by Sir John Webb,
and the Webb family being staunch Catholics, it is very
probable that there was a priest serving their household from
an early date. But even before this time the district would
appear to have been a centre of Catholicism, as there is a
long list of recusants for Hampreston Parish in the year 1592,
showing that there must have been a priest living and working in the neighbourhood. At Moors, in the Parish of West
Parley (the present West Moors), three miles north-east of
Stapehill, lived Venerable William Pyke, the heroic Dorsetshire carpenter, who in 1591 followed his spiritual father,
Venerable Thomas Pilchard, to martyrdom, preferring to be
butchered alive at Dorchester rather than deny his faith.

At Canford in the year 1621 was born Father Anthony
Bonville, S.J. (alias Terrill), who was received into the Church
before his fifteenth year by the famous missioner, Father
Thomas Bennett, S.J. (alias Blackfan).[1] Father Bennett
must therefore have been working in the district soon after
1630. Father Bonville became professor in several colleges
on the Continent, and finally Rector of the College of Liége,
where he died in 1676, described as ' a man of extraordinary
piety, talent, learning, and prudence.' There is preserved
at Stapehill a notable relic (two leg bones) of the Companions
of St. Ursula, which was sent by Father Bonville from Liége
in 1668 to Father Valentine Upsall, S.J., in England. The
authentication given by the Abbess of the ' Collegiate Church
and Noble Monastery of St. Cecilia at Cologne ' is copied in
Father Bonville's handwriting, together with an attestation

---

[1] Foley, *Records of the English Province of the Society of Jesus*, Vol. III,
p. 420.

signed by himself (*Antonius Terillus, Soc. Jesu Sacerdos*), and stating that he sends this treasure as a gift (*thesaurum hunc dono mitto*) to the Rev. Father Valentine Upsall, S.J., in England. Father Upsall, better known as Father John Robinson (alias Taylor), suffered fourteen years' imprisonment for the Faith, and was condemned to death at York in 1652, but either he was released or his sentence was commuted to banishment, for he was again working on the mission in the Yorkshire district in 1655. There is no record of the last twenty years of his life, but he died in the ' College of St. Thomas ' in 1675, at the age of seventy-eight, after forty-nine years on the English Mission.[1] It is possible, therefore, that this venerable confessor of the Faith may have lived at Stapehill during the closing years of his long life. The relic was probably given by the Jesuits to the Cistercian nuns on the occasion of their arrival at Stapehill, which took place on the Feast of St. Ursula, 1802.

The earliest recorded missioner resident at Stapehill was Father Michael Jenison, S.J., who lived there from 1686 to 1690. From that time Stapehill was served regularly by the Jesuits, who were even able to carry on a small school in this secluded spot. Hutchins, in his *History of Dorset*, published in 1774, speaks of ' Stapehill, a little hamlet, where a few years ago was suspected to have been a Popish seminary.' Doctor Oliver, in his *Collections*[2] has preserved a record of how ' bigotry magnified enormously ' this school. ' The following narrative,' he writes, ' which I copied from Brice's Exeter paper, called the *Post Master, or Loyal Mercury*, published October 2, 1724, must delight the lovers of Munchausen adventures : '' From Wimborne, in Dorsetshire, *they* write, that a Catholic seminary, which had long subsisted in the neighbourhood of that town, was by *accident* discovered some time ago, which has obliged the person concerned in it to break up housekeeping and remove. The place was exactly suited to the design, it being out of the way of any great road, and altogether *incog*. 'Twas found out by some gentlemen that were hunting, who came upon

[1] Foley, *op. cit.*, Vol. III, pp. 49–59.
[2] *Collections illustrating the History of the Catholic Religion*, etc. (1857), p. 41.

them before they were aware, and surprised some of the youths that were walking at a distance from the house. There were about *sixty rooms in it, handsomely fitted up, which are all underground ;* so that nothing but a bit of farm-house appears, which has till now been a cover to the rest. The masters, students and other employed made the family about *three hundred in number ;* but they are all now gone to their respective friends ; and 'tis thought 'twill be very difficult for them to fix so much to their satisfaction again in this county.'' '

The legend of underground passages, connecting Stapehill and Canford, has persisted as a local tradition down to our own times.

It has been stated[1] that many of the Jesuit missioners are interred at Stapehill, but no trace of their tombs is to be found. There are, however, two Fathers of the Society buried in the old parish church of Hampreston. These are Fathers Charles and Richard Caryll, cousins, and members of the ancient Caryll family of West Grinstead. The Carylls were connected by marriage with the Webbs of Canford, and this may possibly have had something to do with the unusual occurrence of the burial of Jesuits in a Protestant church in the middle of the eighteenth century. Father Charles Caryll served Stapehill from about 1738 until his death in 1745, at the age of sixty. A stone over his grave bears the following inscription : ' Here lyeth the body of Mr. Charles Caryll, S.J., who died the 12th day of June, 1745.' Father Richard Caryll succeeded his cousin at Stapehill, and died on February 18, 1750, aged fifty-eight.

During the residence of Father Charles Caryll at Stapehill the following entry occurs in the account book of the College :[2]

' 1739–40, June 2. Gave one shilling and about three dozen of strong beer to a great number of people that came from Wimborne and the neighbourhood for assistance when the heath was set on fire, which fire came close round this house, so that the hedges adjoining to it and cherry trees

---

[1] Foley, *op. cit.*, Vols. V, p. 817, and VII, Part II, p. 822.
[2] *Ibid.*, Vol. III, p. 539. ' Richard ' should surely read ' Charles,' according to the dates given.

were burnt, and the whole house wonderfully preserved only through God's special protection, and by virtue of an Agnus Dei ; the fire stopping exactly where it was thrown, to the admiration of all, and the thatch not taking fire, though extremely dry, and so near that the men could not stay on it to lay over it a wet blanket.'

Besides its memories of the penal times, Stapehill has far older monastic associations near by, in the ancient market town of Wimborne, or Wimborne Minster, which lies three miles to the south-west, at the confluence of the River Stour and its tributary the Allen, formerly called the Wyn. Once a Roman settlement, Wimborne became a place of considerable importance under the West Saxon kings. Early in the eighth century, possibly in 705, St. Cuthburga, sister of the great West Saxon king, St. Ina, together with her sister, St. Cwenburga, founded an abbey there. It became a most flourishing house, being, as was common at that period, a double monastery of monks and nuns, under the government of an Abbess. Wimborne was famous for the strictness with which enclosure was observed. ' The two monasteries,' writes Montalembert,[1] ' rose side by side, like two fortresses, each surrounded by battlemented walls. The priests were bound to leave the church immediately after the celebration of Mass, bishops themselves were not admitted into the nunnery, and the abbess communicated with the outside world, to give her orders to her spiritual and temporal subjects, only through a barred window.' At one time the nuns alone numbered no less than five hundred.

In the year 721 St. Richard, the holy West Saxon king, or rather prince, setting out on pilgrimage to the Holy Places, placed his daughter, St. Walburga, in the care of St. Cuthburga, and not long afterwards Walburga was joined by her cousin St. Lioba. Both were near relatives of Winfrid, afterwards the great St. Boniface, who, during his missionary labours in Germany, kept up a close correspondence with his friends in the English monasteries, especially at Wimborne. When he became Bishop, he wrote to the Abbess Tetta, St. Cuthburga's successor, begging her to send him some of her

[1] *Monks of the West*, Eng. trans. (1867), Vol. V, p. 303.

nuns to help him in his work. In response to his appeal,
St. Walburga, St. Lioba, and about thirty others set out from
Wimborne for Germany, where St. Walburga's brothers,
SS. Willibald and Winibald, were already labouring. This
was about the year 748. These Wimborne nuns played an
important part in the Christianisation of Germany, and
founded the great monasteries of Heidenheim, Bischofsheim,
and others.

King Aethelred, brother and predecessor of King Alfred,
who was killed in 871 fighting against the Danes, was buried
at Wimborne in the Abbey Church. The brass which pur-
ports to mark his grave may perhaps have replaced an earlier
memorial to him. During one of the many incursions of the
Danes, probably at the end of the ninth century, both church
and monastery were completely destroyed, and the Abbey
was never refounded as a monastic establishment. A thousand years later, the same Rule of St. Benedict which had
been kept with so much fervour at Wimborne by the West
Saxon princesses and their companions, was resumed at
Stapehill by the French Cistercian nuns, and is observed at
the present day by their English successors.

The Abbey Church, now the Minster, was rebuilt by
Edward the Confessor in the eleventh century, and became a
Collegiate Church of secular Canons. The present Minster
shows specimens of almost every period of English architecture, but is especially remarkable for its fine Norman and
early Transition work. Ten altars formerly stood in the
church, and it was famous for the number of precious relics
preserved there. One of the last of the deans of Wimborne
Minster was Cardinal Pole, whose mother, Blessed Margaret
Pole, the martyred Countess of Salisbury, held the adjacent
Manor of Canford until dispossessed by Henry VIII.

The new Catholic Church of St. Catherine, opened in
1933, is believed to stand on the site of an old pre-Reforma-
tion chapel dedicated to St. Catherine.

Out of the sixty odd religious houses in the present
diocese of Plymouth, only two were in existence when the
Cistercian nuns settled at Stapehill. These were the English
Carmelites from Antwerp, established at Lanherne since
1794, and the Canonesses of St. Augustine from Louvain,

now at Newton Abbot, who had settled at Spetisbury in 1799. The English Benedictines from Paris were then living at Marnhull, but in 1807 they removed to Cannington in Somerset, and finally to Colwich. Still nearer neighbours were the English Carmelites from Hoogstraet (originally a filiation from Antwerp), to whom Sir John Webb had lent Canford Manor in 1794.

In order to adapt Stapehill for the purpose of a Cistercian monastery, some additions as well as alterations to the existing buildings were necessary, and these were carried out under the direction of the Prior of Lulworth. The original farm-house is still standing and forms part of the conventual buildings, the ground floor being occupied by the Superior's room, and the upper floor by the novitiate. The old chapel used by the Jesuits also remains, and is now the refectory. From this nucleus the whole monastery has grown, being added to at different periods and following no one plan, so that although not large, it presents rather the appearance of a small village than a convent. The remainder of the original buildings, which had only mud walls and were roofed with thatch, have long since disappeared.

While the alterations were being carried out, the nuns resided at Burton House, near Christchurch, which had been kindly lent to them and prepared for their reception by Lady Mannock, a great benefactress of the French refugees. They removed there from Hammersmith in January, 1802, and remained till October, a French émigré priest, Abbé Gilles Viel, acting as their chaplain. Four postulants joined them at Burton House, three of whom were to be among the foundresses of Stapehill.

The last Jesuit missioner at Stapehill was Father John Couche, who, on the arrival of the nuns, removed to the old cottage known as the 'Pilgrim's house,' or 'Pilgrimage,' and continued to reside there for some time, with two pupils. After Father Couche's departure the Pilgrimage was let to ladies desiring to live a retired life, close to the monastery. The first tenant was Madame Marie-Antoinette de Fages-Vaumale, a member of an exiled French Royalist family, a friend of Madame de Chabannes and benefactress of the community. Her brother, Baron Louis de Fages-Vaumale, married Barbara du Moulin, daughter of John du Moulin and Mary Browne, sister and heiress of the last Viscount Montague of Cowdray.   Her parents being dead, she was under the guardianship of her maternal aunt, Lady Mannock, and her great-uncle, Sir Thomas Moore, Bart., of Fawley. After the removal of the nuns to Stapehill in 1802, Lady Mannock lived at Burton House herself, with her uncle and niece.   The marriage of the latter with Baron de Fages took place at Stapehill in August, 1805.   The newly married couple went to live in Jersey, Madame Antoinette de Fages remaining at the Pilgrimage, where she died on April 29, 1837, aged sixty-seven.   Her grave is in the oldest part of the nuns' cemetery.   Sir Thomas Moore died at Burton House in 1807 ; his body was brought to Stapehill and buried in the middle of the nave of the old chapel.   When the new church was built in 1850, and the old chapel became the refectory, the marble tombstone covering his grave was taken up and placed against the outside wall.   It bears the following inscription :

' IHS.   Here Reposeth the Body of Sir Thomas Michael Moore, Bart., the last Heir male of Sir Richard Moore, Bart., of Fawley in Berkshire, who departed this life April 10th, 1807, in the 81st year of his age.   Dying unmarried the title became extinct.

Requiescat in Pace.'

A small slab of marble let into the floor of the refectory marks the place where his remains lie.

CHAPTER IX

BEGINNINGS AT STAPEHILL

' THEY entered their monastery of the Holy Cross of Our Lady of La Trappe, founded by R. P. Jean-Baptiste, on October 21, 1802, and celebrated their entrance on November 13 of the same year. They were then to the number of nine : three professed religious, one received to profession, and five novices.'

So runs the brief entry in the earliest register of Stapehill, in Madame de Chabannes' handwriting. The three professed were Madame de Chabannes herself, Mère Marie Josephine, and Mère Julie Josephine. Mère Marie Josephine (Anne Pierrette de Montron) was the daughter of Antoine de Montron, master shoemaker of Dôle, in Franche-Comté. Born at Dôle on September 7, 1763, she became a Carmelite nun, and when the convent at Dôle was suppressed, took refuge in Switzerland. She entered the monastery of La Sainte Volonté de Dieu on October 10, 1796, received the habit on the 22nd of the same month, and made her profession on November 1, 1797, three days after Madame de Chabannes. Having the opportunity of returning to her former Order, she declined to do so, and in her ' Declaration ' she affirms that she had never in her whole life experienced such delight as she found in the austere life of the Trappist Reform, ' although I had the happiness of being twelve years a Carmelite.' Madame de Chabannes describes her as ' a model of regularity.' She was especially devoted to the sick, and acted as infirmarian during the wanderings and later at Stapehill, where she filled also the offices of Sub-Prioress and chantress. She died on the Feast of St. Benedict, March 21, 1814.

Mère Marie Josephine was the only one of the foundresses who had been Madame de Chabannes' companion in Switzerland. Mère Julie Josephine (Julie Favot) had joined the exiles during their sojourn in Bavaria, in March, 1798, and received the habit the same month. Nothing is known of her early life, except that she was a professed religious, who evidently preferred the hardships and uncertainty of a homeless community to the giving-up of her religious state. She was one of the group sent for the foundation at Orsza, where she made her profession in 1799. Mère Julie Josephine died at Stapehill within a year of the foundation, on October 13, 1803, at the age of forty-six, and was the first nun to be buried in the little cemetery.

The fourth and last of the little group sent to England for the foundation was Sœur Thérèse de la Miséricorde (Mary Emily Lamb). Of Scottish parentage—her father, Robert Lamb, a ship's captain, and his wife, Anne Masterton, were both Protestants—she was born at Edinburgh on May 1, 1769, in the same month and year as Madame de Chabannes. Her conversion must have taken place at a very early age, for at eighteen she was already a professed religious in the convent of the Annonciades Célestes[1] at Sens. She, too, joined the exiles in Bavaria, entering the community at the Château de Durnas on October 20, 1798. After receiving the habit on November 1, she followed the community in all their journeyings, and made a vow of obedience in 1800, solemn profession being impossible owing to the want of a settled abode. She was the first nun professed at Stapehill, her profession taking place in March, 1803, on the occasion of the first Regular Visitation made by Dom Augustin. Designated, obviously, for the English foundation on account of her British origin, Mère Thérèse de la Miséricorde filled many important offices in the community, particularly that of Mistress of Novices, which she held until the time of her death in April, 1831.

The ' five novices ' had all joined the foundresses since their arrival in England. Sœur Marie Bernard (Catherine Barbe Hinde), a doctor's daughter from Yorkshire, entered at

[1] The ' Annonciades Célestes ' (so called, from the colour of their mantles, to distinguish them from the Annonciades founded in 1500 by Jeanne de Valois) were founded in 1604 by Bl. Maria Victoria Fornari-Strata. Cf. Butler's *Lives of the Saints*, ed. Thurston & Attwater (1934), September 12.

Hammersmith in August, 1801, and received the habit at Burton House in January, 1802. Not having the health to keep the Rule, she received the black veil as a choir oblate in February, 1803, and died on October 15, 1811. Sœur Jean-Baptiste, a former Carmelite of Huy in the diocese of Liége, entered at Burton House and was clothed there in January, 1802, but left in 1805, for reasons of health.

The remaining three were in reality postulants received to their clothing, which took place on November 13, the day of the solemn entrance at Stapehill. They made their profession on May 24, 1804, and all three were to prove valuable subjects for the new foundation. Sœur Scholastique (Catherine Jeanne Joseph Wattremez), born in 1758, a native of the diocese of Cambrai, entered at Burton House in August, 1802. She became an excellent religious and a capable housekeeper ; she was also Sub-Prioress from 1818 until her death, which took place on September 21, 1831.

The two other postulants became the first two lay sisters of Stapehill, and their devoted and self-sacrificing lives deserve to be kept in memory. Both were exiled French nuns from Cambrai, who entered together at Burton House in August, 1802. The first, Sœur Madeleine (Anne Elisabeth Quatrelivres), had been a Canoness of St. Augustine at the Abbey of Notre-Dame des Près, and was in her sixty-fifth year when she elected to become a Cistercian lay sister. She was most useful in the kitchen, Madame de Chabannes tells us, on account of her exquisite cleanliness and economy. But she did not shrink from the hardest field labour, and took part in the work of bringing the barren heath lands under cultivation. Professed on May 24, 1804, she died on July 24, 1813, at the age of seventy-five, after more than ten years' faithful service. The other, Sœur Humbeline (Séraphine Joseph le Fèvre), born in 1767, had been a Religieuse Hospitalière de St. Augustin at Cambrai. She was a farmer's daughter, and understood baking and dairy work, as well as field work. Madame de Chabannes records that she ' sustained extraordinary labours for eight years, in clearing the entirely uncultivated land, with only one sister of seventy to help her ' (Sœur Madeleine), and adds that ' not only those who are now living, but all who come after us in the future, owe her gratitude for this.' This land, most probably, was the field now known as St. Benedict's. Professed with her companion in May, 1804, Sœur Humbeline died on May 3, 1825, being one of the most valuable sisters of those early days. She kept the primitive Rule in its full austerity throughout her twenty-two years of profession, notwithstanding her great labours.

Such was the little group of nine who drove the ten miles or so from Burton to Stapehill on that autumn day in late October, 1802, to found the first monastery of Cistercian nuns in England since the Reformation. Three weeks were spent in getting the house into order, and arranging the regular places as far as possible according to the plan of a Cistercian monastery. The community then made a three days' retreat in preparation for the solemn celebration of their entrance. This took place on November 13, 1802, Feast of All Saints of the Cistercian Order, which is regarded as the date of the foundation. The nuns themselves relate the event as follows :

' After having been turned out of our holy retreats, and obliged to abandon our country, to traverse many strange lands in order to find a refuge where we could freely carry out the duties of our holy state, and unable to remain anywhere ; we have at last been sent by our Reverend Father Abbot, Dom Augustin, to England, where Divine Providence has willed to prepare the retreat for which we have been longing, in this Protestant country, once the Island of Saints. After searching for so long, during three years, with so much fatigue and trouble, Lady Arundell has given us this little house, which has been added to and arranged as regularly as our small means would allow, with the help of our Reverend Father Dom Jean-Baptiste, former Prior of the monastery of Lulworth, who has contributed greatly to our establishment, by the great services he has rendered us. Having arrived in this little sanctuary, so ardently desired, penetrated with gratitude, and after making a three-days' retreat in preparation, we have celebrated our taking possession of the house with great solemnity, for the first time, on November 13, Feast of our Holy Fathers, and have undertaken for ourselves and for all who come after us, to renew the memory of it on the same day. . . .' Dom Jean-Baptiste said Mass, and immediately before the communion came to the grille holding the ciborium in his hands. The community knelt down, and Madame de Chabannes recited in the name of all a solemn act of thanksgiving and renewal of vows. After Mass, the *Te Deum* was sung, the antiphon *Inviolata*, in honour of Our Lady, and another in honour of the Holy Cross. The chronicle continues : ' This house has been established under the title of Our Lady of the Holy Cross, by a choice of predilection of our Reverend Mother Augustin with the consent of the community.' The Feast of the Invention of the Holy Cross was chosen as the Patronal Feast of the house, that of the Exaltation of the Cross being a day of special devotion.

November 13 is still observed as a holy-day, and a solemn *Te Deum* is sung at Benediction on that day in thanksgiving for all the graces bestowed on the house since the foundation.

A few weeks later, early in December, Dom Jean-Baptiste performed the ceremony of the solemn blessing of the house and all the regular places.

Poverty and hard work mark the beginnings of most religious foundations, but they were to be the lot of the foundresses of Stapehill to perhaps an exceptional degree. The community was devoid of temporal resources, except for the pension granted by the British Government to those among them who were French refugees. The little farm was their only other source of support, but the soil was poor and unproductive, the nuns were unaccustomed to labours of that kind, and could not afford to pay for much hired labour. But they had the heroic spirit of the early Cistercians, and gave themselves unsparingly not only to tilling the land already reclaimed, but even to the thankless task of clearing with the pick-axe parts of the heather-covered moorland which then surrounded the monastery on three sides, as well as draining the low-lying meadows in the valley. Madame de Chabannes herself used to fill the carts with manure between four and five in the morning, after the Vigils, so that they should be ready for the workman when he came at six.

The monks of Lulworth showed themselves true fathers

and brothers to the little community, helping them both spiritually and temporally as far as their own meagre resources would allow. Père Antoine was appointed confessor to the nuns, and came over on horseback every Saturday to hear their confessions, spending Sunday at Stapehill, and riding back to Lulworth on Monday. In the early days he was always accompanied by a lay brother, bearing a barrel of milk, and this continued until the nuns received the welcome present of a cow. The Brothers made the nuns' shoes, and the nuns in return washed and mended the altar linen from the monastery.

During the week, Mass was said for the nuns by a French émigré priest, the Abbé Alexandre Cochet, to whom the care of the small congregation of surrounding Catholics was entrusted after the departure of the Jesuits. He lived in a small thatched cottage close to the chapel. The Abbé Cochet afterwards founded the mission of Burton Green, where he settled in 1811, being succeeded at Stapehill by the Abbé de la Porte, who remained until 1826. The old cottage was then demolished.[1]

A few months after the foundation, the community had the joy of receiving a visit from Dom Augustin de Lestrange, their Father Immediate, who arrived on March 16, 1803. Dom Augustin made the Regular Visitation, and gave an inspiring address in Chapter, urging the religious to zeal for the Divine Office, for silence and for manual work. He also blessed the little cemetery and received the profession of Mère Thérèse de la Miséricorde.

In October of the same year, Madame de Chabannes had the sorrow of losing Mère Julie Josephine, so that at the end of the first year at Stapehill the numbers were reduced to eight, no postulants having as yet presented themselves.

In September, 1804, the Vicar Apostolic of the Western District, Dr. Sharrock, O.S.B., paid his first visit to the Priory. He gave permission for Exposition of the Blessed Sacrament on certain feasts, and for Benediction on the first Friday of each month, by special request of Madame de Chabannes, ' in order to beseech the Divine Heart of Jesus for the needs of the Church, of our whole Order, and the

---

[1] This cottage stood on the site now occupied by the infirmary kitchen.

conversion of the unhappy country in which we live.' The Bishop also examined and authenticated all the relics in the possession of the community.

In spite of the efforts of the nuns, the difficulties of English farming evidently proved too great, and at the end of two years Madame de Chabannes made the following proposal to the community : ' that seeing how little knowledge she had of agriculture, and how impossible it was for her, by reason of the enclosure, to visit all the land of the little farm of the monastery, they should engage a farmer, who should live near the house, to superintend the farm, and inform the Reverend Mother of whatever needed to be done, in order to cultivate the land well and render it fruitful.' The farmer, by name Charles Hock, was duly engaged, the community undertaking to maintain him in health and sickness and pay him ten guineas a year. He seems to have proved a faithful servant to the community, and the farm gradually became a small source of income, the nuns, of course, continuing to do most of the work themselves. In 1808, moreover, Lulworth was able to spare an excellent Irish lay brother for Stapehill—Brother Patrick—of whom Madame de Chabannes writes, after his death in 1823 : ' For fifteen years he edified us by his love for his holy state, and his regular and laborious life. Our monastery has sustained a real loss by his death ; he took such great pains to cultivate our little farm, which he greatly improved.'

During the first five years, though one or two postulants entered, they proved to have no vocation, and not a single novice received the habit. Madame de Chabannes must have needed all her indomitable courage and confidence in Divine Providence to pursue her enterprise, which seemed doomed to failure. The first English subject received was a young girl from Lulworth, Mary Slade, who entered as a *sœur donnée* in October, 1804. She received the habit as a choir novice in February, 1807, taking the name of Sister Juliana, and proved an excellent choir nun and a useful member of the community. Two other good subjects received the habit in the same year, 1807—Sœur Brigitte Le Brun, a former Benedictine lay sister from Belgium, and Sœur Séraphique Huet, Religieuse Hospitalière at Mons before the

H

Revolution. The latter had entered at Darfeld in 1806, had completed her novitiate and received the votes for her profession, but owing to the unsettled state of affairs on the Continent had asked to be transferred to Stapehill, where she entered in December, 1807. Madame de Chabannes describes her as ' a pillar of regularity ' and ' fitted for any employment.' With these three novices began a small but steadily increasing stream of vocations, and the Order began to take root in England once more.

In September, 1808, Bishop Collingridge, Coadjutor to Bishop Sharrock, made his first visit to Stapehill. He said Mass and gave Holy Communion to the whole community, afterwards addressing them on the happiness of the religious state.

At this period the community were in great anxiety, owing to the long silence of the Father Immediate, Dom Augustin. The state of affairs on the Continent rendered regular communication impossible. On this account, the profession of the three novices was long delayed ; finally, however, Dom Maur, Prior of Lulworth, received their vows on October 15, 1809, by special delegation from Bishop Collingridge. A few years earlier, Dom Augustin had obtained permission from Napoleon for the establishment of Trappist monasteries within the Empire, and several foundations had been made. But this favourable attitude of the despot was to be of short duration. Napoleon, having subdued the nations, now wished to render the Papacy itself subject to him. Unable to bend Pius VII to his wishes, he resorted to violence, and on May 17, 1809, Rome was occupied by a French army. The Pope responded by excommunicating Napoleon. The Emperor did not shrink from laying violent hands on the Pontiff himself, and on July 6 Pius VII was forcibly removed from Rome and imprisoned at Savona. Christendom remained silent ; scarcely a voice was raised in protest, so completely had Napoleon terrorised the European powers. Dom Augustin, however, was fearless, and his loyalty to the Holy See at this crisis is in accordance with the greatest traditions of the Order of Cîteaux. He was one of the first to visit Pius VII in his prison, and this drew on him the suspicion of the

Emperor. In 1810 Napoleon required the clergy of Italy to take an oath of fidelity to the Constitutions of the Empire. Misled as to the real implications of this oath, the Trappists of Cervara, near Genoa, had signed it. On hearing of this act, Dom Augustin obliged the monks to make a public retractation of it, which they did on May 4, 1811, promising instead entire submission to the Emperor in all that did not affect their conscience. In consequence, Napoleon ordered the arrest of Dom Augustin, and the suppression of all the houses of La Trappe within the Empire. The Abbot was taken prisoner at Bordeaux, where he was despatching a colony of religious to America, but he succeeded in escaping from the hands of the police and returning in safety to Val-Sainte. As soon as the French Government knew of his whereabouts, orders were sent to the French ambassador in Switzerland to arrest him wherever he was, and take him to Geneva, where he was to be executed as a State criminal. But Dom Augustin had not waited for this order, and was already on his way through Germany in disguise. All attempts to seize his person having failed, his enemies spread the report that he had been arrested at Hamburg and shot immediately. They hoped thus to spread fear and discouragement among the religious subject to him. This report reached Stapehill, and the community offered the prescribed suffrages for the repose of the soul of their beloved father. The latter, however, had made good his escape as far as Riga, whence he took ship for England, arriving at Stapehill on January 4, 1812.

The joy of the religious on seeing him again, after nine years' absence, may be imagined. He made the Regular Visitation, blessed and erected the Stations of the Cross in the chapter room, and gave the habit to a postulant.

From England, Dom Augustin proceeded to America to organise the groups of monks and nuns who had preceded him thither. But while engaged in this work, the news reached him of the downfall of Napoleon. He hastened to return to Europe with his religious. The period of exile was over, and the Trappists were able to return freely to France and to the other countries of the Empire. Twenty-one monks had left La Trappe in 1791 ; in 1815 they returned to France six hundred strong, to resume there the regular observance which had continued uninterrupted throughout that stormy epoch.   This is but one more demonstration of the truth of Montalembert's dictum, that ' monks, like oaks, are immortal.'   The storm had not only failed to uproot the great tree, but had even strengthened its growth, and caused it to throw out fresh branches.

In the midst of these labours, Dom Augustin found time, on his return from America, to make another Visitation at Stapehill, in July, 1815.   It was during this Visitation that the colour of the scapular of the choir nuns was changed from tan to black.   Dom Augustin at the same time gave permission for milk to be put in the portions of the community and dessert to be served, when Christmas Day fell on a Friday.

During the early years children were received at Stapehill, to be educated and trained for the religious life.   They wore a ' little habit ' made of linen, with a hood to draw over the head.   Most of these children afterwards entered the novitiate, but several died young, being remarkable for their saintly piety.   Of one of them it is related that she habitually saw Our Lord in the Sacred Host at Holy Communion, under the form of a beautiful infant.   This became known through her innocently remarking one day to her Mistress : ' How very beautiful the Divine Infant looked to-day.'   The Mistress was unable to conceal her surprise, and the child said : ' I thought, Mother, that *everyone* who went to Holy Communion saw the Divine Infant as I do.'   When she understood that it was not so, she remained silent.   This child, known as ' little Sister Rosalie,' died in 1828 at the age of twelve, having been six years in the house.   Another of these little oblates was Theresa Harding, who, as a child of twelve, was brought by her parents to see Madame de Chabannes. The Reverend Mother playfully allowed her to try on the ' little habit,' and once she had put it on, nothing would induce her to take it off or to go home with her parents. The latter knew that she had already the desire to consecrate herself to God, and being themselves profoundly pious, they allowed her to remain.   She received the name of Sister Bernard, and died on July 4, 1827, at the age of fifteen, ' having no desire to live except to be consecrated to

God.' This child was the granddaughter of that remarkable old baronet, Sir Harry Trelawny, who, by turns Presbyterian minister, Anglican clergyman and Prebendary of Exeter Cathedral, was received into the Church in 1826, at the age of seventy, was ordained priest by Cardinal Odescalchi on Whitsunday, 1830, and died at Lavino in 1834. His two daughters, Miss Trelawny and Mrs. Harding, had long been Catholics and benefactors to Stapehill, and Sir Harry's own name appears as a benefactor as early as 1814. After 1828 no more children were received at Stapehill, the institute of the *Tiers Ordre* being in that year suppressed in France.

CHAPTER X

'OUR LADY OF THE HOLY CROSS'

At the end of fifteen years of labour and poverty it seemed that the new foundation was beginning to be solidly established. It might have been expected that the difficulties inherent in all such beginnings would now lessen, and that a time of prosperity could be hoped for. The exact contrary was the case; one trial after another was to fall upon the little community, and the title of ' Our Lady of the Holy Cross ' given to the monastery at the outset was to be fully verified in the course of its history.

It will be remembered that it was through the efforts of the then Prior of Lulworth, Dom Jean-Baptiste de Noyer, that the nuns had come to Stapehill, and the generous kindness of his community to the new foundation had known no bounds. Dom Jean-Baptiste had been succeeded in 1801 by Dom Marie-Bernard Benoît, and on the death of the latter in 1805, Dom Maur Adam was chosen Prior. Dom Maur, dying in 1810, designated as his successor Dom Antoine Saulnier de Beauregard, and foretold the great increase of the community which was to come about under the latter's rule. Anne-Nicolas-Charles Saulnier de Beauregard was born on the Feast of St. Bernard, 1764. Doctor of the Sorbonne and Canon of Sens, ordained priest in 1789, this brilliant and promising young ecclesiastic came to London in 1794, in company with other refugees. Hearing of the Trappist monastery at Lulworth, he determined, notwithstanding the entreaties of his friends and patrons, to become a monk there, and was the first to enter the novitiate, in June, 1795, at thirty-one years of age. He gave himself to his new life with all the ardour of a St. Bernard, and made his profession in June, 1796. In 1802 he was appointed confessor to the nuns of Stapehill, who enjoyed the benefit of his wise and holy direction until his appointment as Prior in 1810. From that time onwards he acted practically as Father Immediate to the nuns during the prolonged absences of Dom Augustin, and was delegated by the Bishop to receive professions. To the end of his life Dom Antoine remained a friend and benefactor to the community of Stapehill, and his memory was held in benediction by the nuns. A bust of him stands in the library.

In 1813 the Priory of St. Susan, Lulworth, was raised by the Holy See to the dignity of an Abbey, and Dom Antoine was solemnly blessed as Abbot by Dr. Poynter, Bishop of the London District. As Abbot he remained the poor and humble monk he had ever been. He always wore a wooden pectoral cross; the plain gold one he had bought under protest he wore only once, and then gave it to his friend, Mgr. Flaget, the saintly Bishop of Bardstown, U.S.A. The ring he habitually wore was of steel, with a death's head instead of a precious stone; this ring was buried with him.

Dom Antoine was not to remain long in the peaceful exercise of his office. For some years Protestant prejudice had been busy circulating evil reports against the community, and in 1815 the calumniators were reinforced by an apostate monk named Power, from Waterford, who cast off his faith together with his habit, and read his abjuration publicly in Blandford parish church. He drew up a long list of charges against the monks, and these, naturally, made a strong impression on Protestant public opinion in the neighbourhood. The matter was brought to the notice of the Government, and Dom Antoine was summoned to London to answer the accusations. The apostate refused to appear, and the whole case fell to the ground, Dom Antoine being completely exonerated from all blame by the Prime Minister, Lord Sidmouth. The affair, however, did not end here. Lord Sidmouth took occasion to impose on the Abbot a fresh restriction—that only French subjects were henceforth to be received into the novitiate. Dom Antoine could not accept this condition, and the Prime Minister, reminding him that the monks had only been tolerated in England in the character of French refugees, required him to remove his community to France, where it was now possible for religious to live in peace. To this Dom Antoine was compelled to agree, though with reluctance, for he foresaw that the tranquil state of affairs in France was not to be of long duration. Having obtained the unwilling consent of Mr. Weld, he succeeded in purchasing the ancient Cistercian abbey of Melleraye in Brittany, and the community of Lulworth embarked at Weymouth on July 10, 1817, on the government frigate, *La Revanche*, sent by Louis XVIII for their transport. The monastery of St. Susan, which had been their home for over twenty years, fell in ruins during the following winter, leaving only the cloister walls surrounding the little cemetery where still lie the remains of the monks and lay brothers who died there, twenty-seven in number.

Up to this time Stapehill had been in the normal position of a house of Cistercian nuns, that is to say, in the proximity of a monastery of monks of the Order, who supplied priests for the spiritual direction of the nuns, and lay brothers for the external service of the monastery. Now, it was the only Cistercian house in England. But although the monks had crossed the Channel, they continued to render spiritual and temporal assistance to the nuns as hitherto. Père Palemon, who had succeeded Dom Antoine in 1810 as confessor to the nuns, remained at Stapehill as resident chaplain, and the good Brother Patrick also stayed behind. Still, it must have been a heavy trial to Madame de Chabannes no longer to have Dom Antoine close at hand, with his wise counsel and fatherly interest in the growing community. At this period many of the exiled French communities returned to their native land, and it may be wondered why the nuns of Stapehill did not do likewise. In the life of Dom Antoine[1] it is recorded that he thought of purchasing for them an old abbey at Châteaubriant, not far from Melleraye, but that ' Providence disposed otherwise.' It appears that Madame de Chabannes declined the offer, and chose to remain in England. She seems to have had a firm conviction that the English foundation was willed by God and would promote His glory ' in this unhappy country, formerly the island of saints,' as she expressed it, and that it would lead to conversions, several having already taken place at Stapehill. She was filled with zeal for the conversion of England, and

[1] *Vie du R. P. D. Antoine* (Paris, 1840), p. 76.

felt that she and her community owed a debt of gratitude to the nation which had so hospitably received them and supplied their wants. Possibly if she could have foreseen the trials that were in store for her she might have decided otherwise—for the next seven years were to be a veritable *Via Crucis*.

On May 3, 1818, less than a year after the departure from Lulworth, the monastery of Stapehill was all but destroyed by a disastrous fire. The following account of the event is taken from the old French chronicle of the house. ' In the year 1818 Divine Providence was pleased to afflict our Monastery with a terrible calamity. On May 3, the Feast of the Invention of the Holy Cross, our Patronal Festival, between ten and eleven o'clock at night, through an unforeseen accident, the exterior buildings of our house caught fire, and in the space of two hours the guest-rooms, the wash-house, the Brother's room, the bake-house, and finally the barns, stable, and cow-sheds, were reduced to ashes. Having but little help, we were able to save hardly anything from these places, which contained the provisions for our subsistence, much linen, furniture, quantities of wood and straw, all the tools for the farm work—all these became the prey of the destructive element. It was only by a miracle—we can truly say this, for it was acknowledged even by Protestants who came the next day to see the ruins—that the whole house was not reduced to ashes, for the flames stopped close to a pile of dry wood, and if that had caught fire, the chapel and monastery would have been entirely consumed. No one, moreover, was injured, amid the great confusion and consternation. We owe our deliverance to the protection of the Blessed Virgin, to whom our Reverend Mother Augustin and the community had recourse by fervent prayer, while the flames were raging most violently ; promising her that if she came to our aid, we and all those who should come after us, would sing the *Ave Maris Stella* every year on the same day. . . . Reverend Mother then felt inspired to throw a relic of the True Cross into the midst of the flames, and from that moment they subsided, and soon afterwards the fire was completely extinguished. A few days later, while clearing and turning over the heaps of ashes, we found the

Relic intact, only the glass having been scorched, without even being broken. . . . We continued our task until eight o'clock at night, and this prolonged labour lasted the whole week. We were forced to engage men for several nights to guard the house, for it was quite open, and many curious people came to see the ruins. We could not even ascertain that the fire was completely extinguished, for the beams and joists were still smoking, there being a shortage of water, as we had only one pump, the other having been burnt at the beginning.'

No natural explanation could be given for the sudden cessation of the conflagration, and all believed that the house had been miraculously saved from destruction. Every year, on May 3, the *Ave Maris Stella* is sung after Vespers at the altar of Our Lady of Dolours, in thanksgiving.

Although the main buildings were uninjured, the loss caused by the fire was nevertheless very great, the damage being estimated at £1,400. In a few hours the work of years had been destroyed. Good friends, however, were not wanting to the community in their hour of need, and many persons whose names even were unknown to the community, Protestants as well as Catholics, gave liberal alms for the work of restoration. In gratitude to these benefactors, two annual Masses were established, with General Communion— one on the Feast of the Transfiguration, for their intentions, and a Solemn Requiem on May 4 for those deceased.

It was not until 1821 that the work was completed, and the new buildings solemnly blessed by Père Palemon, those destroyed by the fire having been replaced, and some new ones added, in view of the growing numbers of the community. The accommodation, however, was still very inadequate, and it became necessary to prepare plans for a further enlargement of the monastery. A new wing was planned, to include a dormitory and work-room, and on the Feast of St. Bernard, 1822, the ceremony of laying the foundation-stone took place. Père Palemon performed the ceremony, assisted by the Rev. John Coyne, P.P., of Newry in Co. Down. This holy Irish priest was a great friend and bene-factor of the community, and from 1820 onwards sent many postulants, both choir and lay. His visits to Stapehill were

frequent ; on this occasion he had come for the clothing of
his sister, Bridget Coyne, who received the habit as a choir
novice on the Feast of the Assumption, taking the name of
Sister Winifred.[1]

On the eve of the feast, Père Palemon and Father Coyne
planted a wooden cross on the spot where the foundation-
stone was to be laid. The following morning, at four o'clock,
immediately after Lauds, the two priests, in sacerdotal
vestments, accompanied by the whole community, went in
procession to the site. A mason was waiting, with the stone
ready squared, a cross having been cut in each corner, and
an inscription which ran as follows :

Reverenda Augustina Priorissa de la Trappe
Hic me posuit
Die Sancti Bernardi, 20 *Aug :* 1822.

Père Palemon intoned the antiphon *Signum salutis*, and the
chantress gave out the psalm *Quam dilecta tabernacula tua*
(Ps. 83), which was sung in alternate choirs, Père Palemon
meanwhile sprinkling the site with holy water. He then
blessed the stone, with the appointed prayers, and Madame
de Chabannes placed under it a silver medal of the Sacred
Heart, chanting the invocation : *Cor Jesu, Rex et centrum
omnium cordium, miserere, miserere nobis.* Medals of the
Holy Family and of St. Benedict were added by Mère
Scholastique, the Sub-Prioress, and Mère Thérèse de la Miséricorde, the only survivor of those who had come to England
with the Foundress. Madame de Chabannes then placed
the stone in position, saying the usual prayer ' In the faith
of Jesus Christ,' etc., and sealed it with the seal of the
monastery, Mère Scholastique and Mère Thérèse also sealing
it in their turn. The psalm *Miserere* was then chanted, with
the antiphon *O quam metuendus*, followed by the canticle
Fundamenta ejus, while Père Palemon again sprinkled the
entire site with holy water.

---

[1] Sister Winifred made her profession on September 8, 1823, and died
suddenly on March 7, 1824, at the age of twenty-three, while Fr. Coyne
was on a visit to Stapehill. Mme de Chabannes was able to declare after
her death that she had not committed a single fault since she entered the
house, and describes her as a soul very united to God, and of a great
exactitude and love for all her duties.

The loss of the neighbouring community of Lulworth, and the material destruction caused by the fire, were followed by still greater trials, threatening the very existence of the community itself. Although many postulants were received, the number of deaths became so great that the community, instead of increasing, was actually decreasing. Already in 1811 the first English lay novice, Sister Lutgarde (Mary Cane), died a saintly death at the age of twenty, having made her vows on her deathbed. Born of Protestant parents, she had been baptised at Stapehill in 1807 at fifteen, and entered the following year. In 1813 the good old Sœur Madeleine went to her reward, to be followed in 1814 by the oldest of the foundresses, Mère Marie-Josephine. In the same year another young lay sister died, and in 1815 a young choir nun, Mère Rosalie, only a year professed. But it was in 1817 that the mortality became alarming. In that year there were seven deaths—three choir nuns, one lay sister and three oblates. Among them were two of the most promising of the younger religious—Mother Juliana Slade, already spoken of, who was the first English choir nun professed, and who died at thirty-two, after twelve years of profession, and Mother Bernard Curr, aged twenty-seven, described by Madame de Chabannes as ' a model of recollection, endowed with great talents, and having made great sacrifices for God.' Her father was a wealthy Yorkshire manufacturer, and her sister a nun at the Bar Convent, York.

Several other deaths followed within the next few years, and when Dom Augustin made the Visitation in 1820, Madame de Chabannes begged him to send some professed religious from another monastery of the Order to help to build up the community. Dom Augustin agreed to this request and sent four choir nuns from the monastery of Mondaye in Normandy. This monastery had been founded in 1815 by Madame de Châteaubriand, formerly Superior of the monastery of Valenton in the diocese of Versailles. After the suppression of Valenton she had succeeded in keeping her little community together, and after various vicissitudes they had re-established their regular life in the old Premonstratensian Abbey of Mondaye (*Mons Dei—Mont-Dieu*), near Bayeux. They had been placed by their Bishop under

Dom Augustin's jurisdiction, but they followed the Regulations of de Rancé. In the practice of penance, however, they went far beyond the strictest observance of La Trappe, and their poverty amounted almost to destitution. The community had gained a high reputation for regularity and fervour, and they continued their austerities until 1827, when some mitigations were imposed on them by ecclesiastical authority. In 1845 the community was transferred to La Cour-Pétral, in the diocese of Chartres.

Père Palemon went to France to escort the four religious who had been chosen. They arrived at Stapehill on June 19, 1820, and on the 21st, which was the Feast of Corpus Christi, they were solemnly received into the enclosure. Having been given the Kiss of Peace, they took the rank of their profession, and were incorporated into the community, who were greatly edified by their regularity. In this year there were also six choir and two lay novices, all English and Irish, so that the future of the community seemed now to be assured.

Another Visitation was made by Dom Augustin in October, 1822. On All Saints' Day he received the two lay novices to profession, and two days later gave the habit to four postulants, two choir and two lay. Assisted by Père Palemon and Father Coyne, he also blessed the new dormitory and work-room, recently completed.

The mortality, however, continued to increase, especially among the young choir religious and novices. Like St. Stephen of old, Madame de Chabannes saw her best and most promising children cut off, one after another, by the hand of death. Many died soon after their profession, others in the very year of their novitiate. Of the four nuns who came from Mondaye in 1820, two died in 1823—Mère Thérèse le Fèvre, aged twenty-five, and Mère Félicité Rogerie, aged thirty-two—while the third, Mère Véronique Guiber, died in 1824, aged forty.[1]

There was, indeed, a consoling side to these deaths, for all these young religious died with intense joy and confidence. They had come to the monastery only to seek God, and death

---

[1] The last of the Mondaye nuns, Mère Joseph le Clerc, died in 1861, at the age of eighty, having been professed fifty-eight years.

was the shortest means of coming to Him, so they welcomed death with simplicity of heart, rejoicing to be so soon united to the one object of their love. Of several of them, besides Sister Winifred Coyne, their Superior could affirm that they had not a single fault to reproach themselves with since they entered the house. There was Sister Clare Lennon, one of Father Coyne's spiritual children, ' endowed,' Madame de Chabannes tells us, ' with a charming character and an extraordinary love of her holy state and all her duties ' ; Sister Agnes McDonnell, ' of a singular simplicity, innocence, and union with God ' ; and many others, who went to God in all their early fervour and innocence.

But the grief of the Superior was intense. Madame de Chabannes herself speaks thus of St. Stephen in one of her conferences : ' Fearing the entire destruction of his little flock, his heart is pierced with sorrow ; nevertheless, firmly fixed in God, he remains unshaken, and like Abraham, still hopes against hope.'   Here we get a glimpse of her soul and the invincible hope and confidence which carried her through these trials.

The years 1823 and 1824 were the darkest hour of trial ; seven deaths occurred in the former year, and five in the latter. The community was now reduced to the number of nine professed religious. Comment was inevitably aroused, and the mortality was naturally ascribed to the excessive severity of the reformed observance. It will be remembered that the Reform of La Val-Sainte had not only gone beyond the Regulations of de Rancé in austerity, but even, in certain respects, beyond the primitive Constitutions of Cîteaux and the Rule of St. Benedict itself, especially in the severity of the abstinence, the curtailment of the hours of sleep, and the couch of bare boards without even a straw mattress. Although the Reform had been praised and encouraged by Rome, the *Règlements de la Val-Sainte* had never received the formal approbation of the Holy See even for monks, and for nuns had received no approbation at all, owing to the unsettled state of the times. The epoch of the Revolution was, as has already been pointed out, extraordinary, and the heroic penance practised almost without effort in an age of persecution and martyrdom, proved impractic-

able when conditions became normal again. The sage
principle of St. Benedict—' that the strong may have something to strive after, and the weak may not be dismayed '—
had been lost sight of, and if the foundations made after the
Revolution were to take root and prove stable, the observance must be made accessible to subjects of average strength.
Racial and climatic differences, too, must be taken into
account ; for what is possible in one country may prove
impossible in another. Mitigation, in one form or another,
was inevitable, especially for the nuns, and after Dom
Augustin's death, as will be seen, became universal.

The reports which were in circulation regarding the deaths
at Stapehill reached the ears of Bishop Collingridge, who had
succeeded Bishop Sharrock in 1809 as Vicar Apostolic of
the Western District. The Bishop resolved to inquire into
the matter, and early in 1824 he visited Stapehill, and without disclosing his intentions demanded of Madame de
Chabannes a list of all the persons who had died in the
house since the foundation in 1802. This list he forwarded
to Rome, together with his own observations. Neither the
community nor the Regular Superiors had been informed of
this. In July of the same year, Bishop Collingridge reap-
peared at Stapehill in the capacity of Visitor delegated by
the Holy See, and was received with the usual ceremonial.
He proceeded to hold chapter, and began by causing Père
Palemon to read the Rescript he had obtained from Leo XII.
This document ran as follows :

From an Audience of His Holiness held the 26th May, 1824.

Our Most Holy Lord, Leo XII, by Divine Providence,
Pope, in accordance with a request presented by me, the
undersigned Secretary of the Sacred Congregation of Propaganda, having maturely examined the circumstances of
the monastery of Trappist nuns at Stapehill, near Wimborne, in the County of Dorsetshire, and according to his
great wisdom having seriously considered the necessity of
mitigating the severity and austerity of the rules under
which the nuns in that religious house now live, by which
severity and austerity it happens that the nuns cannot
long support life, and for that reason, the preservation of

the monastery is in great danger, and even greater evils may arise ; having withdrawn all power over that monastery from Père Augustin de Lestrange, Superior of the same monastery and Abbot General, has subjected the monastery, during the good pleasure of the Apostolic See, to the jurisdiction of the Right Rev. Peter Bernardine Collingridge, Bishop of Thespiæ and Vicar Apostolic of the Western District in England, whom he also charges to undertake the visitation of the monastery without delay, and to correct in the rules what he in his prudence may think necessary to be corrected, and also, in the name of the Apostolic See, to forbid Père Augustin de Lestrange the foundation of another monastery of the same Order and Institute.

In fine, His Holiness orders the Right Rev. Vicar Apostolic Collingridge, having finished the visitation of the monastery in question, to send an account to the Sacred Congregation of the Propagation of the Faith, and to refer to it all the corrections which he may judge necessary to be made in the rules.

Given at Rome, at the Offices of the Sacred Congregation, on the day and in the year above named.

PETER CAPRANO, ARCHBISHOP OF ICONIUM,

Secretary.

The Bishop then addressed the community, explaining his mission and declaring that in his opinion it was one with which no Bishop had ever before been charged ; for human weakness was such that, although religious communities often began with the purest intentions of serving God, insensibly they relaxed from their first fervour, and the duty of Bishops and Visitors was to recall them to their former aspirations, and to restore what had become relaxed through human weakness. He, on the contrary, had come to moderate a Rule which was believed to be beyond the powers of a sex which possessed more courage than strength, and to do so on behalf of persons who would willingly continue to observe it in all its rigour.

The Bishop then saw each member of the community in private, including the lay sisters, and was astonished to find that not one of them regarded the Rule as too severe.

He promised to make no fundamental changes, and to alter it as little as possible. What he really did was to substitute for the Regulations of Val-Sainte those of the Abbé de Rancé, making certain modifications in the latter, which he considered necessary in order to adapt them for women. Most of Bishop Collingridge's regulations concern the food of the community and of the sick, and are decidedly more austere than those laid down at the present day in the Constitutions of the Cistercians of the Strict Observance. The religious were to sleep on straw mattresses, and were never to take less than six and a half hours' consecutive sleep ; this exceeded by half an hour the time prescribed in the Order during the summer, when the meridian or siesta is taken after dinner. They were to be allowed to walk in the garden for half an hour after meals. This provision of Bishop Collingridge's was afterwards made obligatory by the General Chapter for the nuns of the Order, and incorporated in the Constitutions of 1835. There were no other mitigations of importance, but very exact regulations as to the reception of novices and ascertaining that they had sufficient health to keep the Rule. The election of the Prioress was henceforth to be triennial. In accordance with this, Bishop Collingridge proceeded to hold an election, at which Reverend Mother Augustin was unanimously re-elected. This election appears to have been merely a formality necessitated by the institution of triennial elections, and there is no reason to think that the Bishop had any wish to depose Madame de Chabannes from office. On the contrary, it will be seen that she repeatedly asked him to accept her resignation, which he as often declined to do.

An extraordinary chapter was held to close the Visitation, the Bishop being accompanied by Père Palemon, who read the new Regulations to the community. Bishop Collingridge then gave a discourse, after which he enjoined the religious, by the authority he had received from the Holy See, to observe these Regulations, and in whatever they did not provide for, to follow those of the Abbé de Rancé—'and forbade and prohibited us the Regulations of the Reverend Father Dom Augustin our Superior and Father Immediate, which we had practised up till then,' as the old chronicle

I

expresses it, recording the facts briefly and without comment, yet not without a certain eloquence in its very brevity. The next remark is still more expressive : ' The community manifested their submission by their silence.' They were, in fact, dumbfounded. Rome had spoken, and they had no choice but to obey, but the blow was a heavy one, and came, moreover, totally without warning. The little community, isolated as it already was, in a Protestant country, was now cut off, not only from the Reform of Val-Sainte, but from the Order of Cîteaux itself—and this separation was to endure for more than ninety years, although the observance of Stapehill throughout that period differed in no important respects from that of all the nuns of La Trappe. Bishop Collingridge had merely anticipated, in the case of Stapehill, a modification which, as we have seen, was inevitable, and which, ten years later, was to be imposed on all the monasteries of the Reform. Already, in fact, on the return to France in 1815, Darfeld and its dependent houses had given up the *Règlements de la Val-Sainte* and resumed those of de Rancé. The French nuns from Darfeld had founded in 1818 the Monastery of St. Catherine at Laval, which was placed under the jurisdiction of the Abbot of Port-du-Salut, founded from Darfeld in 1815. The Regulations of de Rancé were followed at Laval, as by the monks of Port-du-Salut. Leo XII, however, judging these Regulations too severe for women, ordered the Bishop of Le Mans to introduce some mitigations into them on behalf of the nuns. These mitigations were drawn up by the Bishop in 1819, in consultation with the Father Immediate, the Abbot of Port-du-Salut, and they are reproduced practically word for word in Bishop Collingridge's Regulations. It seems probable, therefore, that the Bishop had been previously informed of this similar instance of mitigation imposed on a community of Trappistines by the same Pontiff, Leo XII, only five years earlier, and had based his action thereon. It can only be regretted that he did not act as the Bishop of Le Mans had done, in concert with the Regular Superiors, instead of taking such a drastic step.

Immediately after the Visitation, Bishop Collingridge, in accordance with the Rescript, sent his report to Rome, together with the new Regulations he had drawn up. The result was a Decree of the Sacred Congregation of Propaganda, dated April 25, 1825, approving the corrections in the Rules, and placing the monastery under the jurisdiction of the Vicar-Apostolic for the time being of the Western District, during the good pleasure of the Holy See. In the letter to Bishop Collingridge which accompanied the Decree, great praise was given by the Sacred Congregation to His Lordship's prudence for the happy termination of the affair.

Courageous as Madame de Chabannes had shown herself in face of so many previous disasters, and the apparent failure of her work, this final blow seems almost to have proved too much even for her. This 'eldest daughter of Dom Augustin' had up till now always been able to count on the fatherly counsel and guidance of the venerated Abbot. Since the restoration of peace on the Continent, regular intercourse had been once more possible, and his visits had been frequent. This had, to a great extent, made up for the loss of the monks of Lulworth. Moreover, in spite of the isolated situation of Stapehill, the bond which united the community to the whole Order secured to them all the benefits of the wise system of Cistercian government : uniformity of observance, maintained by Regular Visitations ; and the certainty of a constant supply of Cistercian priests and lay brothers for the spiritual and temporal assistance of the community. Now, however, the little foundation was completely cut adrift, and Madame de Chabannes, with her prudence and foresight, saw only too plainly the probable consequences. The remaining twenty years of her life were to be spent in the courageous effort to maintain the existence of the house, in spite of all, struggling single-handed against difficulties of every kind, not the least of which was continual and extreme poverty. Her conviction that God willed the English foundation, gave her strength, and Providence undoubtedly watched over the destinies of the community in a remarkable way.

At first, however, she felt the situation too much for her. As has been said, she offered her resignation to Bishop Collingridge, but in spite of her importunities he was firm

in refusing it. An intimate correspondence took place at
this time between Madame de Chabannes and Madame
Elisabeth Pietta, the saintly foundress and Superior of the
Monastery of Ste.-Catherine at Laval. Unfortunately,
Madame de Chabannes' letters have not been preserved,
but several of her correspondent's are extant, and give us
some insight into the state of mind of the Superior of Stapehill at this crisis. Madame Elisabeth writes : ' It is with
great wisdom, and doubtless by the inspiration of the Spirit
of God, that His Lordship your Bishop has constantly
refused to accept your resignation, for where could anyone
be found who would be capable of replacing you in the office
you hold ? If, however, Divine Providence should change
Its dispositions in your regard, not only do I offer you,
my most worthy Reverend Mother, a corner of my house,
but the entire house, and also the charge of governing it,
for I should think myself only too happy to be able to end
my days under obedience—and what obedience ! that of
the Mother of all the nuns of the Reform of La Trappe ! '
In spite of her desire to retire into obscurity in some monastery abroad, Madame de Chabannes did not remain
inactive under the trial. She consulted Madame Elisabeth
regarding the possibilities of appealing to Rome through
the intervention of the Abbot General of the Order of
Cîteaux, with a view to being placed under the jurisdiction
of an Abbot of the Reform of La Trappe—the ' Old Reform '
as it was now called, to distinguish it from the Reform of
Val-Sainte or ' New Reform.' We do not know whether
these steps were taken ; if so, they came to nothing. But
there was another possibility in view. For some years past
there had been a project on foot of making a foundation
in Ireland. The greater number of the subjects received at
Stapehill were Irish, and it may well have seemed that there
was a good opening for a Cistercian community in that
country. Father Coyne, who has been already mentioned,
appears to have been the chief promoter of the idea of
sending a colony to Ireland. In the Rescript of 1824,
quoted above, a clause was expressly inserted, enjoining
Bishop Collingridge to forbid Dom Augustin ' the foundation
of another monastery of the same Order and Institute,' and

on the authentic translation of the Rescript, signed by the Bishop, the latter has added, in his own handwriting, the words 'in Ireland' immediately after the above clause. From this it would appear probable that one of the Bishop's motives in having recourse direct to the Holy See was to prevent the proposed Irish foundation, the preparations for which were by that time well advanced. The house and property known as Violet Hill, near Newry in Co. Down, had, in fact, been purchased for the nuns by the subscriptions of benefactors, and had already been put in order and arranged for their reception. Seeing only too clearly the difficulties in store at Stapehill, now that they were cut off from the Order, Madame de Chabannes conceived the idea of removing the whole community to Violet Hill. During the winter of 1824–1825, Father Coyne, travelling on the Continent, visited the Monastery of Ste.-Catherine at Laval, and was the bearer of letters and messages between Madame de Chabannes and Madame Elisabeth. He spoke to the latter of the projected foundation, and told her that Madame de Chabannes herself was thinking of going to Ireland. The project, however, came to nothing, no doubt owing to Bishop Collingridge's opposition, the community having been placed by the Holy See under his jurisdiction. Violet Hill became a hostel for boys, who were boarded for £10 per annum and attended a 'seminary' in the town of Newry. One of these boys, Terence Donnelly, came to Stapehill as a servant or familiar in 1826, and served the community faithfully for many years. In 1834, the property of Violet Hill was purchased by Dr. Blake, Bishop of Dromore, and is now the Diocesan Seminary.

CHAPTER XI

END OF DOM AUGUSTIN'S REFORM

THE community of Stapehill were never to see Dom Augustin again. Under the year 1827, the chronicle records that ' Our Reform has suffered an irreparable loss in losing the Reverend Father Abbot Dom Augustin, who had been the preserver and we may say the restorer of it. He died at Lyons, as he was returning from Rome, on the Feast of Our Holy Father St. Stephen, after five days' illness, having received all the Sacraments, and is buried there in the choir of our Sisters. As a last proof of his fatherly affection, he sent us, seven days before his death, Père Joseph, priest and monk, who remained with us six months and then returned to the Monastery of Bellefontaine. He left at his death twenty-two houses of which he was the Founder and Father ; his great confidence in Divine Providence enabling him to surmount every obstacle.'

The last years of the great reformer had been clouded by misrepresentation and calumny. Like all dominant personalities, Dom Augustin had enemies, and these made it their business to spread all kinds of accusations against him. In 1825 he was summoned to Rome to answer the charges, which, however, completely fell to the ground. A statement was drawn up by the Secretary of the Congregation of Bishops and Regulars, exonerating Dom Augustin from all blame, and testifying to his character and virtues, especially his obedience and humility, his simplicity, charity, mortification, and regularity. Moreover, the Holy Father, Leo XII, showed him marked kindness. But the *Règlements de la Val-Sainte* had not yet received formal approbation, and many questions both of jurisdiction and of observance were awaiting settlement. The whole future of the Reform was at stake, and Dom Augustin, awaiting

at Rome the long-delayed decisions, felt that his strength
was failing him. Nevertheless, during the vacation of 1826,
he went to Naples to discuss with the King the establishment
of a monastery in that kingdom.   On his way back he visited
Monte Cassino, where he was taken seriously ill, and received
the Last Sacraments.   Believing death to be at hand, he
addressed a circular letter to all his children, monks and
nuns, by way of a spiritual testament, and concluded it with
these words : ' I beg of you all in general and each one in
particular, as if this letter were addressed to him only, to
pardon me all my failings in your regard, which have arisen
from my imperfection, but not from my indifference or want
of love for you.'   He then carefully enumerates the houses
to which this letter is to be sent, and his children in England
are not forgotten.

Dom Augustin recovered, however, from this attack, and
returned to Rome.   Foreseeing clearly that the austerities of
Val-Sainte would be mitigated after his death, he wrote once
more to his communities : ' If you are obliged to diminish
something in the austerities prescribed by St. Benedict and
St. Scholastica, strive to compensate for these mitigations
by a greater fidelity and a more ardent zeal in practising the
interior virtues which the Rule recommends, and above all,
the chapters on obedience and humility.   Let these be the
principal object of your meditations and resolutions.'

Dom Augustin finally left Rome in June, 1827, and after
visiting several of his houses, arrived at the Monastery of
Vaise, near Lyons.   The bells rang as he approached ; ' they
seem,' he said, ' to be tolling for death.'   The same evening
he was taken ill, and after receiving the Last Sacraments,
and awaiting death for five days with perfect serenity and
confidence, he gave up his soul to God at daybreak on the
Feast of St. Stephen, July 16, while the nuns were singing the
Te Deum in choir.   No less than a thousand monks and nuns
mourned his loss as that of a true Father in God.   That,
indeed, was Dom Augustin's true character.   He had all the
qualities needed for his great mission—energy, enterprise,
initiative, the genius for organisation, indomitable courage
and perseverance ; yet Madame de Chabannes, than whom
none knew him better, wrote truly of him that it was, above

all, his confidence in God which enabled him to surmount all obstacles. His chief defect, and the only one of the accusations made against him which was really grounded on fact, lay in the too autocratic character of his government. This was due in part to his natural temperament, accentuated by the exceptional circumstances of the period. The Chart of Charity could not be carried out, and in default of the annual General Chapter, he maintained uniformity of observance by centralising authority in his own hands. This meant a limiting of the power of the local Superior, and was the cause of most of the opposition to him within the ranks of the Order itself. But nothing could be further from the truth than to represent Dom Augustin as a fanatical reformer, a harsh ruler, imposing on others severities which he did not practise himself. He was, above all, a father, and a most tender and loving father, beloved by his children. His life was one of complete self-sacrifice in the service of those under his charge. He wore himself out with labours and journeyings on their behalf, thinking nothing of dangers and hardships as long as he could encourage and console his religious in their vocation. The 'Visitation Cards' or exhortations given at the five Visitations he made at Stapehill, show nothing of harshness or rigorism, but breathe the true spirit of monastic tradition—zeal for the Work of God, first and foremost ; the love of silence and of manual labour, and finally, fraternal charity. As in the early days of Val-Sainte, charity was still the reigning virtue of the Reform, and Dom Augustin's virtue of predilection. His words to the monks who left France with him in 1791 had been ' *Diligamus nos invicem,*' and to the end of his life the Gospel text most frequently on his lips, and which was evidently the inspiration of his whole life, was that one which so perfectly sums up the spirit of the Rule of St. Benedict : ' As long as you did it to one of these My least brethren, you did it to Me.'[1] To wound charity, he says, again quoting Scripture, is to wound God Himself in the apple of His eye ; whereas ' he who has the happiness of abiding in charity and of perfecting himself therein, will abide in God and enter more and more deeply into His heart.' In 1822, after blessing the new

[1] Matt. xxv, 40.

buildings, which will enable the nuns to sleep and work all together, he tells them not to limit this advantage to being united merely in body, but to maintain among themselves a still more close and intimate union of hearts, as they have been gathered together by God from different countries into a single family : ' Then will they know that you are truly my disciples, if you love one another tenderly and constantly.'

At each of his Visitations he urges the nuns to zeal for the Divine Office, the Work of God. They are to count themselves happy if, like the candles which burn and consume themselves on the altar in honour of the thrice-Holy God, they also burn with zeal for God's glory, and consume their strength in singing His praises, thus doing what the angels do in heaven, and beginning to do here below what they themselves will do for all eternity. Novices who do not show this zeal are on no account to be received as choir religious, since they lack the most essential qualification for the choir. And this zeal is to show itself in a practical manner, by punctuality at the Offices and by giving their whole voice to the singing or recitation, above all to the singing of the Mass. The pauses in the psalmody are to be well observed, and the singing and recitation of the psalms are on no account to be precipitated, for this gives disedification and shows a want of reverence for the Majesty of God.

Silence is looked upon by Dom Augustin as, above all, a means to interior recollection and converse with God. ' We only observe this strict silence towards creatures in order to converse more continually with our Creator. Make your life, then, a continual prayer.' ' We should be occupied unceasingly with God in the depths of our hearts.' Especially are they to keep themselves in the Presence of God during their work, and to aim at performing all their actions in a truly interior spirit. Here he becomes insistent. ' In vain shall we keep ourselves carefully separated from the world, in vain shall we devote all our time to holy exercises, in vain will our lives be full of austerities ; if all this is not animated with the interior spirit, all will be as nothing, and will never render us pleasing to God ; nay, it will even perhaps only serve to nourish our self-love, and we shall end by finding ourselves empty-handed at the hour of death.'

Manual labour, he reminds the nuns, was the first penance imposed by God Himself on all mankind ; it is the one most pleasing to Him, since it is of His own choosing, and those who have made profession of penance would be under an illusion if they ran after other penances and rejected this, which should be the first and, as it were, the foundation of all the others. ' Our Divine Lord Himself only took up the wood of the Cross on Calvary after He had laboured at the wood in St. Joseph's workshop.'

Here are the authentic marks of the true Cistercian life, as taught by the great Abbot to the early religious of Stapehill.

On the death of Dom Augustin, Dom Antoine, Abbot of Melleraye, was appointed by Leo XII Visitor-General of all the monasteries of La Trappe, both of monks and nuns. As mentioned above, there were now two Trappist observances existing side by side in France, since the houses dependent on Darfeld had abandoned the Regulations of Val-Sainte and resumed those of de Rancé. After the death of Dom Augustin, at the desire of the Holy Father, all the practices peculiar to Val-Sainte were relinquished by the monasteries of that Reform, which from henceforward observed the Rule of St. Benedict according to the primitive Constitutions of Cîteaux. In his report to the Holy See, Dom Antoine, in a spirit of conciliation, counselled the adoption of the Regulations of de Rancé as a basis of uniformity of observance ; but he considered these Regulations in some respects unsuited to the times, particularly in the restriction of the hours of manual labour, most of the monasteries being now in extreme poverty and obliged to live by the labour of their hands. The chief difference, in fact, between the two observances lay in the horarium, especially as to the duration of the manual labour and the hour for the repast—the two chief points in which de Rancé had been unable to restore the full rigour of the primitive Rule. Gregory XVI, who became Pope in 1831, greatly desired the union of the two groups, and in 1834 decreed that all the Trappist monasteries of France should be formed into a single congregation entitled ' Cistercian Monks of Our Lady of La Trappe,' thus giving the first official sanction to the popular appellation of

' Trappist.' The Congregation was to be governed by a Vicar-General, who was to be the Abbot of La Grande Trappe, and all were to follow the Rule of St. Benedict and the Constitutions of the Abbé de Rancé, but with certain limitations, which in practice left the monasteries free to follow their own usages, adopting either the horarium of St. Benedict or that of de Rancé. The Trappistine nuns were to form part of this Congregation, and at the first General Chapter, held in 1835, their Constitutions were drawn up, and were approved in the following year by the Holy See. The chief points in which these Constitutions differed from those of the monks were : (1) certain mitigations in the fasting and abstinence ; (2) the institution of the ' promenade ' (a silent walk in the garden after dinner) ; and (3) the triennial election of the Superior, whether Abbess or Prioress. This amounted in substance to what Bishop Collingridge had regulated for Stapehill in 1824, so that while separated from the Order, the nuns in England were following almost exactly the same observance as their Sisters on the Continent.

But the unification brought about by the Decree of 1834 was not to prove durable. In reality, by the provision made for the two divergent observances, it defeated its own end, and carried within itself the seeds of disunion. In 1847, Pius IX judged it necessary to revoke his predecessor's act, and the official separation of the two observances was re-established and regularised. Henceforward, there were two Congregations of Trappists, each governed by a Vicar-General, acting as delegate of the Abbot of Cîteaux—the one, following the Regulations of de Rancé, the Vicar-General being the Abbot of Sept-Fons ; the other, following the primitive Constitutions of Cîteaux, and having as Vicar-General the Abbot of La Grande-Trappe. There was also the Congregation of Westmalle, comprising the monasteries of Belgium, and following the same observance as Sept-Fons. Once more, the difference between the Congregations lay only in minor questions of horarium, and all were equally fervent and flourishing. In fact, the nineteenth century was one of the greatest periods of expansion the Order has ever known ; foundations not only multiplied in France and the other countries of Europe, but spread to America, Asia, Africa, and the Far East ; and everywhere the name of La Trappe was a synonym for the highest ideal of austerity and contemplation. Nevertheless, the best minds in each Congregation were always desirous to return to the unity of the Order as established by St. Stephen, but it was not until the last decade of the century, under Leo XIII, that this unity was achieved, as will be described in a later chapter.

The Reform of Val-Sainte, therefore, was not destined to continue in its original form, but it had done a great work, in counterbalancing the evils of the day, and recalling to a decadent civilisation the heroic examples of the earlier ages of monasticism. By its means, the Order of Cîteaux not only maintained its existence, but had new life infused into it, and was able to enter on a new phase of its history, carrying into the modern world of the nineteenth century its ancient traditions of prayer, penance, and labour. The outcry raised against Dom Augustin and Val-Sainte, as against de Rancé and La Trappe a century earlier, was the echo of that raised against the early Cistercians—*non cessabant titubare*—for the folly of the Cross is at all times a stumbling-block to the world. Human nature is ever filled with a kind of horror at the spectacle of those who take their faith literally and push supernatural principles to their logical conclusions. Yet Incarnate Wisdom has said : ' If any man will come after Me, let him deny himself and take up his cross daily and follow Me.'—' He that can take it, let him take it.'

CHAPTER XII

THE monks of Lulworth had prospered since their return to France. They were fifty-seven in number when they left England in 1817 ; twelve years later they were one hundred and ninety-two in community, including French, English, Irish, Spanish, Belgians, Italians, Scottish and Swiss. The Abbey of Melleraye was situated in the most desolate and sterile part of Brittany, and the land was almost entirely uncultivated. Under Dom Antoine's guidance, however, a complete transformation took place, and the hitherto barren soil produced magnificent crops, to the astonishment and envy of the neighbouring farmers. The monks had brought with them from England up-to-date machines and methods of agriculture, to which their success was due, and it was with Melleraye, according to the historian of La Trappe,[1] that the agricultural reputation of the Trappists began.

After the Revolution of 1830, however, Dom Antoine saw signs of a coming storm. He who had pronounced the funeral oration of the Duc de Berri in 1820, and had entertained the widowed duchess in 1829, was not likely to find favour with the new dynasty. Moreover, the agricultural prosperity of the Abbey had aroused the jealousy of the local trades-people. Once again, calumny did its work, and Melleraye was denounced as an establishment of foreigners, whose aim was to ruin French industry. In 1831 a decree of suppression of the monastery was issued, and the English and Irish monks were expelled from the country. Sixty-four of them landed at Queenstown on December 1, 1831. Father Vincent Ryan had been sent to Ireland by Dom Antoine in 1830 to endeavour to make a foundation, and

---

[1] Gaillardin, *op. cit.*, p. 446.

after great difficulties had just obtained from Sir Richard Keane, a Protestant, a grant of six hundred acres of barren mountain land near Cappoquin, in County Waterford. There the exiled religious settled, and founded the Abbey of Mount Melleray, the first stone of which was laid on August 20, 1833, the Feast of St. Bernard. Early in 1835, Father Norbert Woolfrey was sent into England by Dom Vincent, now Abbot of Mount Melleray, to obtain alms from English Catholics, and at the same time to investigate the possibilities of an English foundation. He was hospitably received at Grace Dieu Manor in Leicestershire by Mr. Ambrose Lisle Phillips, who welcomed the project with enthusiasm, and himself purchased for the monks a large tract of land in Charnwood Forest, adjoining his own estates. In the same year, 1835, a group of six monks, headed by Father Odilo Woolfrey, Father Norbert's brother, took possession of a small half-ruined cottage on the estate, and thus laid the foundations of Mount St. Bernard Abbey. In 1836, the saintly Father Bernard Palmer, who had entered at Lulworth many years previously, came from France to be the first Superior of the new Abbey. Thus, three hundred years after the dissolution of the Cistercian Abbey of Garendon in 1536, a new Cistercian abbey was founded almost on the same lands, and by the generosity of a descendant of the de Lisles, who had formerly been great benefactors to Garendon.

The history of Lulworth is only one more illustration of that constant law of monastic history, by which persecution becomes the seed of future expansion. Driven from England to France, and again expelled from the latter country, the English and Irish monks returned to found Mount Melleray and Mount St. Bernard ; Mount Melleray in turn gave rise to New Melleray in the United States in 1848, and Mount St. Joseph, Roscrea, in 1878. Thus it came about that Stapehill was no longer the only Cistercian community in these islands,[1] and in spite of their separation from the

---

[1] Later still, in the present century, England was to receive another colony of Cistercian monks, when, in 1929, eleven choir monks and three lay brothers from the monastery of Chimay, Belgium, took possession of the monastic island of Caldey. The foundation is already a flourishing community, and was erected into a Priory in 1934.

Order, the nuns were still to find spiritual fathers and brothers in the monks of Mount Melleray and Mount St. Bernard.

In the meantime, Père Palemon remained as chaplain, and from 1826, when the Abbé de la Porte left Stapehill, took charge also of the congregation, which at that time numbered between thirty and forty souls. On the departure of the Carmelites for France in 1825, the congregation of Canford had been united to that of Stapehill. Sir John Webb, who had established the Carmelites at Canford in 1794, had died in 1797. His daughter and heiress, Barbara, Countess of Shaftesbury, died in 1815, and the Manor then came into the possession of her daughter, Lady Barbara Ashley-Cooper, who had married the Hon. W. F. Spencer Ponsonby (created Lord de Mauley in 1838). The Ponsonbys rebuilt the Manor House and made it their residence, and the Carmelites had to find another home. Accompanied by their chaplain, the Abbé Marest, they sailed for France in September, 1825, settling first at Thorigny and afterwards at Valognes.[1] The Abbé Marest had been ordained at Winchester during the Revolution, and for many years was stationed at Wardour. In 1817 he was appointed chaplain at Canford, and with his long experience in England, and close connection with the Arundell family, he proved a valuable friend and adviser in business matters to the nuns of Stapehill.

There was now no longer a public chapel at Canford, but Lady de Mauley had a private chapel, in which Mass was said on Sundays from Stapehill when she was in residence. This was made possible by the fact that at this period there was usually at least one retired priest living at Stapehill as a boarder, paying a pension to the community. Three of these priests are buried in the cemetery, the first being the Abbé François Langlois, a simple and holy old French priest, greatly beloved by all, who died on May 13, 1834, aged seventy-two. Just before his death he entrusted to Père Palemon an old stocking which he had kept hidden, containing the sum of five hundred pounds, which the good

[1] In 1870 this community returned to England and founded the Carmel of Chichester.

Father had saved for the nuns. His name has ever been
kept in grateful remembrance by the community, and an
annual Mass and four Offices of the Dead were established
in perpetuity for the repose of his soul. On January 14,
1842, died the Abbé Jacques Normand, another French
émigré priest, at the age of eighty-two, and on March 10,
1844, a Benedictine, Rev. Richard Towers, O.S.B. The
Abbé Normand was residing at Stapehill as early as 1827,
and was delegated in that year by Bishop Collingridge to
preside over the election of the Prioress, which resulted
again in the unanimous re-election of Madame de Chabannes.
He was commissioned at the same time to make the Canonical
Visitation.

In the following year, 1828, the Bishop made the Visitation in person, remaining several weeks in the house. He
exhorted the religious to exactitude in observing the new
Regulations, appealing to the authority of the Holy See
in support of the changes he had introduced. This was
Bishop Collingridge's last visit to Stapehill. He was taken
suddenly ill on February 10, 1829, received the Last Sacraments, and died within half an hour.

There are few events of interest to record during the next
ten years. In January, 1829, the community had the
happiness of receiving a friendly visit from Dom Antoine,
who showed them much affection and interest, and promised
to do all in his power to restore the Priory to the jurisdiction
of the Order. His efforts, however, were to prove fruitless.

In 1831, Madame de Chabannes had the sorrow of losing
the two Mothers who were her chief support—Mère Thérèse
de la Miséricorde, the last survivor of her companions in
exile, and Mère Scholastique, who had come to Stapehill
with the foundresses, and had received the habit on the
day of the solemn entrance.

In 1835 died a venerable Mother whose history deserves
recording. Margaret Barnwall was born in Dublin in 1756,
and was professed at the Benedictine Monastery of Our
Lady of Consolation, Cambrai (now at Stanbrook) in 1776,
under the name of Dame Bernard. In October, 1793, the
community, twenty-two in number, were expelled from
their monastery and taken in open carts to Compiègne,

where they were imprisoned, being joined in the following year by the Carmelites who were martyred in Paris in July, 1794. The Benedictines, however, Dame Bernard among them, escaped to England in 1795, and took up their residence at Woolton, then at Salford near Evesham. Dame Bernard was Novice Mistress for some years and was greatly beloved by her community, but she had a strong desire to embrace a stricter observance of the Rule of St. Benedict, and for years petitioned to be allowed to join the Cistercians at Stapehill. At last the consent of the Abbot President was given, and she entered the novitiate in 1825, in the seventieth year of her age, and within a year of her Golden Jubilee. Soon after her arrival, Madame de Chabannes wrote to her former Abbess, Mother Christina Chare : ' Our Sister Bernard is happy. She desires and hopes to persevere in her generous enterprise, if it is the Will of God. Her conduct since she has been in the house has been most edifying.' She made her vow of stability in November, 1826, and lived for ten years an exemplary life as a Cistercian, ' a model,' writes Madame de Chabannes, ' of the most perfect charity, humility and obedience.' She died, as she herself had predicted, on the Feast of her holy Patron, August 20, after a painful illness most patiently borne. She was the last survivor of the Benedictine Dames who had been driven from Cambrai by the Revolution.

From 1828 to 1838 no Visitation was held at Stapehill. Bishop Baines, who succeeded Bishop Collingridge in 1829, paid several friendly visits, and showed kindness to the community, but he never made a Canonical Visitation or inquired into the state of regular observance. In 1838, however, he delegated Dr. Gentili to make a Visitation of the Priory. Dr. Gentili remained a fortnight in the house, gave several exhortations in Chapter, and won the confidence and esteem of the community by the charity and patience with which he fulfilled his mission. Among other improvements, he obtained an organ to accompany the chant, this through the generosity of Mr. Lupton of Liverpool, father of Sister Philomena, a promising young choir religious who died in 1840 at the age of twenty-seven. It was at this Visitation, and in response to Dr. Gentili's urgent appeal

K

for prayers for the conversion of England, that the custom
of singing the *Parce Domine* after Vespers for that intention
was adopted, a custom which is still kept up.

A Visitation was made in 1840 by the Rev. Joseph Dwyer,
likewise delegated by Bishop Baines.

In the autumn of 1842, Stapehill was visited by Queen
Adelaide, widow of William IV, who, during her residence
at Bushey Park, used to spend the shooting season at
Canford Manor. Driving near the Priory one afternoon
with some of her suite, the Queen Dowager sent on Lord
Denbigh to inquire whether she would be allowed to enter
the enclosure and go over the monastery. This being one
of the privileges of Royalty—the Princess Charlotte had
similarly visited the monastery of Lulworth—Madame de
Chabannes received the Queen in the parlour, and admitted
her into the enclosure, together with her entire retinue.
They were shown over the house by Mother Mary Joseph
Troy, and were deeply interested in all they saw. Queen
Adelaide afterwards wrote the following account of her visit
in a letter to Queen Victoria :

CANFORD HOUSE,

October 31, 1842.

. . . 'I wish you could see the convent to which I went
the other day. The nuns belong to the Order of the Cistercian Trappists. They are not allowed to speak amongst
themselves (what a relief my visit must have been to them !)
and they eat neither meat nor eggs, nor butter, nothing but
milk, vegetables and rice. They look healthy and there
were several young, rather pretty ones amongst them. One,
the best looking of all, took me affectionately by the hand
and said, "I hope the air agrees with you here, and that
you feel better" and then she added, "Come again, will
you, before you leave this country ? " She told me she was
born in Ireland and had a German grandfather. She seemed
to be a favourite amongst them all, for when I bought of
them their works and asked them to make up my bill, they
called Mother Mary Joseph to summon it up, and she said
to me, "Do not stay for that, we will send you your things
with the bill." Two hours after my visit to them I received

my things with a wealth of flowers besides, as their gift to
me : on the paper attached was written, " To the Queen
Dowager, from the Reverend Mother and her community."

' This old Reverend Mother, the Abbess, was very infirm
and could not get up from her chair, but she spoke very
politely and lady-like to me in French. She has been forty
years in her present situation and comes from Bretagne.
The Chaplain of the Convent is also an old Frenchman, and
there are several other French nuns amongst them, one
who had been condemned to be guillotined in the Revolution
and was set at liberty just at the moment the execution was
to have taken place. I should like to know whether these
good nuns resumed at once their silence when I left them or
whether they were permitted to talk over the events of
that day.'

About a week after this visit, the Duchess of Kent, mother
of Queen Victoria, was received at the Priory. Queen
Adelaide had kindly sent a donation of fifty pounds to the
community, and wishing to make some little acknowledg-
ment in return, Madame de Chabannes sent her, through the
kind offices of the Duchess, an illuminated manuscript, a
paraphrase of the Lord's Prayer, the work of one of the
religious. The Royal party stayed about a month at
Canford, during which time they frequently attended the
services at Stapehill.

The Queen Dowager was probably little aware how much
her kindly gift was needed. The community was at that
time at the lowest ebb, as far as temporal resources were
concerned, and wealthy benefactors seldom came the way
of the obscure Dorsetshire monastery. The tide, however,
was beginning to turn, for Providence had recently brought
to Stapehill one who was to be a true friend in need to the
religious—a priest, moreover, of their own Order.

CHAPTER XIII

SPIRIT OF MADAME DE CHABANNES

PÈRE PALEMON was now growing old and infirm, and it became imperative that he should have a younger priest with him to assist him in his duties. In May, 1840, Dom Vincent Ryan, Abbot of Mount Melleray, visited the Priory and brought with him Father Andrew Hawkins, a holy and zealous Cistercian priest whose name is inseparably bound up with the history of Stapehill, for to him was due the building of the present church and monastery.

Francis Hawkins, afterwards Father Andrew, was born at Wardour in 1795, of an excellent Catholic family which gave four of its members to the Cistercian Order. In that same year, Francis' uncle, Father Stephen Hawkins, entered the novitiate at Lulworth, being one of the first three novices to enter, together with Dom Antoine and Père Palemon ; he died at Mount St. Bernard in 1856 at the age of eighty-nine. Father Andrew entered at Lulworth in 1808, as a boy of twelve, and while still a novice accompanied the monks to France in 1817. He made his profession at Melleraye on July 11, 1819, with his brother James (Father Eugenius), who had followed him to Lulworth in 1813, and the two brothers were ordained priests together at Nantes in 1822. Their sister, Mary Anne Hawkins, entered at Stapehill in 1820, at the age of eighteen, and was professed on March 19, 1822, under the name of Sister Bernard. She died on May 30, 1823, to the great grief of the community ; Madame de Chabannes describes her as ' a subject fitted for any employment,' and Father Coyne, in a letter of sympathy, writes : ' I must confess I am most afflicted by the death of Sister Bernard. I loved her most dearly, and I expected she would one day be a pillar of La Trappe.'

Father Andrew became one of Dom Antoine's most

capable helpers, but in 1831 he was arrested with the other British subjects. He was their leader and spokesman, and drew up the protestation they made to the British Consul at Nantes ; he was afterwards, however, set at liberty. He went to America for a time, perhaps with a view to investigating the possibilities of a foundation, and then returned to Mount Melleray, whence he came to Stapehill. He was filled with compassion at the state of poverty and ill-health in which he found the community, and above all at the dilapidated and insanitary condition of the monastic buildings. Full of zeal and activity, he determined to improve matters without loss of time. He told the nuns that they must appeal to their relatives and friends to help them rebuild the monastery ; ' as for the chapel,' he said, ' that is my affair, I will be responsible for that.'

The result of the appeal to the friends and relatives of the community made it possible to erect a new building, containing a dormitory for the lay Sisters ; this was completed in 1843. Meanwhile, Father Andrew was collecting funds for the church he had set his heart on building. But before the first stone was laid, the holy Foundress had been called to her reward. Madame de Chabannes had for some years been very infirm, and on June 13, 1844, the Octave day of Corpus Christi, she breathed her last, to the great sorrow of all her children. After her death, her body, clothed in the Cistercian habit, remained exposed in the chapel for three days, so that all might satisfy their devotion by visiting her holy remains. For she was believed by many to have been a saint, and had the reputation of having wrought several miraculous cures, both during life and after death, though unfortunately no details of these have been preserved. She was buried in the little cemetery according to the Cistercian Rite, her body, still clad in the white cowl, with a wreath of flowers on the head, being laid in the grave by her children with loving reverence. Six months later, her remains were exhumed, in the presence of the medical attendant, Dr. Stewart (a Protestant) and several of the community. They were found intact, and showed no signs of corruption when the damp earth was removed from the face and habit by the infirmarian, Mother Juliana.

This fact was attested by Dr. Stewart, a Cistercian priest, Father George, who was present, the Mother Prioress and Mother Juliana, and two workmen. The body was then placed in a coffin, and re-interred in a vault specially prepared for it in the middle of the cemetery, and surmounted by a graceful stone cross, about twelve feet high, supported on a base with three steps. The inscription on the steps runs as follows :

'IHS. In memoriam Reverendæ ac Domnæ Matris nostræ Rosaliæ Augustinæ de Chabanne, Fundatricis ac Gubernatricis hujusce Monasterii per XLII annos, Crux Ista Erecta est. At hic in Pace Exuviæ ejus requiescunt, Immutationem ac Gloriosam Resurrectionem expectantes, Per Dominum Nostrum Jesum Christum. Obiit Die xiii Junii, Ecclesiæ Sacramentis Munita, A.D. MDCCCXLIV, Professionis LVII, Ætatis LXXVI. *De Profundis clamavi ad Te, Domine.* R.I.P.'

A truly Cistercian silence surrounds, in death as in life, this great and saintly religious. Nothing of her inner life has been left on record ; like the Psalmist, she ' kept all her strength for God.' It was in silence that she found this strength to endure to the end amid the many and heavy trials that beset her path. Hers was indeed a soul refined in the crucible of suffering, and the whole course of her life was nothing but a progressive series of detachments, the outward indication of the purifying action of God within her soul. To her natural energy of character was added a high degree of the gift of fortitude, enabling her to undertake great things for God, and to endure all contradictions in carrying them out. This fortitude, combined with an intense spirit of faith and an unbounded confidence in God, made her, indeed, the ' valiant woman ' of Holy Scripture, able to lead others and inspire them with her own courage and confidence.

Though no personal records exist, some of the conferences Madame de Chabannes gave to her nuns have been preserved, and from these we can gain some idea of the spirit which animated her. Perhaps if we wished to sum up in one word the character of her spirituality, it would be in the word *virility.* Nothing could be further removed from any kind of sentimental piety ; she fed her children on the bread of the strong. It is a spirituality based wholly on compunction and the fear of God, and steeped in the old monastic tradition. Madame de Chabannes knew well that to be a perfect religious it is first of all necessary to be a perfect Christian, and she did not shrink from speaking to her nuns on such subjects as temptation, sin and the Four Last Things—for, as St. Benedict recommends, she kept ever before her eyes the judgements of God.[1] A somewhat stern doctrine, perhaps, to modern minds, yet quite in keeping with the spirit of the Holy Rule. She puts before aspirants the *dura et aspera* in no veiled language ; they certainly knew what to expect, and she is careful to forewarn them that ' it is quite a different thing to hear or read an account of our practices and austerities, and to feel and go through them.' ' You will find sufferings, difficulties, weariness, repugnances, but it is in the midst of these combats that you will find God.' Yet, as in the Holy Rule, we get flashes of sweetness, hints of the good things God has prepared for them that love Him. She quotes St. Bernard's saying : ' The world sees our cross, but not the unction that renders the cross sweet.' The cross, in fact, is the sum of all her teaching, and we realise, in reading these conferences, the full significance of that ' choice of predilection ' which had dedicated the monastery under the title of the Holy Cross. This was the devotion she recommended to her children ; they were to be the crucified spouses of a Crucified Lord, and she is never weary of reminding them of what this means.

' Do not forget that true devotion to the Cross consists in bearing generously the crosses God sends us.'

' To content ourselves with adoring and venerating this precious Cross, and yet to shun the occasions of bearing it, would be an illusion.'

' You have come here to seek the Cross, and you must not rest content with finding it before your eyes to adore and venerate, but it must be in your heart and mind, and in

[1] In one of the early account books occurs the following entry, in Madame de Chabannes' handwriting : ' Aug. 16th, 1827, day of the election. I have made up the accounts from Aug. 10th, 1824. May God give me grace to prepare myself for those which I owe to Him after so long an administration ! '

all the members of your body by mortification. This prospect
would terrify cowardly souls, but those who take Jesus
Crucified for their Spouse should count those days the
happiest on which they have most to endure, for those are
the days which unite them more closely to Him whom alone
they should love.'

' As (Jesus Christ) willed to perpetuate in His Church the
sacrifice of His Body and Blood . . . so also He willed that
the sacrifice of His Heart and Will should continue to the
end of the world, doing by His members who compose the
Body of which He is the Head . . . what He is no longer in a
state to do Himself. He has obliged us by our profession to
imitate His renunciations, poverty, ignominy, suffering, and
humiliations, in order to perpetuate and complete His
Sacrifice, so that we may say with St. Paul : '' I fill up those
things that are wanting of the sufferings of Christ." '

And again : ' The sacrifice made by a religious soul is a
holocaust—nothing is excepted, nothing exempt ; the mind,
the heart, the will, the body by exterior penance.' This she
repeats constantly.

A conference for the Feast of the Sacred Heart reveals
something of the affective side of her piety, but here again
she is careful to remind the nuns that ' the love of Jesus
does not consist in a few passing feelings of love, but in
constancy and generosity in making the sacrifices which
that love demands.' Always there is this spirit of intense
realism, which is so characteristic of St. Benedict, and is
really one form of Cistercian simplicity. No room is left
for illusions or pious dreaming ; all must be reduced to
practice. It is the same when she speaks of prayer. Prayer
is not to be of the heart or lips only, but ' the *prayer of action*,
of our body, soul, and will, our whole being, in fact—the
body by external penance, the soul by the total surrender
of our will.' Certainly, no form of false mysticism could
have taken root in Madame de Chabannes' community.

Another characteristic note is her insistence on the spirit
of faith ; she warns the religious of the danger of becoming
familiar with holy things, and so losing the reverence so
insisted on by St. Benedict. And faith is to be the basis of
that mutual charity which comes before all else. ' Be sure

that all your penances that are so much talked of in the world, if they are void of charity, will be without merit for Eternity.' The religious ought to ' reproduce in their conduct the lives of the first Christians, who were but one heart and one soul.' They are to ' bow to each other with affection, like Sisters destined by their vocation to begin their beatitude in this world by the union of their hearts.'

Now and then there are flashes of a somewhat caustic wit, for Madame de Chabannes was a true Frenchwoman and, moreover, a Gascon. Speaking of reverence for the Cross, she exclaims : ' I know some who have such respect for crosses that they are afraid even to touch them.' She gives no quarter to any of the little foibles of the religious, and if she appears at times somewhat severe, this can hardly be a matter for surprise. Inured to hardship as she herself had been, in the prisons of the Reign of Terror and on the frozen plains of Russia, she may perhaps have found it hard to tolerate the weaknesses of those who had been through no such stern school. Her daughters, however, loved her with devoted affection. Children also loved her, and an old woman who died in 1919 had happy recollections of her childhood in Madame de Chabannes' last years, when the Reverend Mother used to sit in the harvest field with a group of privileged children round her, an immense apple-pie in the midst, made in an earthenware milk pan. Needless to say, the pie soon disappeared.

The death of the Foundress marked the close of the first period in the history of the Priory, the destinies of which she had guided for forty-two years, through so many vicissitudes and difficulties of all kinds. The election of the new Prioress was held in July, 1844, and resulted in the choice of Mother Mary Joseph (Charlotte Troy) who had been Mistress of Novices for several years. Born in Ireland in 1804, of Protestant parents, she was received into the Church in 1827, entered at Stapehill in 1830, and was professed in 1832. Bishop Baggs, who had just been appointed to the Western District, on the death of Bishop Baines, presided at this election, and at the same time made the Visitation and gave a few days' retreat to the religious. He is described in the chronicle as ' a very amiable and holy Bishop, and much regretted at his death, which occurred the following year.'

Bishop Baggs was succeeded by Dr. Ullathorne, who presided at the election of 1847, when Mother Aloysius (Anne O'Brien) became Prioress. Bishop Ullathorne also made a Visitation, and at the same time laid the foundation stone of the new church, on May 28, 1847. This was Bishop Ullathorne's only visit to Stapehill, as he was translated to the Midland District in the following year.

In 1850, the community had the privilege of a Visitation made by the saintly Dom Bernard Palmer, first Abbot of Mount St. Bernard, as delegate of Bishop Hendren, Dr. Ullathorne's successor. It was the first Visitation made by a Cistercian Abbot since Dom Augustin's last visit in 1822, nearly thirty years earlier.

At the election of 1850, Mother Mary Josephine (Marguerite Campion) was appointed Prioress. By her gentleness and charity she won the affections of all, and became a true Mother to the community, being elected and re-elected until her death in 1871. She was then in the sixtieth year of her age and the thirty-second of her religious profession. Her body was laid to rest in the same vault as that of Madame de Chabannes, of whom she was a worthy successor. During the latter years of her life she was constantly ill, but the community would not hear of her resignation, and with the approval of Bishop Vaughan, Mother Cecilia, the Sub-Prioress, assumed to a great extent the government of the house. On Mother Josephine's death, Mother Cecilia (Blanche Keats) was elected Prioress, and was likewise re-elected until her death, in 1882. She also was much loved by the community as a wise yet gentle Superior. In spite of her delicate health, she continued to the end to fulfil her duties, and held Chapter for the last time only two days before her death.

CHAPTER XIV

THE most urgent problem with which Father Andrew was
faced was the building of the Priory church, the old chapel
of the Jesuits being now in a ruinous condition and, moreover, quite inadequate for the needs of the community and
of the congregation. In a letter of appeal addressed to the
Catholics of France, Father Andrew thus describes this old
chapel as he found it in 1840 :

' On my arrival I found only a poor chapel which served
both for the community of Trappistines and for the neighbouring Catholics, and could only contain a small number
of the latter. It was horribly damp, as eight or ten steps
led down to it, and it was in such a state of dilapidation
that more than half of it collapsed soon after my arrival.'
' It then became necessary,' he goes on ' to consider seriously
how to find the means of repairing this disaster, and of
building another chapel, in proportion to the needs of the
congregation ; but for that, I had no other resources but
Divine Providence and the inexhaustible charity of the
faithful. I set to work courageously.'

Since that time, it had become a matter of even more
pressing necessity. The chapel had long been too small
to contain the religious, a number of whom had to be accom-
modated in an adjacent room in the old building. The latter
was now being demolished ; the community, therefore,
were obliged to occupy the whole of the chapel, Mass being
said for the people in the schoolroom, which then stood
opposite the Pilgrimage. This room was quite inadequate
to accommodate the congregation, which greatly increased
in Father Andrew's time, owing to the number of conversions made by him. His purpose, then, was to build a
church in which the Divine Office could be worthily carried

out, and in which ample space should be reserved for the congregation.

To this project he devoted himself heart and soul, trusting in Divine Providence, since human means were entirely lacking. In those days, the building of a Catholic church was a bold undertaking, especially in a remote country district, and it was hardly to be hoped that sufficient funds could be raised among the Catholics of England. Father Andrew, who had spent fourteen years in France, determined to appeal to the generosity of that country as well. For half a century the relations between French and English Catholics had been close; France could never forget the generous hospitality Protestant England had shown to her persecuted priests and religious, as well as to many of the laity during the period of the Revolution. The Church in England had benefited by this hospitality, and in every district there were French émigré priests in charge of missions and otherwise assisting the Vicars Apostolic. Some of these priests, as well as many of the religious, had returned to France after the restoration of the monarchy; others had preferred to remain in England and continue their apostolic work. But the friendly interest of French Catholics in the progress of Catholicism in England continued, and after the Emancipation in 1829, the 'Catholic Revival' was much talked of on the Continent. In 1838, Father Ignatius Spencer and Ambrose Lisle Phillips founded in Paris an association of prayers for the conversion of England. The fame of the Oxford Movement, culminating in Newman's conversion in 1845, roused this interest still further, and a more favourable moment could hardly have been chosen for an appeal on behalf of an object likely to further the 'conversion of England.' Moreover, the community of Trappistines was not only French in origin, but still numbered several French religious among its members, and the Foundress, Madame de Chabannes, had only just died, so that there were friends and relatives of the religious in France who would be willing to contribute to the building of the monastery church. Father Andrew was not satisfied with appealing by letter, but determined to go himself and quest for alms. The years 1845, 1846, and 1847 he spent entirely in France, making his head-quarters in Paris, at the house of an excellent Catholic family of the name of Lafond. M. Edmond Lafond gives the following account of Father Andrew's mission :

' For three whole years he travelled all over France, from province to province, from town to town, from door to door, soliciting our alms with an ingenious and indefatigable charity, getting up lotteries and bazaars, and preaching sermons at which he appeared in his beautiful Trappist habit. He thus collected quite large sums, which he passed on at once to the community, keeping nothing for his own needs. But fortunately he lodged in an hospitable house which regarded his presence as a blessing, and indeed it was impossible to see his kind and gentle countenance without believing that God was with him. His Anglo-French speech had an inexpressibly naïve charm, so true is it that charity is beautiful and beautifies all who possess it in their hearts. . . .'

The acute political differences which were dividing France at the time mattered little to Father Andrew ; he begged from all alike—Republicans and Royalists, Legitimists and Orleanists—and his appeal was seldom refused. He was kindly received at the Tuileries by Queen Amélie, consort of Louis-Philippe, who presented a large oil painting for the church, and the statues—a Pietà flanked by two kneeling angels—now on the altar of Our Lady of Dolours in the nuns' choir ; also the five plaster medallions of angels bearing the instruments of the Passion, surrounding the altar. Father Andrew likewise approached the Duc de Bordeaux (' Henry V '), more usually known as the Comte de Chambord, who had visited Stapehill in 1843, while staying at Lulworth Castle, and obtained from him the gift of a handsome silver-gilt ciborium, richly chased, round the foot of which runs the following inscription : ' Donné par M. le Comte et Madame la Comtesse de Chambord, au couvent de Stapehill, le 8 décembre, 1847,—Priez pour nous ! Priez pour la France ! '

Only three months later occurred the Revolution of February, 1848, and the abdication of Louis-Philippe, who like his predecessor, Charles X, took refuge in England.

These events came as a blow to Father Andrew's hopes, for much of the help he had been promised was no longer forthcoming. He remained, however, in Paris for some time, soliciting help for a bazaar which was to be held in Manchester in the following year. The church was by this time nearly completed, but a considerable sum was still required, and for this Father Andrew issued a further appeal, supported by a letter he had received from the Prioress, Mother Mary Joseph Troy, in which she gives a moving picture of the state of poverty in which the community found itself at that time. 'Since the heavy winter rains,' she writes, ' our poor house is in such a state that I do not think it will remain standing another winter. . . . We are reduced to such a state of poverty ourselves by the total failure of our potato crop that we have not a single one to eat, and nevertheless they formed three-quarters of our subsistence. How are we to buy bread for nearly fifty people, without counting the poor, when we have not five francs in the house ? . . .'

While Father Andrew was thus engaged in Paris, M. Lafond paid a visit to England, in May, 1848, armed with letters of introduction to Stapehill and Mount St. Bernard. He has recorded his impressions of his English tour in a little volume entitled *De la Renaissance Catholique en Angleterre*, on the title-page of which it is stated that it was to be sold for the benefit of the unfinished chapel of the Trappistines of St. Mary's, Stapehill, in England. We give a translation of his description of Stapehill, abridging it slightly here and there, as although the style is somewhat quaint, it gives an interesting picture of the Priory at that period—the old monastery as it had been during the long years of Madame de Chabannes' rule.

' . . . I had already arrived at Stapehill while I was still looking for it. A pretty little girl tending her cows, dropped me one of those deep English curtsies which cause the shortest petticoats to touch the ground, and opened a wooden gate in a quickset hedge enclosing a lovely meadow dotted with trees, through which some buildings could be seen. We entered an avenue of newly-planted firs, while I looked in vain for the steeple and cross of the monastery, forgetting that the poor chapel was still unfinished. I soon perceived its half-built brick walls and Gothic windows framed in white stone, through which appeared a stretch of serene blue sky. I examined these unfinished buildings with as much interest as the pious Æneas those of the rising Carthage. Nothing which has God for its object is small, and the humblest of our chapels with the belief in the Real Presence is as interesting to the Catholic heart as the most splendid cathedral.

' My coachman stopped at a little covered porch whose arched doorway seemed to me to be the right entrance to the convent. I rang the bell to beg for hospitality like a real legendary pilgrim. The Sister portress appeared, and scarcely had I shown her Father Andrew's letter when she exclaimed that they had been looking forward to my visit, and that a letter addressed to me at the convent awaited me.

' The Sister ushered me into the parlour, a little low-ceilinged room, and left me while she went to inform the Reverend Mother. Left alone, I examined everything in the room with interest, and looking out of the small-paned window saw a little silent courtyard, round which ran a wooden gallery forming the entrance to the cloister. . . . I was aroused from my daydreams by the arrival of a little old white-haired man, his head inclined on his right shoulder, dressed in an old overcoat which appeared to date from the emigration. He declared himself my fellow-countryman, which I at first doubted on account of his speech, half English, half French, but in the end I noticed that French words predominated. . . . The good Père Palemon and I soon became the best of friends, and we began speaking French, more or less well, with the Sister portress, who had been a long time with Madame de Chabannes and had learnt a few words of our tongue from her. This Sister was called Marie-Thérèse ; never was great name more humbly borne, but perhaps it was not less precious in the sight of God.[1]

' At length, Madame Mary O'Brien, the Superior of Stapehill, did me the honour of coming to the parlour with the Sub-prioress and one of her nuns. The latter was in

[1] Sister Mary Teresa, choir oblate, was portress for forty years ; she died in 1876, having made her vows on her death-bed.

the world Miss Charlotte Troy, in religion Sister Mary Joseph. I recognised her at once as being an Irishwoman by her almost French vivacity and the cordiality of her greeting. . . . They plied me with questions about Father Andrew and his good fortune in being so well received in Paris, but I assured them that in spite of all, he thought only of the day when he would be able to return to Stapehill. Sister Mary Joseph spoke the most and I understood her best. . . . She appeared so gay and happy that it did me good to see her. . . . The sound of a bell was heard and these ladies left us. I saw them crossing the courtyard to regain the cloister and resume their life of silence, prayer and work. . . .

' I remained in the parlour where Sister Marie-Thérèse had laid the table for supper.

' Père Palemon introduced me to the two other Trappists who lived with him : Père Jean-Baptiste, a good old man of eighty, and Father Francis Walsh, a young Irish priest, quiet and grave, who served the mission.

' We soon got acquainted. After supper, which consisted of tea and brown bread and butter, as it was still raining, we spent the evening by the fire. Père Palemon spoke to me of France which he had not revisited since 1792, of the revolutions there, about which he had the strangest ideas. We spoke also of the state of the entire Christian world, shaken to its foundations, and commented on the beautiful remark of Fénelon : *L'homme s'agite, et Dieu le mène*, and we ended with the conclusion that the Cross which had already saved the world was still its only salvation.

' It was pleasant for me, an exiled traveller, to meet in this corner of England with a common faith and similar ideas, and to be able to speak freely of religion and politics, the two greatest subjects a man can converse upon, since the one concerns his earthly and the other his eternal interests.

' At nightfall we retired. Father Francis escorted me from the parlour and out of the convent. After crossing a little garden we reached a small brick house where he lodged and where I was to stay with him. He gave me a poor little cell, very clean and warm, whose one window looked out over a charming countryside, gently sloping to beautiful meadows divided by quickset hedges and great oaks which, from their number and the luxuriance of their foliage, looked in the distance like a vast forest. I remained a long time leaning on my window-sill contemplating the scenery, over which the twilight was gathering. The storm had ceased, and the sun had set amidst crimson clouds ; it was a calm and peaceful evening which made me think of that song of eventide in which Wordsworth compares Nature to a nun in adoration before God :

> ' It is a beauteous evening, calm and free ;
> The holy time is quiet as a nun
> Breathless with adoration. . . .'

' The following day was Whit Sunday. Before the High Mass I visited the chapel in course of construction. It was a pleasure for me to see it after having so often heard it spoken of by Father Andrew. Its pure, simple Gothic style satisfied my artistic taste ; the blending of brick walls picked out with white stone looks well. . . .

' Père Palemon said Mass in a little school temporarily serving as a chapel and too small for the congregation, part of which has to remain outside. . . . After Mass he offered to show me the neighbourhood, and first the exterior of the nearly completed monastery, of brick, like the church, and monastic in its simplicity. He pointed out the cemetery, overlooked by the window of his room : " an excellent view," he said, " which daily reminds me : ' Brother, thou must die ! ' "

' We visited the convent farm, extremely fine, and well kept by an Irishman who knows his work and is most devoted. Père Palemon made his parochial rounds among his little Catholic flock, in my company. . . . These good people, on seeing a Frenchman from Paris, eagerly asked : " When will our Father Andrew come back ? " Never have I seen a man more loved and respected. Père Palemon told me that he had a special gift for drawing hearts to him and a persuasive manner which no one could resist. . . . Returning through the heather which the Trappists are going to clear and cultivate, I wanted to climb the hill which has given Stapehill its

L

name. It is a narrow promontory, bare and wild, where Madame de Chabannes caused four fir trees to be planted which have grown very well, and whose sombre plumes wave proudly against the horizon. From it there is a pleasing and widespread view; but this green English countryside always seems a trifle monotonous, dotted here and there with brick cottages that some traveller has compared to pieces of toast in an enormous dish of spinach.

' On returning to the parlour, Madame O'Brien sent me word that I could be admitted into the nuns' choir for Benediction if I wished. I joyfully accepted this exceptional favour and followed Père Palemon, who crossed the cemetery, where I cast a glance at Madame de Chabannes' tomb. We then entered a little sacristy, where I caught sight of an old nun who was arranging the vestments.[1] Père Palemon smiled and pointed me out to her; I saw her bow and intimate by signs her great pleasure at seeing me. Père Palemon told me she was one of the last French religious who had followed Madame de Chabannes, and that she was charmed to see a compatriot, while regretting that the Rule did not allow her to speak. . . .

' We entered the low, damp, half-ruined chapel which, please God, will soon be replaced by the new church. I was shown into the sanctuary, separated from the nuns' enclosure by a green curtain, only partly drawn aside at the moment of Benediction. A choir of invisible voices always makes a lively impression by its mysterious harmonies, but above all when it is a religious chant executed by women's voices. The Trappistines sigh rather than sing the psalms, and I recognised Sister Mary Joseph's voice at once; she was behind me, hidden by the curtain, and soon left her place to go and play the organ. The muffled sounds of the organ, joined to the plaintive chant of the psalms, threw me into a religious ecstasy; it seemed to me as if heaven were half opened and that I enjoyed a foretaste of the angels' songs. . . .

' Perhaps all these monastic details will sound very trivial and childish, but to me who saw them being accomplished they appeared great because done for God. I there

---

[1] This was Mère Albérique Guillemin, who entered in 1822 and died in 1850 at the age of seventy-two.

perceived how the smallest good action is of more worth and more useful by the example it gives, than the finest oratory or the sublimest literature. . . .

' At Stapehill I realised all the great and beautiful things that the love of God can operate in souls. . . . On days of sadness and discouragement I shall remember this little monastic world, so calm, simple, and kindly, because sure of its aim which it ever keeps before its eyes ; I shall recall with emotion my silent cell, my ecstasies in the church and on hearing the organ, my morning walks round the enclosure of the little convent, amidst meadows sparkling with dew, beside elder-bushes in flower mingled with wild roses.'

Father Andrew was able to send home from France the sum of £2000 ; the rest of the funds required for the church was raised in England and Ireland. The architect to whom the work was entrusted was Mr. Charles Hansom, who afterwards designed so many of our best known Catholic churches. The foundation stone was laid by Bishop Ullathorne on May 28, 1847, and the church was finally completed in the summer of 1851, free of debt, to the great credit of Father Andrew's indefatigable zeal and persever-ance. The solemn consecration took place on July 16, 1851, Feast of St. Stephen, and was performed by Bishop Hendren, now Bishop of Nottingham, on behalf of Dr. Errington, who, although already appointed to the See of Plymouth, had not yet entered his diocese. The ceremony was an impressive one, and attracted large numbers, as there were but few consecrated churches in England at that period. The following account is taken from the report published in the *Catholic Standard* at the time :

' The church was crowded in every part, and many were unable to obtain admission. Soon after eleven o'clock the procession moved from the school-room in the following order :

' Thurifer and cross-bearer and assistant acolytes, with lighted torches ; six boys in cassocks and surplices, bearing large bundles of lilies ; clergy two by two ; the Lord Abbot of Mount St. Bernard, in mitre and cope, attended by one of his monks in the Cistercian habit ; Right Rev. Bishop Norris attended by his chaplain, the Right Rev. Bishop of

Newport and chaplain, the sub-deacon of the Mass, Rev. Mr. Woollet, the Deacon, the Rev. Mr. Brindle ; the assistant priest in cope, the Rev. F. Laurenson ; the Lord Bishop of Nottingham in chasuble, with mitre and pastoral staff, train-bearer, mitre-bearer.

' The procession, guided by the Hon. and Rev. W. Clifford, as master of ceremonies, went along the north aisle of the chancel, and entered by the West door ; having arrived at the Sanctuary, the High Mass commenced ; the sermon was preached by the Right Rev. the Bishop of Newport. At the offertory a collection was made by Miss Doughty and Miss Weld, assisted by Mrs. Weld and Colonel Macdonald. It amounted to £57.'

The church is of brick, with stone facings, the interior being plastered. It is in the Early English style, and belongs to the architectural revival inspired by Pugin. It is a hundred feet in length and fifty in height, and consists of two parallel naves, divided by an arcade of seven fine arches, extending the entire length of the church. One of the naves forms the monastic choir, while the other is reserved for seculars, and each has its own sanctuary and altar. The first two arches are left open, only a light screen dividing the two sanctuaries, so that both altars can be seen from some parts of both naves. The remaining arches are filled in by panelled wainscot, rising to a height of nine feet from the ground, and surmounted by large glass windows, thus completely separating the nuns' choir from the outer church.

The choir of the religious is divided by a screen into two parts—the upper choir, containing fifty stalls for the choir nuns (thirty with desks in front of them, to hold the great folio psalters, antiphonaries, and graduals used by the Cistercians, and twenty lower stalls in front of the desks)—and the lay choir, containing thirty stalls for the lay Sisters. At the west end is the belfry tower, from which the summons to prayer is heard day and night over the surrounding countryside. The great bell, weighing 1150 lb., was blessed by Bishop Vaughan in January, 1856, the second and smaller bell being added some thirty years later.

The secular part of the church consists of a nave, with

ample seating accommodation for the congregation, and a side aisle on the north, containing the Lady Chapel and the Baptistry.

The stained glass windows are the work of Hardman of Birmingham, and though crude in colouring, are the best that was being produced at that date. The window over the altar in the nuns' choir was presented by Mr. Hardman as a memorial to his family; it represents Our Lady of Dolours, with St. Anne and St. John to the right and left. On either side of this window are two stone statues, of Our Lady and St. Joseph respectively (the latter being the gift of the architect, Mr. Charles Hansom), resting on carved stone brackets. In the window over the altar in the secular part of the church, Our Lady is seen holding the Divine Child, with St. Stephen Harding and St. Bernard on either side, while the west window represents St. Joseph, St. Patrick and St. Bridget. The altar was painted and decorated by Father Robert Smith, formerly President of Sedgley Park School, who had become a monk of Mount St. Bernard.

Père Palemon, who had so long served the old chapel, did not live to say Mass in the new church. The first Mass celebrated in it was the Solemn Requiem sung by the religious for the repose of his soul. He died on May 19, 1851, in the eighty-second year of his age and the fifty-fifth of his religious profession, having been confessor to the nuns for forty-one years and resident chaplain for thirty-four. Born at St. Malo in 1770, of noble family, Nicolas Rousselin was an ecclesiastical student at the outbreak of the Revolution, and was thrown into the same prison in Paris as Madame de Chabannes. We do not know whether it was to her that he owed his Cistercian vocation, but escaping to Jersey, he thence made his way to Lulworth, and began his novitiate with Dom Antoine in 1795.

While living at Stapehill, Père Palemon was universally revered for his sanctity, and especially for his gentleness and patience, which remained imperturbable through every trial. He was devoted to the poor and sick of the neighbourhood, and beloved by them in return. A friend wrote of him a few days after his death: ' The dear old Père Palemon

departed this life on Monday morning last, at seven o'clock
—a glorious change for one who in this world has followed
our Beloved Saviour with humble submission to the crosses
of this life, to a bright and immortal change. His memory
will ever be cherished in my bosom with affection. Con-
sidering his age, and the race he has run, I feel disposed to
say *quiescit in pace* rather than *requiescat in pace*. Would
that my end would be like to his when death shall summon
me to the tomb.'

Père Palemon was laid to rest in a small vault adjoining
that of the Foundress, under the memorial cross.

After the completion of the church, Father Andrew continued, with unwearying devotedness, to collect funds for
the purpose of improving and completing the monastic
buildings. During the next fifteen years, thanks to his
efforts, the present monastery gradually took shape, being
added to little by little as funds permitted. The old chapel
was first repaired and now served as the refectory and
kitchen ; rooms were also built over it, these being occupied
for some years by the chaplain, and afterwards converted
into a dormitory. The adjoining block which forms the
infirmary was next erected. Funds were still wanting,
however, to carry out fully the proposed plan, which included a building comprising parlours, guest-rooms and
chaplain's quarters, to form the new front of the Priory,
and thus complete the quadrangle, three sides of which—
the church, infirmary, and dormitory—were already built.
This quadrangle was to be surrounded by the cloisters.
Authorised by Bishop Vaughan, Father Andrew made
another journey to Ireland in 1859 to collect funds, and in
1861 was able to send the sum of £334 to the Mother Prioress,
while a further sum of £326 9s. was subscribed in England
for the same purpose.[1] The foundation stone of the new
guest-house was laid on May 8, 1860, and that of the
cloisters on Whit Monday, 1861. When these were completed, the Priory assumed its present appearance, the main
entrance being in the new front, while the old buildings
beyond, together with the cemetery, were all now within

[1] The total amount collected by Fr. Andrew for the church and monastery, from 1847–1866, was over £8000, most of which was in small donations.

the enclosure. In spite of demolitions, enough of the old monastery still remains for it to be possible to reconstruct it in imagination as it was when M. Lafond visited it, surrounding the old courtyard, which stands as it were back to back with the new quadrangle.

The cloisters, though very simple, with their red-tiled pavement and raftered roofs, give a truly monastic character to what is otherwise a somewhat heterogeneous group of buildings, with no pretence to architectural beauty, and marked only by poverty and simplicity. The school, sacristy, and farm buildings were also erected by Father Andrew Hawkins.

During the latter years of his life, Father Andrew became extremely deaf, and was no longer able to hear confessions; it was, therefore, necessary for him to have an assistant. Several young priests succeeded one another in this capacity for short periods, until in 1861 Father Magine was appointed, who remained until shortly before Father Andrew's death. This holy Cistercian priest died on May 1, 1866, after twenty-six years of self-sacrificing labour on behalf of the humble monastery to whose service he had devoted himself. He was buried in the little cemetery within the enclosure, close to the cross under which lie the remains of the Foundress and Père Palemon.

The new cemetery for seculars at the end of the avenue was opened in 1856, the first to be buried there being Canon Tilbury, on June 14 of that year. After that time only chaplains, lay brothers and a few special benefactors were buried in the nuns' cemetery. The last secular priest to be buried there was Canon J. H. Abbot of St. John's, Norwich, who for over forty years was a friend and frequent visitor at Stapehill. He died suddenly in the parlour on April 5, 1868, aged sixty, thus obtaining the fulfilment of a long-cherished wish of his, to die at Stapehill and be buried in the nuns' cemetery.

CHAPTER XV

LATER YEARS

At the restoration of the Hierarchy in England in 1850, Stapehill was included in the diocese of Plymouth, being situated in the extreme east of that long and straggling diocese. The first Bishop of Plymouth, Dr. Errington, does not appear to have visited Stapehill. In 1855 Dr. Vaughan succeeded Bishop Errington, and in him the community were to find a true Father in God, such as they had not had for the past thirty years. Bishop Vaughan was consecrated at Clifton on September 16, 1855, and installed at Plymouth on the 25th of the same month. On November 13 he paid his first visit to Stapehill, blessed the great bell, and professed four novices. Distant as the Priory was from Plymouth, Bishop Vaughan's visits were frequent from that time onwards, and he showed the most kind and fatherly interest in everything that concerned the well-being of the community, both temporal and spiritual. He made the Canonical Visitation regularly, and his ' Visitation Cards ' show his detailed knowledge of Cistercian observances, as well as his intimate personal acquaintance with the community. This close relationship continued throughout the forty years of Bishop Vaughan's administration, and the community owes a deep debt of gratitude to this loved and venerated Bishop.

In 1863 Stapehill was again visited by a Cistercian Abbot, Dom Bartholomew Anderson, Abbot of Mount St. Bernard, who was delegated by Bishop Vaughan to make the Canonical Visitation in his stead.

Dom Bartholomew found that the religious were still practising certain customs peculiar to the Reform of Val-Sainte, which had long been discontinued in the Order, such as saying the *Miserere* prostrate in the Chapter room after

Compline, and prostrating on the knuckles after each of the invocations at the end of the *Salve Regina*. These he ordered to be given up. One custom, however, from the Regulations of Val-Sainte—that of the yearly renewal of vows at the Offertory of the Mass on the Feast of the Purification—was retained, and continued to be observed down to the year 1933.

On the death of Father Andrew Hawkins in 1866, Father David Walsh was sent by the Abbot of Mount Melleray, Dom Bruno Fitzpatrick, to succeed him as chaplain at Stapehill. Father Walsh had been a novice at Mount Melleray, but was unable to make his profession on account of weak health. He was an immense Irishman, six foot seven in height, and with a heart, it was said, as large as his stature. This genial and kindly priest won the affections of all, Protestants as well as Catholics. He died at Stapehill on January 13, 1878, aged sixty-six, his Requiem being attended by a large number of priests, as well as by many of the laity. The two chief mourners, who by special permission were admitted into the enclosure for the burial, were a Protestant clergyman, Rev. Mr. Garland of Stone, and General Sir Edward Greathed of Uddens, also a Protestant, who wrote afterwards in his journal : ' Everyone will feel the loss of Fr. Walsh ; he identified himself with the interests of all around him, and I much regret his loss.'

Father Walsh was buried in a vault next to the grave of Father Andrew Hawkins, two carved stone crosses of similar design commemorating the two priests. He was succeeded as chaplain by Father James Hayes, a professed monk of Mount Melleray, who remained five years at Stapehill, being recalled to his monastery in 1882.

Father Stephen Barron, another professed monk of Mount Melleray, also lived at the Priory from 1868 to 1882, assisting Father Walsh and Father Hayes, and helping the community in many ways. He obtained for them a complete set of the Cistercian liturgical books—ten each of the great folio psalters, antiphonaries and graduals, two Missals and two martyrologies. Until then, the martyrology used in Chapter—the only copy which the community possessed—was one which Madame de Chabannes had

brought with her from Saint-Antoine, and which must have
accompanied her in prison and through all her journeyings.
It is a Cistercian martyrology printed in Paris in 1689, at
the end of which are inscribed the feasts proper to the Abbey
of Saint-Antoine, and the obits of all the Abbesses, the last
name being that of the redoubtable princess, ' Donna Maria
Gabriel Eleonora.'

Father Stephen also obtained from his niece, Mrs. Leonard
of Dublin, the gift of thirty sets of breviaries, which were
greatly needed and are still in use. He returned to Mount
Melleray in 1882, with Father James Hayes.

In September, 1882, Father Austin Collins, of Mount
St. Bernard, was appointed chaplain. Henry Collins, afterwards Father Austin, was born at Barmingham in Yorkshire
on April 28, 1827, being the son of an Anglican clergyman,
Rev. Thomas Collins. His childhood was spent at Knaresborough House, Knaresborough, and in later life he wrote
an account of St. Robert, the hermit of Knaresborough, as
an appendix to his life of St. Robert of Newminster.[1]
Educated at a preparatory school at Stamford in Lincolnshire, and at Rugby, under Thomas Arnold, Henry proceeded to Durham, where he read law, and was afterwards
called to the bar. Under the influence of the Oxford Movement he gave up the legal profession and became an Anglican
clergyman, working for some time in the East End of London.
While still an Anglican, he wrote the two famous hymns :
' Jesus, my Lord, my God, my All,' and ' Jesus, meek and
lowly.' It was his acquaintance with Ambrose Phillips de
Lisle which finally brought him into the Catholic Church,
and his reception took place in the private chapel of Grace
Dieu Manor about the year 1857. Having been ordained
priest, he became chaplain to Mr. de Lisle at Grace Dieu in
November, 1859, taking charge at the same time of the
mission of Shepshed. He at one time thought of becoming
a Redemptorist, but contact with the neighbouring Abbey
of Mount St. Bernard gave him a strong attraction to the
monastic life, and in April, 1861, he left Shepshed and
entered the Abbey. He received the Cistercian habit on
April 20, 1861, made his simple vows on the Feast of the

[1] *The Spirit and Mission of the Cistercian Order* (1866).

Purification, 1863, and was solemnly professed on October 11, 1869. His connection with the de Lisle family continued after he became a monk; he was a frequent preacher at Grace Dieu, Shepshed and Garendon, and on March 9, 1878, delivered the funeral oration when Ambrose Phillips de Lisle was laid to rest in the church of the Abbey he had founded. It was during the twenty-one years he spent at Mount St. Bernard that Father Austin published most of his historical, ascetical and mystical works; he also translated or edited several mediæval mystical treatises, which were thus rendered for the first time accessible to the modern reader.

Over thirty years of Father Austin's long life were to be spent at Stapehill, where he arrived in September, 1882. Reverend Mother Margaret Dillon was then Prioress, having been elected in the preceding July, on the death of Rev. Mother Cecilia. Mother Margaret was re-elected in 1888, and died suddenly on July 16, 1891, two days after the expiration of her second triennium. She was a great lover of Holy Rule, and did much to promote regular observance.

One of the most unfortunate consequences of the separation of the Priory from the Order was the absence of any complete and definitive book of Regulations or Usages, or even Constitutions. For many years the community had only manuscript copies of a compilation from various sources, embodying the customs in use. The result was that it was often difficult to know exactly what observance should be followed. Bishop Vaughan was fully alive to the disadvantages of this, and it was under his auspices that the volume entitled *Use of the Cistercian Nuns of the Strict Observance of Our Lady of La Trappe* was prepared, Father Austin Collins being principally responsible for it. It was published by Burns and Oates in 1886, and was followed by the nuns of Stapehill until recent years. At the Visitation of 1888, Bishop Vaughan said: ' We rejoice greatly in each of you having a copy of the *Usus*. It teaches you the plain path of your duties. Its injunctions are binding on all, superiors as well as the last of the community, nor can they be changed without our authority. From all that we can learn, the observance of what is inculcated in the *Usus* has greatly tended to better observance . . . for on many points it has made what was obscure or uncertain, clear and distinct.' The book had, of course, no official sanction beyond that of Bishop Vaughan himself, but it was entirely drawn from the Constitutions and Usages of the Cistercian Order, with the exception of the modifications introduced by Bishop Collingridge. Most of the latter, moreover, as already pointed out, had since become part of the legislation of the Order.

In 1883, Bishop Vaughan received from Colonel and Mrs. Graham a donation of £500 for the community, which he expended on various much-needed improvements in the buildings. He visited the Priory early in that year to inspect the house, and returned in May with workmen. For the next three or four months he came to and fro at frequent intervals, directing and encouraging the workmen, and sometimes staying for more than a week at a time. Father Austin also obtained donations, and many useful alterations and additions were made. The roof of the dormitories was raised, and ventilators put up, which greatly contributed to the health of the community. A new staircase was constructed, leading to the dormitories ; the lay Sisters' work-room, with the novices' dormitory over it, was built, also a new bake-house and wash-house, calefactory and potato-house ; all these, with many other minor improvements, between July, 1882, and July, 1885. The ladies' guest rooms were built in 1884, at the expense of a benefactor, Miss Pope. It was at this time that the altar of the nuns' choir, which had been erected according to liturgical requirements, was moved back against the wall, in order to allow of a passage for the nuns to leave the choir without passing through the sanctuary. Father Andrew Hawkins had had the church arranged like those of Cistercian monks, with the upper door within the sanctuary itself, and this unfortunately necessitated the change. The grilles, both in the church and in the parlour, were erected early in 1891.

A few months later, Rev. Mother Margaret died, and Mother Alberic Lloyd-Anstruther, a former Benedictine nun of Colwich, was elected Prioress. In the same year, 1891, another Benedictine nun joined the community. This was Mother Walburga Weld, daughter of George Weld, Esq., of Leagram Hall, Lancashire, and granddaughter of Thomas Weld of Lulworth. Professed as a Cistercian in 1893, she became Sub-Prioress, and died in 1899.

Rev. Mother Alberic was succeeded in 1894 by Rev. Mother Agnes Rolls, who had been Prioress from 1885 to 1888, and was again re-elected in 1897 and 1900. Born at Lulworth in 1841,[1] she entered the house before she was fifteen, was clothed on October 21, 1856, and made her profession on St. Bernard's Day, 1861, at the age of twenty. She died on October 3, 1900, only a month after the election, in her sixtieth year. Mother Malachy Ryan was elected to succeed her, and in 1903 Mother Scholastica Shean, who remained in office until 1913, and died in 1923.

Bishop Vaughan's last Visitation at Stapehill was made in 1894. For nearly forty years he had watched over the interests of the community, both spiritual and temporal, but he was growing old and infirm and could no longer make the long journey from Plymouth to Stapehill. His Coadjutor, Bishop Graham, made the Visitation as his delegate in 1896, 1898, and 1899. The good Bishop died on October 25, 1902, much to the sorrow of the community of Stapehill, who lost in him a devoted father and friend. His name will ever be held by them in grateful remembrance. Bishop Graham, who succeeded Bishop Vaughan, was also a kind friend to the community, though his visits to the Priory were less frequent than those of his predecessor.

Father Austin Collins finally left Stapehill in January, 1913, and returned to his monastery of Mount St. Bernard. He was then in his eighty-sixth year, and on arriving at the Abbey informed his Superior, Father Louis Carew, that he had come to prepare for death. Father Louis sent Bishop Keily the following account of his last years and his death, which occurred on January 29, 1919, when he was in his ninety-second year. ' He entered on what was practically a new life for him, with all the zeal and fervour

---

[1] Through her mother, Mary Slade, Rev. Mother Agnes was the great-, niece of Mother Juliana Slade, the first English nun professed at Stapehill, who had entered the house nearly forty years earlier.

of an earnest novice, edifying the whole community by his obedience, humility, simplicity, and devotion in public and private prayer. He strictly persevered in these dispositions to the end, as far as the infirmities of age and health permitted him. It was astonishing how vigorous he was in mind and body until about seven months ago, when his memory became so much impaired that he could no longer venture to say Mass. This privation he felt keenly, for it was a daily joy to him to offer the Holy Sacrifice, which he habitually did about 4 a.m., after assisting at Matins and Lauds in the choir. . . . He was highly gifted, and so redolent of the religious spirit and solid piety as to exercise a charm for those who shared his sentiments. . . . He continued to move about pretty much as usual. I thought it advisable to have the doctor to see him, and he considered that owing to his great age—ninety-one—he might succumb. Accordingly the Last Sacraments were administered, and on the following morning—January 29—he breathed his last whilst his confessor was reciting the prayers for a departing soul.'[1]

Bishop Keily himself gives the following character sketch of Father Austin : ' In appearance I remember him as a fine upstanding man of frank manners, with a remarkably clear look which saw everything without betraying any curiosity. He took a direct interest in any topic, and gave one the impression of having a full and hard-thinking mind. There was, however, a strange aloofness with regard to general topics which let him drop conversation in the impersonal way a receiver is put back on a telephone. This marked independence of everything conveyed the impression of being sufficient without self-sufficiency. It was not the coolness of indifference, for it was all the other way. It all came from the great reality of his life. Father Austin was a very holy man and nothing else. Very little intercourse was necessary in his case to receive a deep and lasting impression of his real holiness, for spiritual things do not always require prolonged experience of life or

---

[1] Quoted in Bishop Keily's Introduction to the new edition of Fr. Collins' *Spiritual Conferences*, published by Burns Oates and Washbourne in 1920, pp. x–xi.

abnormal wisdom to be guessed at. A mere hint, a stray intuition, a seemingly inconsequent act, a mere peep through the chinks of the clouds, may be channels of a very complete information. All sorts of people at Stapehill knew what he was. Wrapped up in contemplation and the intimacies of a Divine life he looked upon all things in its haze. Hence everything in this passing world he would look upon if charity demanded it, but as merely passing.'[1] Nothing need be added to this appreciation, for no one could be better qualified than Bishop Keily to speak of Father Austin, who himself, as the Bishop points out, sedulously cultivated obscurity, and strove to ' efface all tracks.' He informed no one of his approaching departure from Stapehill, but quietly slipped away, sending the Bishop a post card from the station to say that he had gone. With his long white beard and patched habit he was in appearance the very type of the mediæval ascetic, and was a well-known figure in the neighbourhood.

During the summer of 1912, Father Celsus O'Connell, the present Abbot of Mount Melleray and Father Immediate to Stapehill, came to the Priory to act as assistant to Father Austin. After a few months' stay he returned to his monastery, and Father Leo Fitzgerald of Mount St. Joseph Abbey, Roscrea, took his place. On Father Austin's departure in February, 1913, Father Leo remained as chaplain until the following October, when Rev. Edward Damen from Tiverton was appointed chaplain to the community and to take charge of the mission, Father Leo returning to his monastery. Since that date, secular priests of the diocese have acted as chaplains.

In September, 1913, Rev. Mother Scholastica resigned her office and Rev. Mother Maura Perry was appointed Prioress by Bishop Keily. Rev. Mother Maura's long and fruitful rule will rank in the future as perhaps the most memorable chapter in the history of Stapehill, marked as it has been by two achievements of the first importance—the reunion of the Priory with the Order, and the foundation of a house in Ireland.

In 1927, the General Chapter decreed that for the sake of

[1] *Ibid.*, pp. ix–x.

uniformity, all the Superiors of the houses of nuns should bear the title of Abbess, and should wear as the insignia of their office a cross and ring of a simple character. From that date, therefore, the Prioress received the title of Abbess, those of Prioress and Sub-Prioress being now borne by the second and third Superiors respectively.

CHAPTER XVI

DURING the nineteenth century several attempts had been made to bring about the fusion of the three Congregations of Trappists, but without success. Leo XIII, however, had the unity of religious Orders very much at heart, and it was under his auspices that the reunion was finally achieved.

In 1891 the eighth centenary of St. Bernard's birth was celebrated at Fontaines-lès-Dijon, and an immense concourse of Cistercian Abbots, representing all the different observances, was assembled. This gathering gave the final impetus to the movement towards reunion, and the three Trappist Congregations petitioned the Holy See to that effect. In October, 1892, Leo XIII convoked a General Chapter at Rome under the presidency of Cardinal Mazella, representing the Cardinal Protector, Monaco della Valletta. Fifty-five members were present, thirty-two being mitred Abbots, and during eleven sessions the vital questions at issue were freely and pacifically discussed. At the end of the Chapter, by a majority of forty-seven votes out of fifty-two, the three Congregations of La Grande Trappe, Sept-Fons and Westmalle elected to unite into a single autonomous Order, under the title of ' Order of Reformed Cistercians of Our Lady of La Trappe,' having at its head an Abbot General, residing at Rome. The election of the Abbot General resulted in the choice of Dom Sebastien Wyart, Abbot of Sept-Fons, who had taken a leading part in the negotiations for reunion. Formerly an officer in the Pontifical Zouaves, then monk of Mont-des-Cats, secretary for some years to the Procurator General in Rome, then successively Prior and Abbot of Mont-des-Cats, founder of the monastery at the Catacombs of St. Callixtus, Abbot of Sept-Fons and Vicar-General of that Congregation, Dom Sebastien seemed in every way marked out by Providence to be the first head of the newly-constituted Order.

Leo XIII, who had ardently desired the union—*vehementer optat* were his own words—rejoiced in the happy issue of the Chapter. ' This Chapter,' he said, in an address to the Abbots, ' will have the utmost importance in the history of the Order, on account of the admirable concord which has reigned in it throughout, and thanks to which the desired fusion of the various Congregations has been attained—the union of all the members in one body and under the direction of one Superior. This most important fusion will give new life to the Cistercian Order, and will be for it the source of most precious advantages.' And again, ' this work will endure and will prosper.'

A Decree of the Sacred Congregation of Bishops and Regulars, dated December 8, 1892, officially confirmed the acts of the Chapter. The Trappistine nuns formed part of the newly-constituted Order. The Constitutions and Usages, both of monks and nuns, were carefully drawn up and were confirmed by the Holy See. They conformed as closely as possible to the primitive Usages of Cîteaux, with the exception of the rules of fasting, which, at the express wish of Leo XIII, underwent some modification, in order to render them more in accordance with the weakness of modern constitutions. But a Cistercian Prior, not of the Strict Observance himself, was able to declare that ' following almost exactly the rule and usages established in the twelfth century by the founders themselves and by St. Bernard, the monks of the Strict Observance represented the true Cîteaux, the Cîteaux of the Golden Age.'

The work of reunion was crowned by the acquiring, not without great difficulties, of the ancient Abbey of Cîteaux, the cradle of the Order, secularised since the Revolution. It was in 1898, the eighth centenary of the foundation of Cîteaux, that it became once more the property of the Cistercian Order. The Abbot General now became titular Abbot of Cîteaux, and the Apostolic Constitution of 1902 decreed that the Order should be entitled ' Order of Reformed Cistercians or of the Strict Observance,' having its chief monastery at Cîteaux, being on the same footing as the Cistercians of the Common Observance, and enjoying all the privileges and favours conferred in the past on the Order of Cîteaux.

Since that time, the General Chapter has been held year by year at Cîteaux, as it was in the days of St. Stephen and St. Bernard ; all the European Abbots attend yearly, and those outside Europe at fixed intervals. Modern means of transit make it possible for the Chart of Charity to be more fully observed than it has ever been since the early days of the Order, and through the faithful carrying out of the Cistercian system of General Chapters and Regular Visitations, St. Stephen's ideal of unity is now once more attained : ' that all may live united in the observance of one and the same Rule, according to the same customs, and in a common charity.'

The spirit infused into the Order by its founders, and which the Chart of Charity was intended to preserve in its expansion, has thus survived all the vicissitudes of history. Reforms and renewals have had vitality and permanence in so far as they were permeated with this spirit ; in so far as they departed from it they became dead branches. The Feuillants and other congregations and reforms renowned for fervour and austerity died a natural death, but in La Trappe the primitive spirit survived, in spite of an admixture of alien elements, and when the cataclysm came and the monastic Order was all but swallowed up in the general upheaval of society, it was La Trappe which handed on that primitive spirit. It was by the monks of La Trappe that the sacred flame was kept burning, and Val-Sainte transmitted it to modern times. The era of Dom Augustin, like that of de Rancé, was extraordinary, and the state, both of religion and of society, called for an extraordinary remedy. When conditions became normal again, the excrescences dropped off of themselves, and the true Cistercian tradition remained intact—the proof of vitality and healthy condition of any organism being its power to reject any elements which it cannot assimilate and which do not promote its growth. All the legislation of the General Chapters since the reunion shows a constant endeavour to return in all things to the primitive ideals of Cîteaux, thus carrying out the words addressed to all the religious Orders in the schema of the Vatican Council : ' We strongly exhort the Superiors of Orders and all religious carefully to maintain regular observance and discipline, and to show themselves religious not only by their habit, but *by the virtues and spirit which animated their holy founders.*'[1]

The community of Stapehill had, of course, no part in the reunion thus happily achieved at the end of the last century, but they became more than ever desirous of returning to the unity of the Order. It was not, however, until 1915 that their long-cherished aim was realised. In the autumn of 1914, Rev. Mother Maura approached Bishop Keily on the question, and His Lordship most kindly gave his consent to the presenting of a petition to the Holy See, promising to do all in his power to ensure its success. The community having expressed their wishes by an all but unanimous vote, Bishop Keily himself despatched the required documents to Rome, to be presented to the Sacred Congregation of Religious. The petition was favourably received, and on April 29, 1915, the Feast of St. Robert, Founder of Cîteaux, a Rescript was granted by His Holiness Pope Benedict XV, authorising the Most Reverend Abbot General of the Order of Reformed Cistercians to restore the Priory of Our Lady of the Holy Cross, Stapehill, to the jurisdiction of the Order. This was formally accomplished in the following July by Mgr. Augustin Marre, Bishop of Constance, who in 1904 had succeeded Dom Sebastien Wyart as Abbot General. Mgr. Marre showed the most fatherly kindness to the community, and addressed the following letter to Rev. Mother Maura, a letter which filled the hearts of all concerned with joy and gratitude :

' Cîteaux Abbey,

27 July, 1915.

Reverend Mother,

With very great joy, and with lively feelings of gratitude towards the Sovereign Pontiff, who has been graciously pleased to accord you the favour, I hasten to send you the Rescript which places your Convent again

[1] *Schema*, I Constit. de Regul.

under the jurisdiction of the Cistercian Order. In this eighth centenary of the foundation of Clairvaux by Saint Bernard, your dear community is a scion that is grafted once more on the mighty tree of Cîteaux. The reunion will be for your community a source of abundant blessings through the intercession of our glorious Founders and Fathers in Christ. Furthermore, it will be a renewal stronger than ever of loyal fidelity to the spirit and the rules of our holy Order. The ardent desires and patient efforts of your community to attain reunion will thus be crowned with complete success.

May each and all remain faithful to the strict observance of the Holy Rule. May our sainted Fathers intercede on your behalf. With this two-fold hope, Reverend Mother, I give most cordially to you, and to your daughters, my fatherly and choicest blessing, together with the assurance of my love for you all in Our Divine Lord.

(Signed) AUGUSTIN MARRE,
Bishop of Constance, Abbot-General.'

The Right Rev. Dom Maurus O'Phelan, Abbot of Mount Melleray, Ireland, was appointed Father Immediate—the first Father Immediate the community had known since Dom Augustin de Lestrange ceased to hold that office, over ninety years before.

In the year 1922, to the great regret of the Order, Mgr. Marre was obliged to resign the office of Abbot General, owing to failing health. He was shortly afterwards honoured by His Holiness Pope Pius XI with the title of Archbishop of Melitene, and died at Cîteaux in 1927. He was succeeded by Dom Jean-Baptiste Ollitrault de Kéryvallan, Abbot of Melleray, who in August, 1923, honoured the Priory of Stapehill with a short but greatly-appreciated visit. Though it was his first visit to Stapehill, Dom Jean-Baptiste was formerly well known in Plymouth diocese as Superior of the community of Woodbarton, South Devon, where the Abbey of Melleray had established a refuge in view of possible expulsion from France. An unforgettable personality, frail in body but with rare gifts of mind and heart, it was above all by sheer personal holiness that he made an indelible impression on all who came in contact with him. His brief visit to Stapehill will long be remembered. He had promised to come again and make a longer stay, but on February 25, 1929, he died at Rome after a short illness, to the great sorrow of the whole Order.

On September 23, 1928, the community had the sorrow of losing the beloved and venerated Bishop to whom they owed the great blessing of their reunion with the Order. Bishop Keily had been a true Father in God to the community of Stapehill during the seventeen years of his episcopate, and his name will always be held by them in grateful veneration. His visits to the Priory were frequent, notwithstanding the long journey involved, and were always a joy and inspiration to all. The spiritual conferences he gave in the Chapter room will live long in the memories of those who heard them. He had a profound knowledge of religious life, especially that of the contemplative Orders, and understood and appreciated the Cistercian vocation. He especially admired its character of simplicity and unity, comparing it to the lives of the Patriarchs as summed up by the Book of Genesis in the phrase ' walking with God.' In the Canonical Visitations made by Bishop Keily, all his interest seemed to be in the spiritual life of the religious, and each one who went to him felt that she was understood, for he had the gift of reading souls. He always took a special interest in the novices and postulants, and many owed much to his kindly encouragement in the early years of their religious life. In his latter years, when Stapehill was visited regularly by an Abbot of the Order, the Bishop no longer made Visitations, but his informal visits to the Priory were just as frequent as before. The last was in June, 1928, three months before his death, and although in failing health he climbed the stairs to the infirmary to visit a sick Sister, remarking as he did so : ' Wherever I go in this house I feel the Presence of Our Lord.'

Since the reunion with the Order, the community had considerably increased in numbers, and this made it possible to entertain the project of a foundation in Ireland. There had always been a steady stream of Irish as well as English vocations at Stapehill, both choir and lay, and there being already two flourishing monasteries of Cistercian monks in Ireland, Mount Melleray and Mount St. Joseph, many desired the establishment also of a house of nuns of the Order in that country. In the autumn of 1926, the property known as Glencairn Abbey,[1] near Lismore in County Waterford, and about ten miles from Mount Melleray, came into the market. Situated in a solitary spot on the banks of the River Blackwater, amid some of the most beautiful scenery in Ireland, the property consisted of a fine mansion with farm buildings, and a hundred and fifty acres of land, partly arable and partly wooded. It seemed an ideal spot for a Cistercian monastery, and Dom Maurus O'Phelan, then Abbot of Mount Melleray, proposed to acquire it for that purpose. The community of Stapehill having expressed their willingness to make the foundation, the purchase was concluded, and the Abbot and community of Mount Melleray became the owners of the property, of which they made the munificent offer to the community of Stapehill, undertaking to carry out all the alterations and additions necessary for the conversion of the house into a Cistercian monastery. All the required authorisations for the foundation having been obtained, Rev. Mother Maura crossed to Ireland in the autumn of 1927 to inspect the property and advise regarding the plans for the remodelling of the house. These proved very extensive, and included the building of an entire new wing; it was also thought well that the monastery church should be completed before the nuns came into residence. The work extended over several years, and it was not until March, 1932, that the foundation was actually made. The venerated Founder, Dom Maurus, did not live to see the accomplishment of the work he had set on foot, and which he had so deeply at heart. He died at Mount Melleray on July 10, 1931, to the great sorrow of the community of Stapehill, whose Father Immediate he had been for sixteen years. It was reserved for his successor, Dom Stanislaus Hickey, to welcome the Cistercian nuns to Ireland.

On March 8, 1932, the departure from Stapehill finally

---

[1] The house was christened ' Glencairn Abbey ' by a former owner, a Protestant, who enlarged the existing mansion in 1795. There was never a monastery there.

took place. All good-byes were said the day before, and the solemn silence of the night was still unbroken when the little band of fifteen religious left their enclosure to found the first monastery of Cistercian nuns in Ireland since the Reformation. Mass was said immediately after the Vigils, and all received Holy Communion together for the last time. At five o'clock the whole community assembled in choir and went in procession through the cloisters to the enclosure door, headed by Cross and candle-bearers, and reciting the *Benedictus*. The travellers, wearing a black cloak over the Cistercian habit, followed, and, as the community drew up in two lines along the cloister, passed straight through in silence and out of the enclosure door, Reverend Mother Maura, Foundress of the new monastery, walking last. In silence they entered the car which was waiting to convey them on the first stage of their journey.

Thus, on this ever memorable day in the annals of Stapehill, the project which had been so dear to Madame de Chabannes, but which had had to be abandoned a century earlier, was at length fulfilled in God's own time. After a hundred and thirty years of existence, Stapehill had made her first filiation and become a Mother House. In January, 1935, the Irish house became an autonomous community, independent of the Mother House. Reverend Mother Maura had remained in Ireland to guide the rapidly growing community, and at the expiration of her seventh trienniate as Abbess of Stapehill, was unable to return, the state of her health not allowing her to undertake the journey. She therefore resigned her office, to the regret of all, and on January 12, 1935, the Reverend Mother Paula Turner, who had been the first postulant received by Reverend Mother Maura after the latter's appointment in 1913, was elected to succeed her as Abbess of Stapehill. On this occasion the community had the privilege of the presence of His Lordship Bishop Barrett, Bishop of Plymouth, who presided over the election, assisted by the Abbot of Mount Melleray. Shortly afterwards the Priory of Our Lady of the Holy Cross, Stapehill, received the official title of 'Holy Cross Abbey,' by which it is now known.

A week after the election at Stapehill the professed religious of St. Mary's Abbey, Glencairn, made their vow of stability, and on January 31, Reverend Mother Maura Perry was elected the first Abbess by the unanimous votes of the community. Her health, however, was failing rapidly, but with heroic fortitude and endurance she continued to govern the community for the remaining eight months of her life. She was eighty years of age when she died on the Feast of St. Teresa, October 15, 1935. Many years of Mother Maura's life had been spent at Stapehill, yet it was at the monastery of Glencairn that she was to be buried. Thus the daughter house possesses the grave of Mother Maura, as the mother house does that of Madame de Chabannes ; and at Glencairn, as at Stapehill, the tomb of the Foundress will mark the centre of the monastic cemetery.

CHAPTER XVII

CISTERCIAN LIFE : SOLITUDE IN COMMUNITY

In an earlier chapter we gave a brief outline of the type of monastic life organised by St. Benedict in his Rule. It remains to be shown how that life is lived in our own day by the Cistercians of the Strict Observance. We will speak first of those aspects of the Cistercian life which make most impression on modern minds ; of the distinguishing features by which it is characterised among the manifold forms of religious life now existing in the Church.

The special character of Cistercian life as compared with other forms of contemplative life may be summed up in three words : it is a life of *solitude in community*. The Cistercians, it has been truly said, are the cenobites *par excellence*[1]—that is, the religious of the common life. For them there is no external solitude ; everything is done in common. The liturgical prayer in choir ; the spiritual reading in the cloister or chapter room ; the manual work, whether out of doors or in the common work-room ; the meals taken in the common refectory—all these exercises, which fill up a Cistercian day, are done in community. Even the repose at night is taken in a common dormitory, and although each one has a separate cubicle, these are only divided by wooden partitions, the entrance being closed by a curtain. The Cistercian has no cell, properly so called, which she can call her own, and where she can be really alone. There is thus no respite from the exigencies of community life, from the exercise of self-restraint and consideration for others which it demands. To the modern mind this may appear as one of the principal mortifications, and to certain temperaments it may well be a greater sacrifice than any of the bodily austerities. But this was

---

[1] Abbé E. Maire, *Les Cisterciens en France*, p. 228.

not so to the same extent in former times. Human nature, it is true, never changes, and as we saw, St. Benedict was fully aware of the value of constant contact with others as an instrument of sanctification. Still, life in common was simply the normal thing for many centuries. The common dormitory was universal, and most of the varied activities of the monastery were carried on in the cloisters. So that this was no part of the reforming programme of the early Cistercians. It was not until the fifteenth century that the cubicles which had gradually been introduced became in reality separate rooms. In the period of decadence the Cistercians, too, had private cells, but from the seventeenth century the Strict Observance has adhered to the Rule in this matter, so that it is now a distinguishing feature of the Order. For it must always be borne in mind that all austerity is relative, so that while the observances of an Order may remain identical, their effect will be different in different periods, and the emphasis on the various aspects of the life will therefore change. The letter of the Rule has of necessity been mitigated as regards the fasts appointed by St. Benedict, but the balance of austerity is preserved in other ways, and not least by the continual living in community. At the same time this must not be pressed too far. There is no such thing in the Cistercian Usages, whether of monks or nuns, as any regulation forbidding a religious to be alone, and in actual practice it is by no means an impossible thing for a religious to find herself alone, whether at some employment, or at private prayer in choir, or in the garden. It simply means that there is no place or time when such solitude can be counted upon, and that normally all the exercises are done in community.

It is the teaching of St. Thomas[1] that the society of his fellow-beings is necessary to man in the pursuit of perfection, because without it he cannot be exercised in the virtues. St. Thomas is here at one with St. Benedict[2] in regarding the life of absolute solitude as befitting only the soul which has already attained perfection. And that great Thomist, M. Maritain, has pointed out[3] that it is only in the religious

[1] *Sum. Theol.*, II–II, Q. 188, art. 8.
[2] Cf. *Holy Rule*, Ch. I.
[3] *Three Reformers :* Rousseau.

state that a real harmony is achieved between these two, often conflicting, forms of human life. Perhaps that harmony is nowhere more perfectly achieved than in a Cistercian monastery. There is found to the full that social or community life which, says M. Maritain, ' remains the life natural to man, required by his deepest needs.' For community life is a stimulus and an inspiration, and provides the aid of that force of example which is so potent a factor in human life. At the same time it provides a field for the acquirement and exercise of virtue, especially of those specifically Christian virtues of fraternal charity, patience, meekness, humility, obedience—all of which necessarily require a setting for their exercise. In both these ways community life furthers and helps the life of the spirit ; even the very defects inherent in it ' work together,' as M. Maritain says, ' for the good of the spirit '—and how ?—' by the virtue of obedience, of a limitless sacrifice.' Yet that life of the spirit might too easily be swamped by such constant contact with others, were it not for the law of silence. The increased emphasis on common life demands, as a counterbalance, an increased insistence on silence. The soul, thus disciplined by community life, is set free by silence to commune with God unhindered. And silence has, in fact, become the principal feature of the Cistercians of the Strict Observance, so that they are known in the Church as the ' silent Order.' To the outside world this appears, perhaps, the greatest of penances, but it is not so in reality. A contemplative life is essentially a solitary life, a life lived alone with God in the depths of the soul. External solitude, as we have seen, is denied to the Cistercian, yet thanks to the silence there is no more solitary life possible, short of the eremitic life itself. The prevailing silence of a Cistercian monastery forms an atmosphere of prayer in which the soul finds it easy to ascend to God.

In his book of war sketches, *French Windows*, the late Monsignor Bickerstaffe Drew gives a sympathetic description of a visit to the Cistercian monastery of Mont-des-Cats. Of the monk who escorted the visitors, he says : ' Silence was not merely his habit but his atmosphere, and he breathed it, expiring it as well as inhaling : silence was not his prison

but his freedom ; he escaped out of talk into it whenever his
captors let him go.'[1] The character of Cistercian silence
could hardly be more happily expressed. Silence is, indeed,
the very atmosphere of the Cistercian life. We speak of
' the silence of the grave '—a silence due to the mere absence
of life—but Cistercian silence is not of that kind. On the
contrary, it is a silence like that of nature, throbbing with the
energies of an intense life ; not an empty silence, but one
which is full of God—God, who Himself dwells in eternal
silence. It is like that profound silence of which the Book
of Wisdom speaks, in which the Almighty Word leaped down
from the Throne of God—for it is only in silence that the
soul can hear the Voice of God. Silence is to the Cistercian
what the cell is to the Carthusian, and in that interior enclosure the soul is free to speak to God, to listen to God, undis-
turbed by externals. The perfect observance of Cistercian
silence demands a great reverence for the interior life of
others, and we find the Usages of the Order descending to
such details as the noiseless opening and shutting of doors,
the manner of walking, and so on, all of which materially
affect the atmosphere of silence. Yet this external silence is
only a means to the acquiring of the interior silence of the
soul. Beneath the silent exterior goes on the ceaseless war
against self, by dint of which alone is attained that silence
of soul which implies a victory over all inward disturbances—
that PAX which has become the very motto of the children
of St. Benedict, and which is the goal of the contemplative
life, for it is the fruit of perfect charity.

There are many false ideas current regarding the Cistercian
rule of silence, and it may be well to state exactly in what it
consists, and in what it does *not* consist. It should hardly be
necessary to say that there is no such thing as a ' vow of
silence,' or even ' perpetual silence,' in the absolute sense of
the word. All the religious may speak freely to two
Superiors : all may speak to the Abbess ; the choir religious
may also speak to the Prioress, and the novices and lay
Sisters to their respective Mother Mistresses. These officials
are always accessible at certain hours of the day, and can be
freely approached at these times. In certain employments

[1] John Ayscough, *French Windows* (1917), p. 237.

where two Sisters work together, permission may be given to speak for what is necessary regarding the work. The Cellarer, or housekeeper, who directs the work of the lay Sisters, can speak to them concerning the work, and they to her. Apart from these cases the silence is absolute, the religious having no communication with one another, either by speech or writing. All necessary communications incident to daily life are carried on by means of a code of manual signs, which have been handed down from the Customs of Cluny. It is not true that the signs constitute a kind of deaf and dumb language, and actually take the place of speech ; in point of fact they cover only a very limited field, and for whatever cannot be conveyed by signs, the religious must have recourse to a Superior to whom they can speak, and settle the matter through her as intermediary. There is no common recreation, that is, general conversation, even on the greatest feasts. On any occasion when the community are assembled, no one may speak except to the presiding Superior. There are certain evergreen legends current on this subject, but they can easily be refuted by a reference either to the Constitutions or Usages of the Strict Observance, whether of monks or nuns, all of which have been revised in conformity with the Code of Canon Law, and have received the approbation of the Holy See within the last few years. No mention of recreation occurs in any of them, nor has there been any question of introducing it. Nothing is dearer to the Cistercian than her rule of silence, and to touch that rule would be to touch one of the most vital points of the Constitutions.

'What an unnatural life !' some will exclaim. The exact contrary is the truth. We even venture to assert, at the risk of appearing paradoxical, that the Cistercian life is pre-eminently 'natural.' Serious-minded adults in any walk of life do not feel the need of spending several hours a day in recreative conversation. In a Cistercian monastery all are fully occupied, and all are happy and contented ; each one goes about her duties in silence, occupied with her work, and still more with the interior work of communing with God ; no one feels the need or wish for conversation, or even notices the absence of it. Should anyone desire to unburden herself, if only for the sake of relaxation and without any special necessity, she is free, as we have said, to go and speak to a Superior. And provision is made by the Rule for all such communication as is indispensable to the good ordering of the monastery. To those who live the life it seems an ideal combination ; living always in community, a normal human life, and with all the advantages of community life, the Cistercian is yet always a solitary, a contemplative, the law of silence protecting, as it were, the solitude and independence of the soul. When we come to describe the different occupations of a Cistercian day it will be seen that they form such a well-balanced scheme of life that no specific recreation is required, the alternation of spiritual and mental activities with manual labour providing sufficient relaxation for mind and body in turn. And this balance and variety of occupations prevents any kind of strain or tension, so that the silence never becomes burdensome, but on the contrary seems as natural and necessary as the air we breathe.

Another marked feature of Cistercian life, and one which is intimately connected with the rule of silence, is *liberty of spirit*. There is no attempt to force all souls into the same mould ; each one is free to follow her own interior attraction, and is even, in a sense, compelled to do so, since the interior life of her sisters is to her a sealed book. It is often remarked by those who visit a Cistercian monastery that the religious do not seem to bear a common stamp, but preserve their own individuality. If this is true of the exterior it is still more true of the inward life of the soul. While living in constant juxtaposition, each soul is in reality a world in itself, and lives its own life alone with God, who fashions it as He pleases. This will be more clearly seen when we come to speak of the spiritual exercises of the Rule.

But while silence is thus the ' cloister of the heart,' preserving inviolate the interior solitude of the Cistercian, common life is the safeguard against an egotistic self-absorption or a false individualism. As already pointed out, it affords a field for the exercise of many virtues, and above all, of the supreme virtue of charity. It is stated in the *Spiritual Directory* of the Order that one of the qualifications required for the Cistercian life is a ' sociable character.'[1] This may cause some surprise, but if the word is taken in the literal sense it is strictly accurate. A character ' able to associate with others,' fitted for the companionship of others, is most necessary in a life of constant though silent intercourse, while on the other hand, anything like an aloof or morose disposition is the worst possible qualification for a Cistercian vocation. It is charity which oils the wheels in community life, and in Cistercian life there are many opportunities for little acts of charity and thoughtfulness for others. When speech is forbidden, an increased importance attaches to the manner and demeanour of each religious. The old-fashioned virtue of courtesy, which is the flower of charity, is not out-of-date in a monastery. The off-hand, casual manners too common at the present day—not to speak of anything like actual rudeness—are totally out of place. Nor is it sufficient to observe correctly the rules of politeness, and yet to go about with an aloof and distant air, absorbed in self or in one's own affairs. Something much more positive and cordial is required. An affectionate consideration for others, a large-hearted tolerance of their weaknesses, a spirit of generous self-sacrifice, and that constant cheerfulness which implies a constant death to self—all these should be characteristics of the true Cistercian, and experience shows that the more solitary and recollected is the soul, the more does charity radiate from her. For cheerfulness does not mean dissipation, and the continual giving of self to others is only possible in the light of faith, which sees Christ in every soul. Thus the mere external routine of community life demands a very thorough-going self-renunciation. Personal preferences, tastes, ideas, habits, and mannerisms have to be sacrificed, in order to fall in generously with the common life and not to be a trial to others. And this self-renunciation is itself the greatest aid to the interior life of prayer, for it effects that emptying out of self which enables God to fill and possess the soul, while without it all prayer is illusory.

This, then, is the special character of the Cistercian life as distinct from that of other contemplative Orders. ' These

[1] *Directoire Spirituel à l'Usage des Cisterciens Réformés* (Bricquebec, 1910), p. 68.

two essential observances, common life and perpetual silence, thus wedded, combine together,' says a French writer already quoted,[1] ' to produce the ideal contemplative, by providing him with powerful wings . . . and facilitating at one stroke . . . detachment from the world and intimacy with God.'

[1] Abbé Maire, *op. cit.*, p. 231.

N

CHAPTER XVIII

A CISTERCIAN DAY

AT two o'clock the bell for rising rings through the silent dormitories; a few moments later—for the Cistercian sleeps fully dressed on her straw mattress—all are making their way to the church through the dimly-lit cloisters. The church is in darkness, save for the sanctuary lamp. After a few moments' silent prayer before the Blessed Sacrament, the signal is given for the Office of Our Lady. The Cistercian day begins and ends with Our Lady, and her Office precedes the Canonical Office at every Hour except Compline. The first words which break the silence of the night are those of the angelic salutation—*Ave Maria, gratia plena, Dominus tecum*—all meanwhile prostrating on the knuckles; that is, kneeling bowed down with their knuckles on the ground, a ceremony peculiar to the Order, and specially, though not exclusively, reserved for the honouring of the Mother of God. Matins and Lauds of Our Lady are then recited by heart in the darkness. The Cistercian ' Little Office ' does not vary with the liturgical seasons, but always honours especially the Mystery of the Incarnation.

Half an hour's mental prayer follows, forming an immediate preparation for Matins and Lauds of the Divine Office, which begin at three o'clock and are usually over at about four o'clock. On Sundays and greater feast days, the concluding portion at least of Matins—that is, the *Te Deum* and the Gospel, sung by the Superior—and the whole of Lauds, are always sung, while the rest is recited on a monotone. On other days, the whole of the Night Office is recited. On ferias the Office of the Dead follows. The Angelus concludes this first portion of the monastic day, which is known as the Vigils.

The religious then retire to the dormitory to wash, change

their habits, and put their cells in order. After an interval the bell again summons them to choir for Prime, which is the first of the Day Hours and the monastic morning prayer, consecrating the opening day to God and asking His help in all its needs. At Prime and the remaining Hours, Our Lady's Office is first recited, and the Divine Office is always sung. The concluding portion of the Office of Prime is sung in the Chapter room. After the Martyrology follow the prayers asking God's blessing on the labours of the day, for in ancient times this was the hour when work began, all the religious receiving their appointed tasks from the Superior. A portion of the Rule of St. Benedict is then read, and the Abbess gives a commentary thereon, or a spiritual conference. The solemn silence of the night now ends, and this is the first use made of speech, except in prayer. On certain days, ' chapter of faults ' is next held, in which each religious accuses herself publicly of external faults against the Rule or customs, and receives a penance. According to Cistercian usage, the religious may also point out one another's faults in a spirit of charity.

Chapter concludes with the reading of any death notices which have been received, and prayers for the dead. Charity towards the souls in Purgatory has always been a marked feature of the Cistercian Order, and Masses and prayers in abundance are offered for all the departed members, relatives, and associates.

The conventual Mass, whether sung or not, is usually at six o'clock. All the preceding hours, wholly given to silence and prayer, lead up to this central act of the monastic day. Even in those communities of nuns where fewness of numbers or local circumstances make it impossible to have a Missa Cantata except on Sundays and feast days, the daily Mass is still a solemn conventual act, especially in these days of frequent Communion. Immediately before Mass the Celebrant sings what our Catholic forefathers would have called a ' bidding prayer,' in which all the intentions to be included in the Holy Sacrifice are gathered up and placed in the keeping of Our Blessed Lady by the singing of the *Sub tuum*. This is a custom of very ancient date and peculiar to the Cistercian Order. The Communion is preceded by the

beautiful and touching ceremony of the Kiss of Peace. The
server presents the instrument of the Pax to the Abbess at
the grille; she then gives the Kiss of Peace to the first
religious who comes after her, and it is communicated from
one to another, as the long line of white-robed nuns and
brown-clad lay Sisters come up to receive it—the visible
symbol of the *cor unum et anima una*, which should reign in
every community. The Communion itself is a striking
ceremony, as the religious go up in single file on the epistle
side, prostrate on the knuckles one by one, and then kneel
at the square opening in the grille to receive Holy Communion. The one who has just communicated bows profoundly, while the next takes her place at the grille, and then
proceeds slowly down the choir on the Gospel side. A quiet
time of thanksgiving follows the Mass, and at seven what is
known as ' Mixt ' is taken in the refectory.

An interval follows, usually for spiritual reading in the
chapter-room or cloister. At 8.15 Tierce is sung, and at
8.30 the manual work of the day begins. All go from the
choir to the place where the Superior announces the work to
be done; the cowls are then removed and replaced by a
working apron. On Monday morning all take their share in
the weekly washing; on other days there will be sweeping
and dusting and all the necessary work of a house to be
done, vegetables or fruit to be prepared, and these duties
will be followed by many and varied tasks in the garden or
fields, according to the requirements of the season. At
10.45 the bell again rings for the cessation of work; the
religious resume their cowls and return to their reading or
prayer.

Sext is sung at 11.10, and after a few minutes for examination of conscience, the midday Angelus is rung, and the
community go in silent procession to the refectory for dinner
at 11.30, pausing before they enter, for the ceremonial
washing of the fingers. Monastic simplicity reigns in a
Cistercian refectory, and at the same time the gravity and
dignity of a religious function. The long tables ranged round
the walls on a kind of low platform with seats only on one
side; the three Superiors—the Abbess, Prioress, and Sub-
Prioress—presiding at the table at the upper end, under the

large crucifix ; the liturgical prayer which precedes and follows the meal ; the absolute silence, broken only by the voice of the reader, who occupies a pulpit on one side : all gives an air of solemnity to the monastic repast. The religious take their turn week by week to act as reader in the refectory, and to serve their Sisters at table. After dinner the community return in procession to the church, chanting the *Miserere*, and there conclude the prayers of the Grace.

An interval follows, spent in reading and prayer ; a walk may be taken in the garden, or the religious may go and speak to their Superiors. The novices and lay Sisters have an instruction on the Holy Rule and the Usages of the Order, or a spiritual conference, several times a week, from their respective Mother Mistresses. The Office of None recalls the religious to choir at 1.15, and at 1.30 work begins again, and continues until 3.40. In the afternoon there will nearly always be outdoor work, when the weather is fine. This work is of the most varied character, from the potato-planting in the spring, through the labours of weeding and thinning the rising crops, to the seasons of harvest—the haymaking, the setting up of the corn sheaves, the gathering of the potatoes in early autumn, and the final gathering in of the root crops, mangolds and turnips, which continues well into the winter months—while, if there is no field work, there is always the garden to be kept in order.

Work ends at 3.40, and the rest of the day is given wholly to spiritual things. After half an hour's interval, Vespers are sung, the most solemn of the Day Hours, and the liturgical opening of the feast or office of the next day. A quarter of an hour's mental prayer follows Vespers, and the religious then go to the refectory for collation at five o'clock. Another interval for reading and prayer, and a few minutes after six the whole community, choir and lay, assemble in the chapter-room for the public spiritual reading, at which the choir religious take their turn as reader for the week, as in the refectory. After this, the religious go once more in silent procession to choir for the closing Office of the day—Compline, the monastic ' night prayers.' Unvarying throughout the year, Compline is always sung by heart, whether in the dusk of evening or in the winter darkness. It is a perfect prayer for the close of day, with its unchanging psalms, recited deliberately : the 4th, *in pace in idipsum, dormiam et requiescam ;* the 90th, the *Qui habitat*, the psalm of absolute confidence in God's protection, and the overshadowing of His wings. The hymn of evening, *Te lucis ante terminum*, and all the concluding formulæ express the same unshaken confidence and trustful petition for the coming night. With this Office a deepened atmosphere of peace and recollection seems to descend on the monastery. After Compline of Our Lady's Office, the liturgy of the day concludes with the solemn singing of the *Salve Regina*, the last salutation offered to the Mother of God by her Cistercian children. The evening Angelus rings out, and after a few minutes of silent recollection and examination of conscience, the religious file out of choir for the last time. The Abbess stands near the church door, and sprinkles each one with holy water as she passes out. The solemn silence of the night has begun, and will be unbroken until after Prime next morning. Not only will silence from words be kept, but all movements will be quiet and grave, and the usual greeting is omitted when the religious meet one another. In silence they go to the dormitory ; ten minutes later the bell is rung, the lamp which burns throughout the night is lowered, and all are at rest after the long day of work and prayer.

Such is the sequence of the ordinary working day in winter. In summer all take the siesta, or ' meridian,' after the midday meal until 1.30, the hour for repose at night being eight instead of seven. During the meridian the religious may either sleep or read, but absolute silence must be observed. The ' promenade ' appointed by the Constitutions is not binding on those employed in outdoor work, but the religious are always free to walk or sit in the garden during the ' intervals.'

Such is the daily routine of life in a Cistercian monastery ; one day succeeds another with a regularity unbroken except for the recurrence of Sundays and feast days. On these days there is no work, and all the time left free by the choir offices, Mass, and Benediction, is at the disposal of the religious for reading and private prayer. On Feasts of Our

Lady, and on all Sundays throughout the summer, the Missa Cantata is preceded by a procession round the cloisters, chanting responsories and antiphons appropriate to the day. At Benediction, too, the motets sung are in keeping with the liturgy of the feast or season, and always, of course, in plain chant. The Cistercian Order has its own chant, and all the choir books have been revised and brought into conformity with the most authentic manuscripts of the Order.

If it were not a life in which the liturgy holds the first and foremost place, it would be monotonous in its uniformity, but the seasons and feasts of the liturgical year provide an element of constant variety in the unchanging round of psalmody, work, and reading. Then there are the events in the family life of the monastery—days of clothing and profession. The profession ceremony among Cistercian nuns is marked by the simplicity characteristic of the Order. The rite of the Pontifical is not used, the ceremony being identical with that of the monks of the Order, with the addition of the blessing and imposition of the black veil, while the choir sing *Veni, sponsa Christi.* The vows taken are those appointed by the Rule of St. Benedict—stability, conversion of manners, and obedience which includes those of poverty and chastity.

Finally, death comes—the moment for which all life is a preparation. For a Cistercian it is very simple to die, and there is a serenity and sweetness about death in a monastery which robs it of all its gloom. The religious rests on the bier in the midst of her Sisters in choir, clothed in her religious habit, with a crown of flowers on her head as on her profession day. Two of the community watch beside her, reciting the psalter alternately. The burial is very simple. The body is not placed in a coffin, but is reverently lowered into the grave by the Sisters, and as the grave is filled up, all fall on their knees, and with knuckles to the earth, chant three times the last suppliant cry for mercy : *Domine, miserere super peccatrice !*

The life of penance is over, but the life of contemplation has passed from the shadows of faith into the open Vision.

CHAPTER XIX

THE present Constitutions of the Order begin by stating that the ' Cistercians of the Strict Observance . . . strive to attain the perfection of the spiritual life by the way of contemplation and penance.' All the observances of the Order can, in fact, be reduced to these two heads : exercises of contemplation, positively and directly leading to union with God, or exercises of penance which negatively and indirectly tend to the same end, by the removal of the obstacles to that union.

The Cistercian is by definition a contemplative, that is to say, one who applies the whole activity of her soul to God, to the exclusion, as far as possible, of other objects. St. Thomas says that the life of any man can be defined by that in which he delights most and to which he principally applies himself.[1] That which formally makes the Cistercian life a contemplative one is the amount of time given daily to exercises of contemplation. Many modern readers would expect from this to find in the Cistercian horarium long hours devoted to ' contemplation ' in the strict sense of the word—that is, to contemplative prayer, or to such exercises of mental prayer as are apt to lead the soul into the contemplative region. Such readers will have been surprised to find that, on the contrary, a decidedly meagre allowance of time—half an hour in the morning and a quarter of an hour in the evening—is allotted by the Rule to mental prayer made in common. Not private but liturgical prayer is the chief occupation of the Cistercian contemplative. It is in this public, official vocal prayer that the greater part of the hours devoted to prayer are passed. The professional work of the Cistercian is what St. Benedict calls the ' Work of

---

[1] *Sum. Theol.*, II–II, Q. 179, art. 1.

God '—the *Opus Dei*—to which he requires that nothing whatever shall be preferred. And it would not be too much to say that it is in so far as she succeeds in making this work an act at the same time interior and exterior—that is, a contemplative act—that the Cistercian will achieve the end of her vocation and become a true contemplative. All the other elements in her life are to help her to attain to this : silence, self-renunciation in the practice of humility and obedience, holy reading, manual labour—all these are to prepare the soul, directly or indirectly, to become one of the ' true adorers ' whom God seeks to adore Him, not with lip service, but ' in spirit and in truth.'

There is in our own day a great liturgical revival in the Church ; but, full of vitality as that movement is, and happily gaining ground—though as yet but slowly as far as our own country is concerned—it is none the less a revival, and it is to be feared that the liturgy is still regarded by the ' average Catholic ' rather as a cult of faddists and æsthetes than as the normal expression of Catholic piety. In the old monastic Orders, on the other hand, the liturgy is in its own home ; no revival of a bygone age, but a living tradition which has never been lost. These Orders have preserved the full authentic traditions of Catholic worship which have been long since, unhappily, lost to the laity. Up to the time of the Reformation it had not occurred to anyone to conceive of religious life without the choral celebration of the Divine Office. Only at the time of the Counter-Reformation, when the Church was compelled to defend herself against the aggressor, did those religious families spring up, wholly devoted to apostolic labours, and reciting the Divine Office only in private. The monastic Orders happily retain the ancient spirituality of Catholic Christendom, and what was formerly a universal heritage has become the distinguishing mark of the children of St. Benedict.

This older spirituality had certain characteristics from which later schools of devotion have departed. It tended to express itself in external and material forms, and was essentially social and objective in character, whereas the modern type is, on the contrary, more exclusively interior, and markedly individualistic and subjective.

In the Cistercian life the external bodily element is apparent in the manual labour and physical austerity by which the body participates in the act of the soul offering itself in sacrifice to God. But in the liturgy, too, in which, according to the old spirituality, the life of prayer is centred, the body plays an important part. Vocal prayer, the sacred chant, the manifold ceremonial, the use of material objects—all these are made use of in liturgical worship for a twofold purpose : to consecrate the whole of man's being, body and soul, and even the material creation, to the worship of God, and also to give external symbolic expression to interior attitudes of soul.

Again, the liturgy is essentially a collective, social prayer. It would be difficult to exaggerate the importance of this as a factor in the work of sanctification. During those hours when she is engaged in the ' Work of God,' the choral Office, the religious is not praying as a mere individual ; she is praying in and with the entire Mystical Body of Christ, both those members of it who are still on earth, and those already in eternity, and the entire Mystical Body is praying in and through her. It is easy to see how such a prayer, rightly understood, emancipates the soul from the little world of its own individual spiritual life, introducing it into the incomparably vaster and fuller life of the Church ; again, how it demands the sacrifice of egoism in entire self-devotion to the community act of praising God. We are far removed here from sentimental pietism.

Lastly, the old spirituality, which was centred in the liturgy, was essentially objective, and therefore contemplative in character. For the contemplative life does not mean the contemplation of self, but the contemplation of God. There is a fatal tendency among souls who cultivate the spiritual life to devote their energies to endless self-analysis, concentrating all their attention on the removal of specks of dust from their souls. But, as Father Reginald Buckler used to remark, ' it is not pleasant to contemplate a dung-hill,' and it is a more wholesome spirituality which turns its attention from the sorry spectacle of self to the contemplation of the great realities—God, and the truths He has revealed. Such was the spirituality of ancient and mediæval times, and it is still that of those religious families who, as children of St. Benedict, make the liturgy their chief work. The contemplative life thus understood is essentially positive and objective, its chief act being the act of worship or *praise*. For liturgical prayer does not turn the soul inwards in self-inspection, but outwards in praise of God.

It is of faith that God created all things for His glory, and all creation praises God, simply by being what it is—*Cœli enarrant gloriam Dei*. Man, who by his composite nature, stands midway between the material, irrational creation, and the purely spiritual (angelic) creation, gathers up, as it were, this unconscious praise rendered to God by His creatures, and transmutes it into intelligent praise ; he is thus the mouthpiece of creation. After the Fall, the original harmony of this universal hymn of praise was marred, and only with the Incarnation did God receive a praise worthy of Him. The great act of the Incarnate Word during the thirty-three years was the praise of His Father, and after the Ascension He left to His Church the mission of carrying on this work of praise. The Sacrifice of the Cross was not only a redemptive sacrifice, a sin-offering ; it was also a sacrifice of praise, a holocaust. St. Thomas teaches that ' by His Passion and Death, Christ initiated the rite of the Christian religion.'[1] The central act of worship in the Catholic Church is the Sacrifice of the Mass, which perpetuates the Sacrifice of Calvary ; and round the daily offering of the Holy Sacrifice has grown up the liturgy of praise, the Divine Office or Canonical Hours. The Mass is the very core of the Christian religion, and it may, therefore, seem superfluous to speak of it in connection with the life and spirit of any one religious Order. Yet, just because it is the centre of every Christian life, it must also be that of every form of religious life, and it is in a very special way the centre of the monastic life.

It would seem that St. Benedict intended the religious profession—that initial oblation which renders the whole of the monastic life a continual holocaust—to take place at the offertory of the Mass. This is in harmony with the concluding words of the Prologue to the Rule, in which St. Benedict

[1] *Sum. Theol.*, III, Q. 62, art. 5.

lays down the following programme for his religious : ' that per-
severing in the monastery until death, (they) may by patience
share in the sufferings of Christ.'   The sacrifice of the vows of
religion is thus, in St. Benedict's mind, closely united with the
Sacrifice of Christ on the altar ; the religious becomes by the
vows a victim, united to the Divine Victim. All Christians
may, of course, and should offer up their daily life in union with
the Sacrifice of the Altar, and the more complete their self-
oblation, the closer their participation in the Sacrifice. Those,
therefore, who have made the entire holocaust of their whole
being by the vows of religion, have a special share in the
daily Sacrifice of the Church, and it is in her daily contact
with the Divine Victim that the Cistercian finds both the
model of her life of self-abnegation and the strength to carry
it out.

' Look, and do according to the model shown thee on
the mount.'   But if she thus becomes incorporated with the
Victim of Calvary by a life of penance and self-immolation,
it is only in order that, sharing likewise in the Priesthood
of Christ, she may ' through Him, with Him and in Him '
offer the sacrifice of praise.

The two elements in her ascension to God—penance and
contemplation—the two aspects of the Cistercian life—
thus find their supreme inspiration and fulfilment in the
Mass. In all monasteries of Cistercian monks the conventual
High Mass is the central action of the day, and in all the
larger monasteries of nuns the daily Missa Cantata holds the
same place. Even where this is not possible, the community
Mass of Cistercian nuns has, as we have seen, a character of
solemnity.

Although, in the time of St. Benedict, the daily offering
of the Holy Sacrifice was not yet the custom, it is nevertheless true that the origin of the Divine Office is closely
bound up with the Liturgy of the Mass. With the Rule of
St. Benedict the arrangement of the Canonical Hours became
finally fixed ; all the divisions of the day and night were
sanctified by liturgical prayer, which thus came to envelop
the whole existence of the religious. In course of time,
when the daily Mass became the general rule in monasteries,
this life of liturgical prayer found its true focus and centre,

the Canonical Hours forming the preparation for, and, as it were, the prolongation of, the Sacrifice of the Mass.

The Cistercian Order has always held to the original arrangement of the Hours, neither anticipating nor combining Offices, but performing each at its appointed time. The Order never adopted the custom of the midnight Office, which, introduced by the Carthusians and the mendicant Orders, spread to the monastic Orders and became general among Benedictines in the later Middle Ages. Down to the present day Cistercians have kept to St. Benedict's ordinances and rise normally at two o'clock or thereabouts for the Vigils.[1] The other Offices are sung each at the traditional hour, so that, as we have seen, the whole order of the day is regulated by the recurrence of the Canonical Hours. The Cistercian thus carries out to the letter St. Benedict's maxim : *Nihil operi Dei præponatur.*[2] The Divine Office is her first and principal work, to which every other occupation is subordinated, not only in principle, but in actual fact. Each Office is announced a quarter of an hour beforehand by a ' first bell,' reminding the religious to raise her heart to God, in preparation for the work of praise to which she must soon return. Nothing could be better calculated to make the day one of continuous prayer. In the early Church it was the custom to make a pause at the end of the psalmody, for private prayer. The life of the Cistercian between the hours for the Work of God might be compared to those pauses ; it is, as it were, only an interval in the daily round of liturgical prayer, in which the soul prepares herself for the Work of God—either directly, by holy reading and private prayer, or indirectly, by manual work, which maintains the equilibrium of life, and renders the mind more capable of applying itself afresh to Divine things. All is organised in view of the liturgy, for while all the elements of Cistercian life are means of sanctification, the liturgy is at the same time an end as well as a means. And not only

---

[1] The time of rising appointed by St. Benedict varied, it is true, with the season of the year, as also did the length of the hours of the day and night. Abbot Delatte, however, concludes that ' all through the year the time of rising oscillated, it would seem, between the hours of one and three o'clock.' (*Commentary on the Rule of St. Benedict*, Eng. trans., 1921, p. 141.)

[2] ' Let nothing be preferred to the Work of God.'

is the Divine Office the paramount occupation, but the whole of Cistercian life is invested with a liturgical character. The religious go from one exercise to another, even to the work of the fields, in silent procession ; the common meals are sanctified by liturgical prayer ; the weekly functions of reader and server at table receive a liturgical blessing in choir, while the server concludes her week in office by the ceremonial washing of the feet of the community, in imitation of Our Lord's action at the Last Supper. The Abbess, who represents Christ, is everywhere saluted with a profound bow, while two religious, meeting, exchange a less profound inclination. All this detailed ceremonial of monastic life, which appears at first sight so strange to the newcomer, accustomed to the free and easy manners of the present day, is no hide-bound formalism ; it is in reality an extension of the liturgical worship in choir, rendering the whole life one continued act of homage to the Divine Majesty, a perpetual exercise of the ' virtue of religion,' which is so marked a characteristic of St. Benedict's spirituality. The cowl, the choir dress, is worn by the Cistercian not only during the Divine Office, but at all times except during work. On returning from work, the choir religious immediately resumes the white cowl, which signifies the repose of contemplation, and wears it even in the refectory. Thus, as the *Spiritual Directory* of the Order points out, not only the church, but ' every part of the monastery becomes a choir and an altar : a choir where the Divine Office is continued and perpetuated by a life of union with God ; an altar on which, as priests and victims of our own sacrifice, we immolate ourselves by the holocaust of perfect obedience.'[1] Thus Cistercians carry out to the full St. Thomas's definition of religious as those who dedicate their whole life to the worship of God.[2]

A Catholic novelist[3] once wrote : ' The cloistered life, in its perpetual protest against all that is mean and feverish, might indeed be called monotonous, but it is the monotony of the cry before the Throne, itself unchanging—SANCTUS, SANCTUS, SANCTUS, DOMINUS DEUS OMNIPOTENS, QUI ERAT,

[1] English translation : *A Spiritual Directory for Religious*, Vol. I (published at New Melleray Abbey, Peosta, Iowa, U.S.A., 1932), p. 65.
[2] *Sum. Theol.*, II–II, Q. 81, art. 1, ad 5.
[3] Mrs. Craigie (' John Oliver Hobbes ').

ET QUI EST, ET QUI VENTURUS EST.' The idea is true and beautiful; yet men are not angels, and human nature is so constituted that it needs variety, and soon wearies of one never-changing object. The Church, as a wise Mother, has provided for this by means of the cycle of the liturgical year. Year by year she renews the memory of the Mysteries of Christ in their order, from Advent to Pentecost, while the remainder of the year is consecrated to His Mystical life in the Church and in souls. Within this great cycle there is the lesser cycle of Our Lady's feasts, and throughout the year occur the feasts of the saints, in whom is seen the perfection of that transformation into the likeness of Christ which it is the work of the liturgy to effect in souls. The liturgical year is not, of course, peculiar to the monastic Order; all Christians are called upon to participate in it according to their opportunities. But to do so to the full requires, as those who attempt it seriously know well, an application of mind which is difficult in the world. In a Cistercian monastery there is nothing to hinder this application. Not only the order of the day, but the days of the week and the seasons of the year are regulated by the liturgy; the whole life takes its colour therefrom. It is easy for Cistercians to remain in harmony with the feast or season when the liturgical texts are constantly before their eyes, while the public reading in the refectory and before Compline is usually in accordance with the office of the day or season. The very order of the exercises varies with the liturgy. Lent, in particular, has a character all its own, and even apart from the fast, it is impossible to forget that it is Lent. The pictures and statues are veiled from the first Sunday in Lent, and the purple curtain hangs before the sanctuary, as in mediæval times. On Fridays, after Chapter, the religious go in procession through the cloisters, reciting the penitential psalms; Vespers are sung daily before the midday meal, and there is the silent hour of the 'regular reading' appointed by St. Benedict.

There is thus an element of variety in a life which might otherwise indeed be called monotonous. The unchanging psalmody with the recurring *Gloria Patri* is enshrined in the ever-varying setting of the Proper of the Season and the Proper and Common of Saints.

All these spiritual riches, however, will remain a buried treasure unless by study and meditation the religious enters into them and makes them the food and substance of her own interior life. A twofold preparation is required if she is to attain to St. Benedict's ideal of liturgical worship—*ut mens nostra concordat voci nostræ*—' that mind and voice may be in harmony.' There is first a preparation of mind, by the study of the psalms and other liturgical texts ; and secondly, a preparation of heart, by the practice of mental prayer and recollection, so that the soul may be fittingly disposed when she comes into God's Presence to praise Him. Ample opportunity for this twofold preparation is given by the ' intervals ' of the Cistercian horarium, representing the time appointed by St. Benedict for *lectio divina*. And while holy reading and mental prayer prepare the soul to discharge the ' Work of God ' worthily, the liturgy in its turn provides inexhaustible material for prayer, and teaches the soul the true language of prayer, inspired by the Holy Ghost, the Divine Master of all prayer.

CHAPTER XX

'LECTIO DIVINA'

ST. BENEDICT legislates very definitely for the employment of the time left over from the Divine Office, ' to which nothing is to be preferred.' ' Idleness,' he says, ' is the enemy of the soul. Therefore should the brethren be occupied at stated times in manual labour, and at other fixed hours in holy reading.'[1] The term here used by St. Benedict is *lectio divina*—the reading of divine things. This expression conveyed very much more than what we now understand by ' spiritual reading.' To the ancients it meant principally the attentive study of the Holy Scriptures with the commentaries of the Fathers thereon—a study, not for the purpose of learned research, but for the nourishment of the soul and as a means to contemplation.[2] St. Jerome himself says that reading is not to be a labour, but for the delight and instruction of the soul. Reading thus understood is an essential factor in a contemplative life, and without it prayer would evaporate in mere sentiment, or would dry up for want of nourishment. For the law of man's nature is that the will follows the intellect—*nihil volitum nisi præcognitum*—we cannot love God unless we know Him. St. Bernard says that contemplation is miraculous when not founded on previous meditation, and it is reading which provides the food for this meditation which is so indispensable. Reading, then, to St. Benedict and the ancients, meant a very different thing from what it means at the present day. It was not the rapid perusal of one spiritual treatise after another, but the attentive rumination of the sacred texts, allowing the Word of God to sink deep into the soul—a kind of spiritual communion with the Divine Word hidden beneath the writ-

[1] *Holy Rule*, Ch. XLVIII.
[2] Cf. Dr. Gorce, *La Lectio Divina des Origines du Cénobitisme à S. Benoît et Cassiodore*, Vol. I (Paris, 1925).

ten text. Such reading was in itself a meditation, and led naturally to affective prayer, which was intermingled with it, and hence to contemplation. So that from the earliest beginnings of monasticism down to the end of the Middle Ages, the traditional view of reading was as the first of a connected series of degrees, leading the soul up to perfect contemplation. This view is excellently summarised in a short treatise entitled *Scala Claustralium*,[1] written by a twelfth-century Carthusian, Guigo II, in the life-time of St. Bernard. It was for long attributed to St. Bernard himself, and therefore represents the early Cistercian tradition. According to Guigo, Reading, Meditation, Prayer, Contemplation are four rungs of a spiritual ladder leading from earth to heaven. ' Reading is a busy looking upon Holy Writ, with intention of will and understanding. Meditation is a studious searching with the mind to know the hidden meaning, by the guidance of reason. Prayer is a devout desiring of the heart to get what is good and banish what is evil. Contemplation is a rising of the heart unto God with some taste and savour of heavenly sweetness.' Again : ' Reading is without, in the bark ; meditation within, in the pith ; prayer in the desireful asking ; and contemplation in the delight of the great sweetness.' Yet there is no fixed division between these four degrees, but all are so ' linked together ' that they help each other. ' Reading without meditation is idle, meditation without reading full of error, prayer without meditation lukewarm, meditation without prayer of none effect. But prayer with devotion attains to contemplation.' It was a frequent saying of the Fathers, especially of St. Jerome and St. Augustine, that, in reading, God speaks to the soul, while in prayer the soul speaks to God. The interior life was regarded by them as a continual colloquy between the soul and God, a colloquy of which reading formed an integral part. Reading was thus at once the main source of prayer and its constant nourishment.

This, then, was the *lectio divina* which St. Benedict lays down as one of the principal exercises of his Rule, the only

---

[1] *A Ladder of Four Rungs*, edited by Dom Justin McCann, O.S.B. (Parkminster Series, 1926).

occupation, besides the Divine Office and manual work, to which he assigns a fixed time. It was not study with any external end in view, the acquiring of knowledge in order to impart it to others, but reading done solely for the good of the soul of the religious, as an exercise of the contemplative life. When intellectual work came to be substituted by Benedictines for manual work, the distinction between the hours given to the two exercises of reading and work was gradually obliterated, and *lectio divina* became assimilated, to a greater or less degree, to study properly so called. The Order of Cîteaux, however, in retaining manual labour as prescribed by the Rule, has also preserved the *lectio divina* as St. Benedict intended it. The time assigned to reading by St. Benedict is represented in the Cistercian horarium by what are now called the ' intervals '—that is to say, the time left free by the common exercises. The use of these ' intervals ' is very definitely laid down in the Usages. The Usages of Nuns direct that ' during the intervals, all the religious shall make their spiritual reading in the chapter-room or cloister, except those who are detained in their employments, but even the latter must return to the place of reading as soon as they are free. The religious may devote a part of the intervals to prayer. They must, however, bear in mind the importance attached by St. Benedict to spiritual reading.' It would be a serious error, therefore, to regard the intervals as so much ' free time '; nevertheless, within these limits they are at the free disposal of the religious, in the sense that there is no rigid rule laid down for their employment. This is undoubtedly one of the chief characteristics of the Order at the present day, and imparts an element of freedom which is rare nowadays in religious life. Scope is thus left for individual attraction and the following of each one's bent in spiritual reading, the study of the liturgy, and private prayer, mental or vocal. This, in a contemplative life, is an incalculable boon, for no two souls are alike, or can be forced into the same mould. The good use of the intervals depends very largely, therefore, on the individual religious, yet it is the touchstone of the life, for a life of liturgical prayer and manual work might otherwise become a very external and material affair, and anything but a contemplative life. Madame de

Chabannes frequently impressed on her nuns the importance of the intervals : ' Let all diligently employ the intervals in reading or prayer. We are no more free to dispose of these times than of any other. It was in these times that our Fathers sanctified themselves, and it is by the good use that we make of the intervals that we, too, shall sanctify ourselves.'

The main occupation of the intervals, then, is reading, though it is only in Lent that there is a fixed hour for this. This private reading made in common—whether in chapter-room, cloister, or scriptorium, according to local custom—is one of the great traditional features of Cistercian life, and is one of the exercises which demonstrate most clearly the twofold spirit of solitude and common life, so characteristic of the Order. In the words of a Cistercian Abbot : ' (Reading) is for (Cistercians) a professional occupation, a division of the employment of time and of life, one of the objects of their activity. . . . (It) is a work peculiarly monastic, common to all and the duty of all. It is the work of nuns as well as of monks ; in our own days it is even, up to a certain point, the work of the lay brothers and sisters in the monastic Order. With the Cistercians of the Strict Observance in particular, it forms a characteristic of the Order. Desiring, like the early Cistercians, to remain purely and exclusively contemplative, the Order encourages only this kind of reading.'[1]

Cistercians do not, as is sometimes supposed, make a cult of stupidity, neither are they vowed to a life of intellectual starvation. They simply follow an inevitable law of life, without which excellence of any kind would be unattainable—that of sacrificing a lesser good for the sake of a greater. They refrain from dissipating their mental powers on lesser objects, in order to concentrate them wholly on the highest of all objects—God and the truths He has revealed.

A well-stocked library is regarded as an essential feature of a Cistercian monastery. Moreover, in addition to the library, from which all may obtain books by means of a ticket signed by a Superior, there is what is known as ' the common box,' containing books for the common use of the

[1] Dom Anselme le Baïl, *L'Ordre de Cîteaux : La Trappe* (1926), Ch. V.

religious. According to the Usages of Nuns, these are to be ' such as deal with spiritual subjects, and in a certain measure with the study of the sacred sciences,' and are to be ' sufficiently numerous, well-chosen, and renewed from time to time according to need.' The reading of Holy Scripture, always a tradition of the Order, is held in honour by Cistercians, and always forms part of the daily reading. The study of the Divine Office affords a wide field for the employment of the intervals, and an inexhaustible source of nourishment for the soul. As an aid to this study, the learning of Latin by the nuns is warmly encouraged by the Order. There is, moreover, the theory and practice of the chant, and all that belongs to the external performance of the Work of God—all this is included among the duties which fill the intervals.

The primitive Usages of Cîteaux regulate that all may go to the church to pray, ' during the reading-time and all the intervals,' and the present Usages make the same provision, thus clearly showing the purpose of the *lectio divina*. For many centuries no fixed time was assigned to mental or private prayer. At the present day, however, the Constitutions, in common with those of nearly all religious Orders, prescribe a definite time for mental prayer to be made in common in choir—namely, half an hour in the early morning, between Our Lady's Office and Matins of the Divine Office, and a quarter of an hour in the evening, before supper. This, of course, is to be regarded as a minimum, and there is opportunity for the religious who feels drawn to it to spend a longer and even a very considerable time daily in mental prayer. This is wholly in accordance with the mind of St. Benedict, who directs in his Rule that prayer made in common is always to be short, whereas private prayer may be prolonged ' by the inspiration of divine grace.' And it is another instance of the accessibility of the Cistercian life to different types of souls, for while there are no long hours of contemplation, demanding either exceptional powers of abstraction and concentration, or exceptional graces, there is yet ample scope for souls capable of such sustained effort in prayer.

For the ideal of the Cistercian life is that it should be a

life of continual prayer.   The older legislators saw no need
to appoint fixed times for mental prayer, because the whole
day is organised in view of such prayer, which should be the
breath of life to a contemplative religious.   The alternating
occupations of the day are all of them prayer under different
aspects.   The various acts which make up the exercise of
' meditation ' as now understood are not compressed into a
single hour or half-hour, but extend over the whole day,
which thus becomes one continuous prayer, taking various
forms.   The *lectio divina*, as St. Benedict intended it—the
public and private reading which recurs so frequently—
gives the mind the necessary food, which in modern systems
is supplied by the preparation of the subject matter and the
' considerations,' these being, so to speak, a *lectio divina* in
tabloid form, suited to the exigencies of the active life.   But
the Cistercian contemplative lives in constant contact with
divine truth : the world of supernatural realities is always
present to her, and is not hidden from view by the distracting
sights of the world.   Consequently, when the time comes for
the actual exercise of prayer, it is natural that this should be
a simplified rather than a discursive prayer.   A soul living
in the Presence of God in silence, and doing God's Will all
day long by obedience, should not need elaborate preparations or preambles in order to enter into converse with Him.
And that converse is by no means confined to the fixed
half-hour or quarter of an hour, or the moments she is free
to spend in choir, but springs up naturally in the heart of
the religious, during her manual work, and wherever she
may be.   It is just this continuous affective union of the
heart with God, combined with the effective union of her will
with His Will by constant fidelity to Rule and the duties of
obedience, which is the aim of every Cistercian worthy of
her vocation.   This is, indeed, the very soul of the Cistercian
life, which without it would be no more than an empty
routine, a mechanical and meaningless drill.   Nor does this
in any way conflict with what has been said regarding the
Opus Dei, for the Divine Office itself would be mere lip
service if not vivified by this prayer of the heart.

CHAPTER XXI

THE Cistercians of the Strict Observance, in the words of their Constitutions, ' tend to the perfection of the spiritual life by the way of contemplation and penance.' It has been seen that a considerable part of the day is occupied by exercises of a directly spiritual nature—liturgical and private prayer, and holy reading. These form the contemplative side of the life. The chief element in the penitential side is manual labour, to which St. Benedict assigns the remaining hours. For ' penance ' in the Cistercian life does not so much consist in self-inflicted pain by the use of ' instruments of penance,' but is something woven into the very fabric of the life itself, and is therefore less conspicuous and more sanctifying, because it affords less room for self-satisfaction. Contrary to the general belief, there are no startling austerities. In food, for instance, it is not so much a question of rigorous fasts as of the plainness and monotony of an abstinence diet, so that novices in the Order are always told that for the Cistercian, mortification consists, not in abstaining from the food, but in taking the ample quantity required by its unconcentrated nature. This is especially the case in these days, when for so many, as far as mortification of the appetite is concerned, it is rather, as Francis Thompson expressed it, a case of ' would we had the appetite to mortify ! ' Then there is the common life, which, as has been shown, is undoubtedly a very real penance to many, and the most effective of hair-shirts. Moreover, common life preserves all other penances from the subtleties of self-love, and leaves no room for the thrill of self-satisfaction which so easily results from self-imposed austerities. The Cistercian is one of a crowd, lost in the crowd and doing the same as all the others. There is nothing here for man's natural egoism to take refuge in. This is true above all of the manual work which is unquestionably the chief of Cistercian penances, and which, together with silence and common life, is at the present day the distinguishing feature of the Order.

Manual toil—that is to say, such work as involves a real output of physical energy—is the common lot of mankind, and was the penance imposed on man by his Creator after the Fall. ' In the sweat of thy brow thou shalt eat bread ' is the law of human society, and if there are those who are in practice exempt from it, it is because others are labouring for them—if labour ceased, life would also cease. Hence those who are vowed to a life of penance must, of necessity, embrace this penance, inherent as it is in the very stuff of human life. The ideal of a Cistercian community is that it should be self-supporting, and it is laid down in the Constitutions both of monks and nuns (as in the *Exordium* of Cîteaux) that the religious—that is, the choir religious— should live by the labour of their hands, as far as possible. Literally, that is impracticable under present economic conditions, the hours of labour being necessarily too restricted to produce a sufficient output. Cistercians, like others, are compelled to use the products of industrialism, and even to possess capital (collectively, of course). But the principle is maintained, and is carried out as far as local conditions and the personnel of the community permit. A typical Cistercian monastery is like a small village in appearance, with its farm buildings and various workshops and exterior offices. In this, Cistercians aim at carrying out St. Benedict's injunction, that ' the monastery, if it be possible, ought to be so constructed that all things necessary, such as water, a mill, a garden, a bakery, and the various crafts, may be contained within it ; so that there may be no need for the monks to go abroad, for this is altogether inexpedient for their souls.'

This means that, in the mere upkeep of the monastery and the cultivation of its lands, there is usually enough work to employ the time of all the religious, though in these days poverty, and the unprofitable nature of agricultural labours, have compelled many communities to undertake an industry, which must however be of such a kind as can be carried on without detriment to enclosure or regularity.

This brings us to the question of Cistercian poverty. Poverty is differently understood by different Orders. For the Franciscan it means total dependence on Divine Providence, both collectively and individually. For those who follow St. Benedict's Rule it means that nothing may be retained without permission, but the religious is to ' hope for all things necessary from the Father of the monastery ' —that is, the Abbot, who is responsible as a father for his children's well-being. The interpretation of what things are necessary varies according to the different observances. For the Cistercian, individual poverty is complete, and its characteristic note is the absence of superfluity. But in order thus to provide what is necessary, the community itself must possess. And to carry out the ideal of a self-contained, self-supporting community, the monastery must possess land and buildings—it must be rooted in the soil. The law of labour and the vow of stability are closely bound up with this. Although various industries may, and sometimes must be undertaken, the characteristic work of Cistercians is still that of primitive Cîteaux—' agriculture and the rearing of cattle '—and for this, landed property is indispensable. A Cistercian monastery grows, as it were, from the land on which it is founded. One of the titles of praise bestowed on the monks of old was *amator loci*—' a lover of the *place* '—that is, of the monastery—and of the vow of stability which bound him to the place—an exactly opposite ideal from the detachment required of the missionary priest or nun. In mediæval days, this *stabilitas* came easily to men and women who were normally content to spend their lives in the castle or homestead in which they had been born ; but to restless moderns it may well prove a new penitential element of monastic life.

For Cistercian nuns, the present strict laws of enclosure render impossible, in many monasteries, actual field labour carried on as it has been at Stapehill for over a hundred and thirty years. But the statute is still in force regulating that the monasteries are always to be built in solitary places,

far from towns or cities, and there would always normally
be a large enclosure, providing ample facilities for the cultivation of vegetables and fruit (both for the use of the community and even for the market) ; for dairy work, poultry,
and bee-keeping, etc.—all of which would sufficiently occupy
those not retained by necessary indoor work, in the kitchen,
wardrobe, sacristy, and so on. For although agricultural
labour is normal for the Cistercian, it is not essential;
there is, of course, always the work of the house to be done,
and any kind of work may be undertaken, provided it is
simple and useful. The Usages of Nuns lay down that the
religious shall be occupied in ' the simplest kinds of work :
sewing, household duties, gardening, and whatever is useful
to the monastery, avoiding work of a dainty or superfluous
nature.'

Why this insistence on simplicity and utility, and this
exclusion of all fine or recherché work ? The reason is
twofold. First, as said above, the manual work of the
Cistercian is intended to be an exercise of penance, and
though health-giving for the body, is not supposed to be
of a kind pleasing to the natural man. Moreover, it is
performed in the spirit of poverty, and this gives it its
character of simplicity and practical utility. The second
and deeper reason belongs rather to the contemplative
aspect of the life, and is the original *raison d'être* of manual
labour as an occupation for contemplatives, based on its
ascetic value. The contemplative life is by definition that
in which man applies himself chiefly to the contemplation
of divine truth. It is impossible in the conditions of this
present life that that application should be continual.
Nevertheless, the other activities of contemplatives should,
as far as possible, be of such a nature as not to distract the
soul from the main object of its activity. The Fathers of
the Desert found in simple manual work a powerful aid
to prayer. A mechanical occupation, such as the weaving
of baskets, tended to fix the attention ; the same principle
underlies the use of rosary beads in reciting vocal prayers.
It has already been pointed out that the Cistercian horarium
devotes but little time to mental prayer made in common,
just because the aim of the Cistercian is to lead a life of

continual prayer. There is, in fact, nothing which should prove a hindrance to this. The essential characteristic of the Cistercian life is its *unity*. It is not a life of alternating prayer and work, of spiritual and material activities kept in watertight compartments ; rather is it one passed wholly in the Presence of God, making no rigid distinction between prayer and work, but passing easily and naturally from one to the other, seeing in each successive duty the Will of God to be done out of love. It is Nazareth rather than the desert of the Quarantana—the same homely exterior, the round of simple everyday duties, silent, unnoticeable, colourless even, to the casual observer, yet veiling an intensity of interior life, of worship and love, of *ascensiones in corde*, which can go on increasing indefinitely.

In that spiritual classic known as ' Bishop Hedley's Retreat,' the great Benedictine has a chapter on the Hidden Life which expresses perfectly the spirit of the Cistercian vocation. He speaks of the four pillars of the Holy House —Solitude, Obedience, Poverty, and Labour—chosen by Our Lord as the *conditions* for the better carrying on of the essential act for which the soul was created—the loving worship of its God. In imitation of Him, Cistercians choose the same conditions, and for the same object. From this point of view the external act is nothing in itself, except in so far as it serves to make the union of the heart with God as intense and continuous as possible.

Manual work, then, is an integral element, not merely in the external routine of a Cistercian monastery, but in the Cistercian ascetic ideal. It is intended not only as a penance, but as a help to the life of continual prayer at which every true Cistercian is bound to aim, for it leaves the mind free to ascend to God. At the same time, no one is encouraged or allowed to strain after a recollection which is beyond her capacity, or for which she is not yet ripe. In this way, manual labour provides the necessary balance to what might otherwise become a too exclusive preoccupation with things spiritual, and prevents anything strained or feverish. For an enclosed and silent life would be too great a strain on human nature if the time were wholly occupied with mental and spiritual activities, and would in the end defeat its own object. Man is a composite being, made up of body and soul, and both require exercise. The Cistercian life is in harmony with man's nature, and satisfies the essential needs of both soul and body—for to till the soil and praise his Creator is the life natural to man from the beginning. Contact with the soil and the things of nature leads to a sane, wholesome spirituality, freed from illusion and sentimentality—not a hot-house growth but a sturdy plant. And this contact with nature is in itself a very real communion with God, Whose intimate Presence reveals itself in every leaf and blade of grass to the soul that seeks Him, so that while at work the Cistercian finds it easy to raise her heart to God, thus continuing throughout the day the *Benedicite* of the morning's Office in choir.

This, again, preserves to the Cistercian life that character of *accessibility* which St. Benedict desired. His principle, ' that the strong may have something to strive after, and the weak may not be dismayed,' applies equally well to spiritual effort as to bodily austerity. The balance of occupations so wisely planned by St. Benedict, and adhered to by the Cistercians, makes the life possible to very different types of souls. In course of time, however, intellectual work was gradually substituted by Benedictines for manual work, and this balance was lost. It is only the few who are able to support the continual strain of intellectual occupations in an enclosed and austere life, and relaxation inevitably set in. Dom Calmet, the great Benedictine commentator, of the Congregation of St. Vanne, goes so far as to describe the total suppression of manual labour as ' one of the greatest sources of relaxation of discipline.' It is certainly owing to the maintenance of manual labour, and the wholesome variety of occupations, that the Cistercian observance has been able to keep up a higher standard of bodily austerity. Here, again, however, we need to guard against the exaggeration of a principle. There is nothing rigid or arbitrary in Cistercian legislation—there is no rigorous prohibition of the use of the mind, and though manual work is the rule, Superiors are free to utilise intellectual or artistic gifts in special cases, for the good of the monastery, and when there is no risk of injury to the soul of the religious in question. Thus, the Cistercians of the Strict Observance have recently begun the publication of a quarterly review, entitled *Collectanea Ordinis Cisterciensium Reformatorum*, and the present Abbot General, the Most Reverend Dom Herman-Joseph Smets, in a circular letter to the monasteries announcing the project, expressly invited ' those of our monks and nuns, Superiors and subjects, whom God has endowed with the gift of intelligence and great love for our holy Order, to consecrate their talent to enriching the *Collectanea* with serious and solid essays . . . without prejudice to the monastic simplicity we profess, and still less to the spirit and letter of our present Usages.'

Normally, however, the work of the Cistercian is manual work, and that, very often, of an unskilled and mechanical nature. Mechanical as it may be, it is nevertheless far removed from that of the wage-slaves of modern industrialism, whose occupation of machine-tending calls for neither skill nor responsibility, with the result that the real life of the worker is lived wholly in the time when he is not working, work being regarded as a necessary evil, only made tolerable by short hours and high wages. Cistercian labour, on the contrary, however unskilled, is essentially a rational act, by virtue both of the intention which governs it and the actual attention of the heart to God in the performance of it. Such work, humble and simple as it may be, calls for the best energies of the worker, for it is wholly an act of love and worship, and as such demands in its sphere an equal perfection with the work of the liturgy itself. The Cistercian, whether inclining profoundly in choir at the *Gloria Patri*, or bowed down under some humble task in the fields, is in worship and adoration of the Divine Majesty in Whose Presence her life is passed and to Whom her every moment is consecrated. This gives a dignity, a nobility to the smallest things, and makes work which in itself is servile and menial—such as is despised and shirked by so many at the present day—as glorious as the greatest deeds. For has not the Divine Workman of Nazareth forever consecrated humble daily toil ? And as each feature of His Incarnate Life is perpetuated in some portion or other of His Mystical Body, the Cistercian Order, among the religious Orders, perpetuates the life of the home and workshop of Nazareth. In this, surely, it gives an object-lesson to the modern world. One of the greatest achievements of the Order in its early days was the restoration of the dignity of manual labour, which in feudal times was despised as only fit for serfs. It is difficult for us to realise how astonishing to mediæval eyes was the spectacle of the feudal baron turned monk and labouring in the fields side by side with his own serfs, or of the high-born lady serving in the kitchen of a Cistercian cloister. But the lesson is no less needed in our own day, though in another way, and the spectacle of Cistercian labour—labour done, not out of compulsion or for gain, but freely and out of love—is scarcely less startling to the modern world.

For in a Cistercian monastery all take their share alike in the common labours of house and field. Menial work is not relegated to the lay Brothers and Sisters. The institution of lay brethren in the beginnings of the Order was intended, as we saw, for the performance of those tasks which would interfere with the supreme duty of the choir religious—the Work of God. Such would be, not only the care of distant granges, but the work of the kitchen and the care of animals, which would necessarily prevent regular and punctual attendance in choir. This is still the case, and in practice it usually results that the lay Brothers and Sisters, who form a comparatively large section of every Cistercian community, are employed in tasks which require technical skill and continued application, while the choir religious—unless they have some special employment—form a body of unskilled labour which can be called upon for any work required. Thus, while the lay Sister spends her laborious days in her dairy or poultry-yard, her kitchen or shoe-maker's shop, the choir religious, summoned twice daily to the 'distribution of work,' may be sent here, there, and everywhere, as need occurs, often working under the direction of the lay Sisters who are the permanent workers on the farm or in the garden. This is, perhaps, one of the most remarkable features in the life of a Cistercian community, though it is very simply taken for granted in practice. ' Nowhere,' says the Spiritual Directory of the Order, ' is religious fraternity more in honour than with us '—' everything is in common among the children of a family—we work by the arms of our Sisters, they chant by our mouths. If there is a diversity of rank and occupation, there is but one body and one soul.' For a community is, as it were, the Mystical Body of Christ in miniature, and though all the members have not the same function, all work together under one head for the glory of God, in a union the world may well envy.

CHAPTER XXII

THE WAY TO GOD

In the preceding chapters we have seen what are the dominant features of Cistercian life in our own day—its special character as a life of solitude lived always in community, this being rendered possible by the practice of silence. We have taken a brief glance at the external routine of a Cistercian day, and have then seen in more detail the manner in which Cistercians carry out St. Benedict's ordering of the three traditional monastic occupations. There is, however, another work, a task which has no fixed hours assigned to it, but is of every hour, and underlies all the external occupations of a Cistercian. This is what St. Benedict terms ' the spiritual craft,' which has to be carried on ' day and night ' in the monastic ' workshop.'[1] In his eyes the religious is ' God's workman '—*operarius Dei* —and if his principal work is the Liturgy—the *Opus Dei*— that work of praise demands a corresponding labour of spiritual discipline and purification to fit the soul for so sublime a function. In St. Benedict's mind, this work of spiritual discipline or ' training '—*ascesis* is the old word— is, as stated in an earlier chapter, co-extensive with the progress of the soul in the fundamental virtue of *humility*. Thus, humility is a general virtue, an attitude of the soul in relation to God and to her fellow-men, and it finds its chief expression in the exercise of *obedience*. It is necessary, therefore, to say a few words on these two virtues, in which all monastic perfection is comprised. Little understood as they are by the modern world, it is in them that the following of Christ must always chiefly consist. ' Let this mind be in you, which was also in Christ Jesus, who . . . humbled

[1] The quotations in this chapter, unless otherwise stated, are from the Rule of St. Benedict.

Himself, becoming obedient unto death, even to the death of the cross.'[1] This, in fact, is the whole programme of monastic life as defined by St. Benedict—to go to God by following Christ in His humility and obedience ; and this, therefore, is the aim of Cistercians, for according to their Constitutions, ' in everything relating to the practice of the virtues' they are to ' follow the precepts of the Rule of St. Benedict.'

In St. Benedict's conception of humility the objective character of monastic spirituality is again apparent. The whole Rule is dominated by the thought of God ; the monastery is a ' school of the Lord's service,' not of self-perfection for its own sake,[2] and humility is to be attained by looking at God rather than at self, by walking in the Presence of God rather than by minute methods of self-analysis. In his chapter on the twelve degrees of humility, St. Benedict shows how this dominant thought of God, having become a practical conviction, gradually penetrates and transforms the whole being of the religious, and becomes the guiding principle of the whole moral life. The basis of humility is the ' fear of God '—not a servile fear, but a reverential fear, springing from the realisation of God's Presence, and influencing the whole conduct. This spirit of reverence or ' religion ' is the foundation not only of all holiness, but of all prayer, and especially of the prayer of the Liturgy.

Possessed by this filial fear, the soul subjects herself to God's commandments, embraces His Will at the sacrifice of her own, even when it is signified to her through human beings who represent Him, and that even in circumstances requiring heroic patience and fortitude. The growing realisation of the greatness of God not only leads to submission of will, but penetrates the soul with the sense of her own nothingness and misery—for humility is truth. Voluntary self-humiliation helps her to attain to profound interior humility, the conviction of her own unworthiness. Finally, humility, now rooted in the heart, takes possession also of the exterior, manifesting itself in the avoidance of

[1] Phil. ii, 5, 8.
[2] Cf. Dom C. Butler, *Benedictine Monachism* (1919), pp. 300–303.

P

singularity, in love of silence, and in the whole bearing of the religious.

Such, in briefest outline, is St. Benedict's conception of that work of self-renunciation which removes the obstacles to God's action in the soul. All the spiritual effort of the religious, then, is to advance in this fundamental humility, which is the fruit of a constant ' looking ' at God, and results in an ever-increasing submission to Him. But St. Benedict is well aware that the principal agent in the work of sanctification is God's grace, and that man's part is only a work of preparation and co-operation. So he is careful to promise his disciples that in the soul thus purified by humility God will pour forth abundantly by His Holy Spirit the sweetness of Divine love. This in reality is the end of all monastic discipline, both interior and exterior—to prepare the soul for the action of the Holy Spirit, who is the Sanctifier and whose Presence in the soul is the source of all contemplation. And while the religious are urged to ' work diligently ' with the ' tools of the spiritual craft ' provided in the cloister, at the same time they are warned to ' magnify the Lord who works in them,' ' knowing that the good which is in them comes not from themselves but from the Lord.'

Monastic humility is thus a comprehensive virtue, an inward attitude of soul governing the whole exterior conduct. The principal outward act of humility is *obedience*, which is the infallible test of whether humility exists in the heart, while at the same time it is the best means of acquiring it, for experience proves that there is no more powerful solvent of human pride than obedience.

The word ' obedience ' has an unpleasant sound in modern ears. We live in an age when the very principle of authority is being questioned, and it is idle to expect that a generation born and bred in such an age will take authority for granted, and embrace without difficulty a life of continual subjection and unquestioning obedience. Yet that is what religious life is, at least, as St. Benedict understood it. No one reading the Holy Rule can fail to realise that for him obedience is the way to God. The one end of monastic life is to ' seek God '—all else is a means to that end, and one of the chief means offered by the Rule

is obedience. It is the great *weapon* in the spiritual warfare :
' To thee, therefore, my words are addressed, whosoever
thou art, that, renouncing thine own will, dost take up the
strong and bright weapons of obedience, in order to fight
for the Lord Christ our True King.' Again, it is the *road*
that leads to God : the religious are to ' return to God by
the labour of obedience,'—' knowing that by this road of
obedience they will go to God.' There can be no question,
therefore, for those who follow the Rule of St. Benedict, of
attenuating or watering down the ideal of obedience to suit
modern ways of thinking. What is needed is rather, to
present it in its loftiest form, and to propose motives which
are wholly supernatural, based on reason enlightened by
faith, and equally removed from sentimentality or mere
utilitarianism. This is exactly what St. Benedict does. It
is obvious, of course, that no community life is possible
without obedience to recognised authority—but to St.
Benedict this is far more than a mere practical necessity :
it is a vital element in the spiritual life, the great means
of union with God. We have seen how spiritual progress
for St. Benedict consists essentially in progress in humility,
in an ever-increasing subjection of the soul to God ; it is,
above all, in the exercise of obedience that this subjection
is both acquired and manifested.

Holiness, spiritual writers are agreed, consists in the
union of the human will with the Will of God. God manifests
His Will in various ways, and not least by the commands of
lawfully constituted authority. All authority comes from
God—' there is no power but from God '[1]—through Christ—
' all power is given to Me '[2]—who in turn delegates it to His
representatives—' he that heareth you, heareth Me.'[3] This
latter text is taken by St. Benedict as the supreme motive
of obedience, and the obedience of his Rule has been well
summed up as ' *Christ's personal order.*' In this light, all is
simple. Obedience, prompt, cheerful and unquestioning, as
St. Benedict requires it, ' befits those who hold nothing dearer
to them than Christ ' ; ' as soon as anything is ordered by
the Superior, just as if it had been commanded by God
Himself,' they not merely obey, but ' are unable to endure

---

[1] Rom. xiii, 1.   [2] Mt. xxviii, 18.   [3] Lk. x, 16.

delay in doing it.'　Obedience is thus the fulfilment of the twenty-first ' instrument of good works '—' to prefer nothing to the love of Christ.'　It has been finely said—' Obedience should not begin until it is an act of faith, nor end until it is an act of love.'　Faith recognises Christ's voice in the voice of the Superior, whatever may be his or her personal qualities, for, as a contemplative nun of our own day, Sister Elisabeth of the Trinity, wrote : ' the truly super-natural soul never sees secondary causes.'　We have an example of this in the life of that great monk, Dom Marmion. Asked the secret of his perfect obedience, he replied : ' It is very simple : I look over the head of my Abbot, and there I see Christ.'[1]　Seeing Christ by the light of faith, the soul lovingly embraces the Will of Christ ; the thing com-manded thus becomes the means of closer union with Christ whom she loves, and as such is wholly desirable, though in itself it may be repugnant to nature.　This is why St. Benedict speaks of *bonum obedientiæ*—' the *boon* of obedience,' —a benefit, a treasure.　Not merely is it of value negatively, as the most effective instrument of combating human pride and self-will (which it undoubtedly is), but it is also a positive good, as uniting the soul to its Supreme Good, God Himself. St. Benedict always regards obedience in this light, as an act of love—' that a man *for the love of God* submit himself to his Superior in all obedience.'　(Third degree of humility.) And this love is a heroic and generous love, involving the total sacrifice of self, for as St. Thomas teaches—' Man can give nothing greater to God than to subject his will to another man's for God's sake.'[2]　There is nothing servile, or merely passive, in obedience thus regarded : it is the free act of the rational creature, submitting his or her freewill to the signified Will of God.　' We all love liberty,' writes Bossuet,[3] ' but let us get to it by . . . the road not of indepen-dence but of dependence. . . . Do you want to be free ? Then free yourself by your own act ; have no will but God's Will.' In a sense, obedience is the freest of all acts, for it implies that the will is completely liberated from all lower attractions

---

[1] D. R. Thibaut, *Dom Columba Marmion*, Eng. trans. (1932), p. 119.
[2] *Sum. Theol.*, II–II, Q. 186, art. 5, ad 5.
[3] *Panegyric of St. Benedict.*

or solicitations, and cleaves with undivided energy to the Will of God. This, of course, is perfect obedience, and is not attained in a day, but at least it is an ideal capable of eliciting generous effort and self-sacrifice on the part of souls truly ' seeking God.'

In the Cistercian Order, obedience regulates the whole existence of the religious, and thus brings all into unity. This is the deepest aspect of that simplicity which we saw to be the keynote of the Order. The ever-recurring bells, marking the divisions of the day, each with its appointed duty of prayer, reading or work, signify nothing else but the Will of God to be done out of love ; the orders of Superiors regulating details, and assigning to each her special task or employment ; all this is a constant check to self-will and the spirit of independence, and renders it easy for a soul of good will to make the day one continuous act of love, by union with the Will of God in each successive duty. For all the different occupations of a Cistercian day, under this general aspect of obedience, as well as each in its own particular sphere, are nothing else but means of ' seeking God.' Hence, in this matter of obedience, as in all else, all reduces to the one vital question, *si revera DEUM quærit*—' if he (or she) *truly* seek God,' and God alone, no matter what the cost. And the cost, once more, is no less than the total sacrifice of self. We must ' give all for all,' as the Imitation says. This, it cannot be too often repeated, is the sole end of Cistercian life, and the essential disposition required of those who would enter upon it. For a soul that truly seeks God will not stop to haggle over details, will not be always questioning this or that, but will generously embrace all, *pro Dei amore.* ' Happy are those,' says Bossuet,[1] ' who carry this desire to its fulfilment, who pursue it even to the final, actual and perfect renunciation.'

Hæc est generatio quærentium Dominum !

[1] *Méditations sur l'Evangile*, La Cène, 83e jour.

CONCLUSION

THE age-long question is still asked : *Cui bono ?* To what purpose is this waste ? What is the use of the cloistered Orders ? Would-be apologists have sometimes pointed to the immense achievements of the monastic Orders in the domain of agriculture, learning, and the arts ; their services to mankind in the material and intellectual order. All that is beside the point. But, in this age of multifarious and feverish activity, their existence requires justification, even in the spiritual order. And, as Christ defended Mary against the complaints of Martha, so in these days the Vicar of Christ has taken up the cause of the contemplative Orders. The magisterial pronouncement of Pius XI in the Apostolic Constitution *Umbratilem* leaves no further room for controversy as far as Catholics are concerned. These are the Holy Father's words :

> ' *they who assiduously fulfil the duty of prayer and penance contribute much more to the increase of the Church and the welfare of mankind than those who labour in tilling the Master's field.*' . . .

The whole of that Apostolic Constitution should be read and pondered. Prefixed to the Statutes of the Carthusians, it was addressed primarily to that venerable Order, but in the Apostolic Letter *Monachorum Vita*, issued a few months later in approbation of the Constitutions of the Cistercians of the Strict Observance, the Holy Father refers expressly to the passage of the *Umbratilem* quoted above, and makes it clear that his teaching has a general bearing, and applies equally to the Cistercian and other contemplative Orders, and that he wishes to impress it on the minds of the faithful, in order to ' excite in them a desire for prayer.'

Nothing could be more opportune than this teaching, in which the Holy Father defines the apostolic and social rôle

216

of the contemplative Orders, the place they occupy in the
ranks of the Church Militant. And the contemplatives
themselves cannot but derive inspiration and encouragement from this authoritative declaration, coming as it does
from the very lips of the Vicar of Christ. Of themselves,
however, they would doubtless more willingly call to mind
the wise and weighty saying of Bishop Hedley : ' Perhaps
the less a monk thinks about converting the world, and the
more he thinks about converting himself, the more likely
will it be that the world will be converted.'[1]

And yet, after all, for the children of St. Benedict at
least, is the conversion of the world their *first* aim ? Have
they not a higher rôle even than that apostolic and social
rôle ? an activity which is wholly God-ward ? A monastic
community, the members of which are living up to their
vocation, undoubtedly radiates a spiritual influence which
is incalculable. But that is not the purpose of its existence.
The Cistercians are children of St. Benedict, and their
supreme work is the Work of God, the liturgy—and the
liturgy, as Guardini has reminded us,[2] does not exist for
the sake of humanity, but for the sake of God. Perhaps,
in these days, we need to beware of a certain tendency
towards utilitarianism, even in the things of the spirit.
Their usefulness to the Church and to the world at large
is not the supreme justification of the monastic Orders.
Great and undeniable as it is, we must not lay too much
stress on it, or regard it as their exclusive or even as their
principal end. Countless religious families exist who are
devoted to the work of the apostolate in all its branches,
and to the alleviation of every form of human misery. Is
it not fitting that others should exist who are wholly
devoted to God alone *for His own sake*, who are ' religious '
essentially, because their whole life is devoted to ' religion '
in the strict sense ; who give their time and strength to
His worship and praise, their minds to the contemplation
of His perfections, their hearts to the attaining of that
purity of love, an instant of which, St. John of the Cross

---

[1] Preface to the English edition of Abbot Tosti's *St. Benedict* (1896)
p. xxiii.
[2] *The Spirit of the Liturgy* (1930), p. 96.

tells us, is of more value to the world than all active works put together ? The good of souls necessarily follows from this ; but it is not the object the religious have in view. They are pre-eminently God-seekers, *monachi* and *moniales*, men and women of unity, seeking God alone in simplicity of heart and simplicity of life. They desire only to live hidden with Christ in God, content to know nothing of results, ' to have no other usefulness than that of adoring God . . . to attain nothing but the essential end of all things, the end of the whole rational creation, the very end of the Church,'[1]

UT IN OMNIBUS GLORIFICETUR DEUS.

[1] Dom Paul Delatte, *Commentary on the Rule of St. Benedict*, Eng. trans., p. 137.

NOTE ON SOURCES

AMONG the works consulted, the writer is more especially indebted to the following :

DOM URSMER BERLIERE. *L'Ordre Monastique des origines au XIIe siècle.* (Maredsous, 1924.)

FR. BEDE JARRETT, O.P. *The Religious Life.* (London, 1919.)

CHRISTOPHER DAWSON. *The Making of Europe.*

PH. GUIGNARD. *Les Monuments Primitifs de la Règle Cistercienne publiés d'après les manuscrits de l'Abbaye de Cîteaux.* (Dijon, 1878.)

REV. J. B. DALGAIRNS. *Life of St. Stephen Harding.* Edited by Fr. Thurston, S.J. (London, 1898.)

WATKIN WILLIAMS. *The " Charta Charitatis " of St. Stephen Harding.* (*Dublin Review*, October, 1928.)

L'Esprit de Simplicité caractéristique de Cîteaux. Rapport demandé et approuvé par le Chapitre Général de 1925 des Cisterciens de la Stricte Observance. (Westmalle, 1928.)

DOM ANSELME LE BAÏL, O.C.R. *L'Ordre de Cîteaux : " La Trappe."* (Paris, 1926.)

DOM J.-M. CANIVEZ, O.C.R. *L'Ordre de Cîteaux en Belgique des Origines au XXe siècle.* (Forges-lez-Chimay, 1926.)

ELIE MAIRE. *Les Cisterciens en France autrefois et aujourd'hui.* (Paris, 1930.)

C. GAILLARDIN. *Les Trappistes, ou l'Ordre de Cîteaux au XIXe siècle : Histoire de la Trappe depuis sa fondation jusqu'à nos jours.* (Paris, 1853.)

ALBERT CHEREL. *Rancé.* Préface de René Bazin. (Paris, 1930.)

ABBÉ HUVELIN. *Some Spiritual Guides of the Seventeenth Century.* Translated by Rev. J. Leonard, C.M. (London, 1927.)

DOM CHAUTARD, O.C.R. *Les Cisterciens Trappistes : L'Ame Cistercienne.* Une des conférences de DRAC donnée à Paris le 28 janvier, 1931. (Abbaye de Sept-Fons, 1931.)

Dom Augustin de Lestrange et les Trappistes pendant la Révolution : Odyssée Monastique. (La Grande-Trappe, 1898.)

H. FOLEY, S.J. *Records of the English Province of the Society of Jesus.*

CANON GEORGE OLIVER, D.D. *Collections illustrating the History of the Catholic Religion in Cornwall, Devon, Dorset, etc.* (1857.)

A Concise History of the Cistercian Order, with its Revival in England at St. Susan's, Lulworth, and Mount St. Bernard, Leicestershire. By a Cistercian Monk. (London, 1852.)

E. LAFOND. *De la Renaissance Catholique en Angleterre.* (Paris, 1849.)

DOM DELATTE, O.S.B. *Commentary on the Rule of St. Benedict.* Translated by Dom Justin McCann, O.S.B. (London, 1921.)

La Règle de S. Benoît traduite et commentée. Cum permissu et voluntate Capituli Generalis, O.C.R., 1907. (La Chapelle-Montligeon, 1908.)

Directoire Spirituel à l'Usage des Cisterciens Réformés ou de la Stricte Observance. (Bricquebec, 1910.) Eng. trans. *A Spiritual Directory for Religious,* 2 vols. (New Melleray Abbey, Peosta, Iowa, U.S.A., 1932.)

ROMANO GUARDINI. *The Spirit of the Liturgy.* (Eng. trans. London, 1930.)

DR. GORCE. *La Lectio Divina des Origines du Cénobitisme à Saint Benoît et Cassiodore.* Vol. I. (Paris, 1925.)

DOM GERMAIN MORIN, O.S.B. *The Ideal of the Monastic Life found in the Apostolic Age.* (Eng. trans. London, 1914.) Ch. VIII. Monastic Spirituality.

A Ladder of Four Rungs, being a Treatise on Prayer by Dom Guy II. Edited by Dom Justin McCann, O.S.B. (Parkminster Press, 1926.)

The Power of Contemplation. The teaching of Pope Pius XI as contained in the Apostolic Constitution *Umbratilem.* (Parkminster Press, 1926.)

J. K. HUYSMANS. *En Route.*

INDEX

The Mayflower Press, Plymouth. William Brendon & Son, Ltd.